# *CATAMARAN RACING*

*SOLUTIONS, SECRETS, SPEED*

# *CATAMARAN RACING*

---

*by Rick White*

with chapters contributed by RANDY SMYTH, HOBIE ALTER, JR., WAYNE SCHAFER, TOM TANNERT, LARRY HARTECK, AND MARY WELLS

*DODD, MEAD & COMPANY • NEW YORK*

Published by Dodd, Mead & Company, Inc.
79 Madison Avenue, New York, N.Y. 10016
Distributed in Canada by
McClelland and Stewart Limited, Toronto
Manufactured in the United States of America
Designed by Nancy Dale Muldoon
First Edition

LIBRARY OF CONGRESS CATALOGING IN PUBLICATION DATA

White, Rick.
Catamaran racing.

Includes index.
1. Catamarans. I. Wells, Mary. II. Title.
GV811.57.W48 1983 797.1'4 83-14083
ISBN 0-396-08193-2
ISBN 0-396-08201-7 (pbk.)

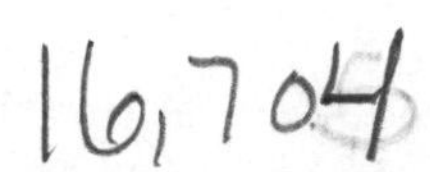

# CONTENTS

# 1

## THE NEO-AGE OF CATAMARANS

SAILING is a sport that, more than most, thrives on theories and experimentation . . . and the theories seem to change with nearly every racing season.

No theory is sacred. No one can provide the surefire formula for successful racing and for guaranteed victories. What works for one skipper will not work for the next.

Yet most of us have a tendency to jump on the bandwagon and at least temporarily try out the techniques that are winning this year, even knowing that the winning sailor will be dethroned the following year by some irreverent upstart with a "new and unconventional" approach.

The important thing is to understand as much as possible

about how and why your boat works and to keep trying different theories and experiments until you find yourself crossing the finish line in first place.

For most of us, that has meant many seasons of studying competitors' transoms, working our way up through the ranks, and generally paying our dues.

But the one common factor I have found among winning sailors is an extremely competitive spirit. Every time they lose, they ask, "Why?" And, more importantly, they listen to the answers to their questions.

In this book I have tried to cover as many "whys" as possible, both for the novice racers and for those seasoned old dogs who may still be able to learn a few new tricks.

It is certain that with each race, each regatta, each season, you will learn something new by racing your boat. But do we race so that we can learn? Or do we learn so that we can race?

In other words, just why DO we race, anyway? It's the question daysailers throw back at us when we ask them, "Why DON'T you race?"

When I asked Wayne Schafer why he races, the old man of the sea answered, "Well, it's fun and competitive. It keeps me excited, stimulated; and I love the camaraderie. I love the thrill of pitting my abilities against someone else—to try to outmaneuver them, outthink them, and just plain outsail them.

"That's kept me going for fourteen years, and I still have not lost the enjoyment of trying to improve my sailing skills."

He adds, "I remember when the Hobie 14 was new; we used to take them out surfing, and we had a ball. But, sure enough, while sitting around out there waiting for a wave, we just couldn't resist the urge to get a race going.

"It's just natural."

Racing is something that does seem natural. It is a way to try out theories and experiments. And it is the best way I know to improve your sailing skills. Without someone to measure against, all your ideas on how to sail a boat faster could be absolutely wrong. They could be right. But until you

*Catamaran racing is a sport for both sexes. Hobie National Champ Paula Alter takes a back seat to no one in sailing abilities. (Photo courtesy of Hobie Class Assn.)*

try them out against someone else, you will never know.

They say ignorance is bliss; but fortunately for the sport of sailboat racing, large numbers of people apparently are not content to be blissful.

The drive to race is the same one that compels joggers to participate in marathons or makes us keep score in tennis or golf, rather than just hit a ball around.

To get into racing is generally pretty easy. The best way to begin is to join an active local fleet of boats in your class. Fleet racing is fun and friendly; it's a good way to meet new people who share your interest in sailing. Besides providing you with a new sport, it also opens up a whole new social scene.

Finding a fleet can be easily done by contacting your dealer or the class association. The fleets usually have a calendar of events for the season, and this will give you an idea of

*Sailing itself attracts the beautiful people, but cats seem to have more than their share. (Photo courtesy of Hobie Class Assn.)*

how active the fleet is. They should have a lot of good local racing scheduled well in advance.

You will love fleet racing, whether you are a beginner or a veteran. This racing offers you consistent competition of the same caliber, giving you a good yardstick against which to measure your progress. You will become familiar with the sailing styles and levels of your competition; this will allow you to experiment with tuning or helmsmanship and get instant feedback on how you are doing with the rest of the fleet.

You also will find that almost all local fleets have skippers who dominate the scene. They will be glad to help you in any way they can to give you confidence and knowledge for future racing; and they are usually very generous with tips on improving performance.

Over a postrace beer is a good time to replay all those little defeats and conquests that make up the game. That provides a natural opportunity to throw out questions like "What should I have done in this situation?"

Sailing and working with the local fleet can be extremely rewarding. By getting heavily into developmental sailing in the fleet, you will acquire a tremendous foundation for becoming an excellent sailor. Local fleets are the stepping stones to larger, sanctioned regattas, leading on up to the districts, regionals, and the ultimate national and world regattas.

Each further step of the way is a new learning process, but you will have the basics. Each further step will pit you more and more against better and better competition, testing your theories and experimentations to the maximum . . . and that is what it is all about.

When you get to be the big frog in your small pond back home, you may enjoy dominating the local fleet, but you will find you are no longer learning as much. At this point, if you wish to continue expanding your skill, you must begin leaving your pond occasionally to learn from new and different competition and racing conditions.

But you need not try for the climb to the top. You can have just as much fun sailing locally. Though the competitors may always be the same, every race is a different situation, and everyone starts out with an equal chance at victory. It is truly a physical game of chess on water, and there are always new moves to be learned.

I'll discuss preparing for a race in depth throughout this book. Here I want to point to mental preparation as the most important element. Although psychology is a field outside my area of expertise, I have seen that everyone has a way to handle competition, stress, and anxiety. Yes, sailboat racing is an outlet for the stresses and anxieties of everyday life, but it also carries with it the pressures of competition . . . along with the fun, excitement, and exhilaration.

You may use the principles of self-hypnosis or meditation, or you may just take a few deep breaths to calm or psych yourself for the race. But find a method that works for you and use it, because racing taxes you both mentally and physically; and the key to success is the ability to concentrate completely on the contest at hand.

This past summer we met a young sailor who introduced us to his girl friend, adding that this regatta would be her first time crewing for him in a race.

After the first race, when we asked how it went, she replied, "I liked it fine." Then, pointing to her skipper, she added, "But I never met THAT guy before." Apparently she was able to adjust to the dual personality, because later that weekend she accepted an engagement ring from him.

Many a Dr. Jekyll has become a Mr. Hyde on the water, but the best prospects for having fun and winning races come from being under control at all times. Try to sail relaxed. You will be more efficient in your handling of the boat, and your decisions on tactics will be more sound. A relaxed mind works much better than one that is tense and panicky.

It is difficult not to lose your cool when a mistake has been made, but the time spent in useless recriminations against yourself or your crew will not undo the damage—it will only cost you additional time and distance until you again focus your efforts and concentration on the present instead of the past.

*Famous surfer turned boat designer, Hobie Alter was one of the catamaran pioneers and an important factor in the popularity and status the boats enjoy today. (Photo courtesy of Hobie Class Assn.)*

Daysailing is fun in catamarans. You can cover greater distances in shorter times than you can in a monohull, which really expands your range for exploration. Cruising along the shoreline or visiting a nearby island is a relaxing way to spend a day.

But if you have a spark of competitive spirit in your bones, sooner or later you will find yourself comparing speeds with other sailboats, or even with powerboats. If another cat comes along, you will find it hard to resist trying to race that other cat, even if your "competitor" doesn't know he's being raced.

Don't fight the urge. After all, racing is natural. And before you know it, you'll be hooked. You won't be giving up your relaxing day. There is nothing like the intense concentration of competition to take your mind off all your other problems. And no relaxation is as wonderful as that which follows a hard-fought race.

*A new and exciting single-hander is NACRA's 18-square meter. (Photo courtesy of NACRA)*

One of the great things about racing a catamaran is the supersensitive feel you will develop for the helm. Cats are so uniquely fast and responsive in their steering that you learn to control the direction of the boat with micromovement flicks of the wrist or fingers. The touch of the tiller is so delicate that the slightest steerage deviation can produce dramatic effects,

*NACRA had its beginnings with this original Tom Roland cat design, probably the fastest catamaran ever sailed. (Photo courtesy of NACRA)*

some pleasant and some not so pleasant. This sensitive touch is best learned on the race course.*

Catamarans, as we know them today, have not been around very long. In the eyes of the old, staunch "monomaran" sailors in this century, we are young whippersnappers with newfangled contraptions. But many of the older classes are dying out rapidly and being replaced by high-performance craft like the cats.

The catamaran has definitely come of age. Those of us who pioneered their designs can be very proud of what has happened in this area of sailing during the past two decades.

*Many sailors who have learned their helmsmanship on a fast-moving boat, such as a catamaran or scow, have moved on to larger, slower-responding boats and totally dominated the field. But the exchange is not reciprocal, for the big-boat sailor moving into a fast, responsive boat usually will fare poorly and will have to relearn his helmsmanship. Cats are the breeding ground for top helmsmen, regardless of what type of boat they may sail in the future.

*The designer of the Prindle cats, Geoff Prindle was still another pioneer in the development of high-performance cats in the United States. (Photo courtesy of Prindle Class Assn.)*

However, please keep in mind that no matter how good the boat may be that you are sailing—it may tack fast, cream on reaches, smoke downwind, point 30 degrees higher or self-right before it gets all the way over—no boat is better than its own class association and boat builder(s). Without a builder or association, you will have these wonderful characteristics all to yourself, with no one to race against.

Many good classes of boats are now dead and gone and others are endangered species because they lack the combination for making a good class. Without a builder, you have no boats; without an association, you have no racing program. Without either, you have no class at all.

Every year new classes of cats are born that may perform

miracles on the sailing scene, but they never get off the ground (or water) in terms of impact on the scene, because they lack the organizational commitment to make them a great class. So support your association and help whenever you can.

Catamarans are the fastest-growing in popularity and most active type of sailboat in the world today. Designs backed up by a substantial builder and a true class association with good, informative newsletters and up-to-date race calendars will flourish. The others will die, leaving us with probably a mere dozen truly great, active classes in the world—and most of those will be cats.

Why not! Catamaran racing is wetter and wilder and calls

*A few wild, wet moments accompany a charge out through the California surf. (Photo courtesy of Hobie Class Assn.)*

*The Alter family of champions. From left are Paula, Hobie Jr., Jeff and Hobie Sr. (Photo by Alistair Black, courtesy of Hobie Class Assn.)*

for more wisdom and quick thinking than any other sailing that exists today.

And best of all, it appeals to people with strong competitive spirit . . . people like you.

# 2

## FIRST TIME

FOR everyone who sails there was always that first time.

I recall my introduction to sailing. It was in a canoe on a small Ohio lake. A friend had rigged the boat with homemade sails and leeboards (they were attached to the gunwales with clamps), and we used a paddle for a rudder. We also used it as a paddle to get back to our car. No air!

One's initial adventure in a sailboat is usually filled with some kind of delight and/or disaster. Thereafter, sailing may be something you look forward to or shun, depending a great deal upon your original experience.

Now it is your turn. So here is a "crash" course in how to take your first spin around the lake and get safely back to your point of departure.

Since you may be sailing any of several different types of cats, I suggest you carefully read your owner's manual for rigging your particular boat.

By the way, when rigging your boat, be sure to look up and carefully watch for power lines or any overhead wires before raising the mast or moving the boat. A number of deaths have been attributed to *not* looking first.

Chapter 12, "Maintenance," provides a good checklist that could prove useful when you are rigging your boat for the first time.

Before doing anything, read Chapter 13, "Safety," which gives you a checklist of equipment you need aboard and tips to make your outing more comfortable, safe, and enjoyable. Also, because the Boy Scouts are right about being prepared, it would be wise to read Chapter 14, "Capsize: Prevention and Cure," before taking that first sail.

Let's take it now from the point where you have your mast up, rudders on, and are looking out at the water wondering what to do next.

## *GETTING READY TO GO OUT*

For your initial outing, choose a day with relatively light air (winds under 12 mph) and little wave action.

1. When ready to raise the sails, position the boat so the bows are pointing straight into the wind. This not only will make it much easier to raise your mainsail, but also will prevent your boat from sailing away without you or capsizing on the beach.

If you will be launching the boat with a hoist or over a wall, it is better to wait until it is in the water before raising the sails. BE SURE YOUR DRAIN PLUGS ARE IN BEFORE LAUNCHING. Again, make sure the boat is tied securely and with the bows heading into the wind.

2. Make sure the sheets are not cleated when you raise the sails and that the sheets are running free through the

blocks. If the sheets are cleated, the sails can fill with air, and the boat may try to sail away or capsize.

3. All necessary and required equipment should be on board (as specified in Chapter 13, "Safety") and stowed away or securely tied down. Be sure to take along a paddle. WEAR your life jackets.

4. If you have never before steered a boat with a tiller, be sure you have the concept firmly in mind: To turn the boat to the right, you will move the tiller to the left; to turn the boat left, you move the tiller to the right.

5. Attach some telltales to the boat. Before leaving the beach and at all times on the water, it is imperative that you be aware of where the wind is coming from so that you can set the sails properly in relation to the wind. You can attach feathers or ribbons to the side stays as wind direction indicators, and/or you may use a bridle fly, which is a ribbon or plastic wind vane attached between the bridle stays below the bottom of the forestay.

Once you are moving, the telltale will be giving you an indication of the "apparent wind" rather than the true wind direction, because the forward motion of the boat will cause the telltale to stream a little farther aft than if the boat were standing still.

6. One basic rule should be kept in mind by the novice sailor: It is easier to sail downwind than upwind. Therefore, at least for that first sail, it is a good idea *to first sail upwind* from your point of departure. That way, if you don't master the art of tacking upwind, you have the comfort of knowing the wind will push you back home safely. If you start out with an offshore wind and can't get back, it is embarrassing to have to ask a passing powerboat to tow you in.

Actually, staying upwind of your return point is always a good habit to get into, so the wind can help you home if something breaks on the boat.

7. Do a few dry-land drills to learn how your sheets, blocks, and cleats work. Familiarize yourself with the main traveler. (The lower set of pulleys through which you sheet your mainsail is attached to a traveler car on a track on the rear

beam of the boat.) This traveler may be set anywhere from the center to far outboard, depending on your point of sail.

For sailing close-hauled or on a close reach, you should try to keep the traveler centered; if you are sailing downwind with the mainsail far out to the side, you may move the traveler car all the way out to that same side. The line controlling the traveler car goes through a cam cleat, and you will cleat it to hold it in the desired position.

For the purpose of this early stage of sailing, it is not necessary to worry much about your luff downhaul tensions, mainsail outhaul tension, or your jib lead settings. The boat will still sail if they are not perfect; and the finer points of these settings are explained at length in other chapters in this book.

## *THEORY AND APPLICATION*

Now, before you take that final big step—leaving dry land behind to set off into that big, wet world out there—let's get some mental images planted in your mind of what makes the boat go forward and how your sails should be set in relation to wind direction.

Anyone can easily figure out how a boat goes with the wind. Huckleberry Finn and Tom Sawyer used a simple piece of cloth set on a cross on their raft and made it down the Mississippi. With the wind blowing aft of you and the sail set perpendicular to the wind, there is no problem of understanding why a boat moves. It's as simple as standing on ice skates with your back to the wind and holding open your coat.

But sailing against the wind is not so easy a concept. You probably already know that a boat cannot sail or "point" any closer than 45 degrees to the direction from which the wind is blowing. Sailing that close to the wind is called "sailing close-hauled" or "going to weather." If you point the bows straight into the wind, the sails will flap or "luff" uselessly. You not only will make no forward progress, you will begin drifting backward. This is called "being in irons." It is a completely neutral position.

If you point the boat directly downwind (180 degrees off

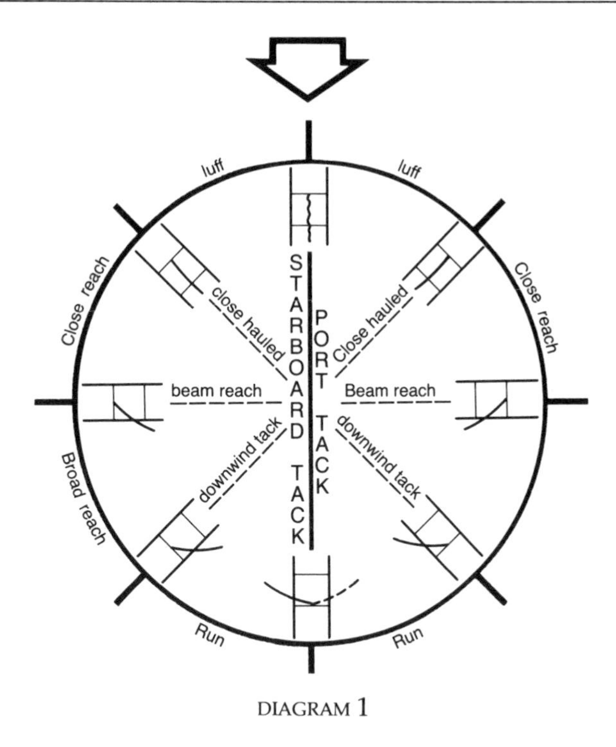


DIAGRAM 1

the wind), the wind will drive you as fast as it is blowing, minus the amount of water drag your hulls are producing.

But you also may sail at any angle from dead downwind up to close-hauled. All those positions in between are reaches. A close reach is just a little farther off the wind than close-hauled. You are "on a beam reach" when the wind is coming from straight off the side of the boat, or perpendicular to the boat. A "broad reach" is the point of sail with the wind coming over the aft quarter of your boat.

The boat goes forward when pushed from behind, so why doesn't it just go sideways when pushed from the side, or even backward when pushed by the wind from the forward quarter?

The answer lies in aerodynamics. The same principles that airplanes learned from birds, sailboats have learned from both.

Suppose you are sailing to weather (45 degrees off the

wind) with your sails sheeted in fairly tightly on the side opposite the one over which the wind is blowing. You will note that the leeward side of your sail is shaped very much like the top of a wing of a bird or an airplane. Both of those flyers have a convex arch on their upper wing surface. Air has to flow faster to get over the curved surface in the same length of time as air going over the bottom so the two currents of air can meet, or rejoin, at the same point after the wing has passed through.

The difference in air speed causes a negative pressure (suction) on the upper surface of the wing and a positive pressure (blow) on the lower side of the wing. The plane and the bird both fly because of the lift (suck) from above and the simultaneous push (blow) from below.

Your sail is the same as a wing, except that it is on a vertical rather than horizontal plane. The wind strikes your sail, causing a negative pressure on the leeward side (the side away from the wind) and a positive pressure on the windward side (the side from which the wind is blowing).

A reasonable question still occurs here: Why does the boat go forward and not sideways in the direction of the lift (or suck)? Because of the friction underwater, most obviously caused by the centerboards and rudders, as well as by the design of the hulls themselves. Due to their resistance to lateral movement, the lift is converted into forward thrust. The boat has no choice but to be "squirted" forward through the water.

Of course, its other alternative is simply to fall over sideways because of the pressure on the sail, but you prevent that by having your weight on the windward side so the boat does not take this easy way out.

Now that you understand what makes the boat go forward, let's discuss how to make it work.

The whole theory of sailing depends entirely upon the angle between wind and sails. The angle of the boat itself is really irrelevant. That is why it is so important to know where the wind is coming from at all times.

Your sails must be set at approximately a 45-degree angle

to the TRUE wind at all times. The boat's heading may change, but the sail will remain fairly close to that same 45-degree angle with the true wind.

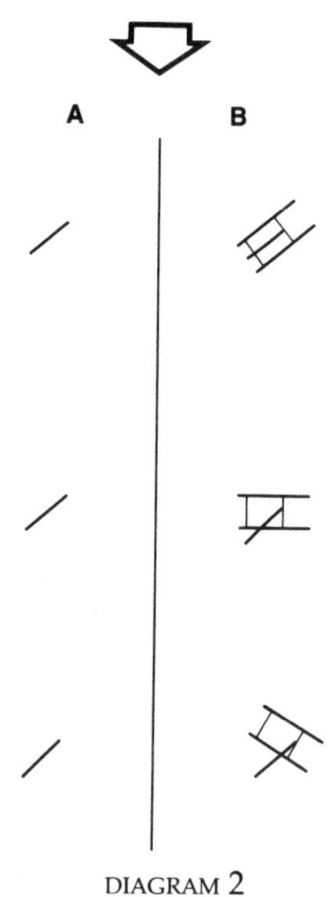


DIAGRAM 2
*The sails in Column A are all set at approximately a 45-degree angle to the wind. The same sails are in Column B, all still at the same angle, but all three boats are heading in different directions, from closed-hauled to a broad reach.*

When you are going to weather, your sails must be pulled in tight to maintain their 45-degree angle to the wind. (See diagram 2.) The reason you cannot point the boat any higher than 45 degrees into the wind is that you cannot bring your sails in any farther. When the angle between wind and sails becomes *less* than 45 degrees, the sails begin to luff. The luffing will increase as the angle is decreased. If the sail is pointing directly into the wind, you will go nowhere, because the sail will be in a full luff.

*What goes up must come down, and these are certainly examples of how not to beach a boat unless you have full coverage insurance. (Boat 22963 photo by Jake Grubb, courtesy of Hobie Class Assn. Boat 888 photo courtesy of Hobie Class Assn.)*

If you are on a close reach, you will ease the sails out a little more to maintain the approximate 45-degree angle to the wind. On a beam reach, your sails will have to be let out still farther.

This process of easing the sail works up to the point of the broad reach (tacking downwind) position. If you sail deeper than that, you will find it is no longer possible to keep your sails at a 45-degree angle to the wind, because the sail cannot go out any farther (due to the mast stays). Past that point, the sail simply acts as a barn door (very inefficient).

If you are just sailing around for the fun of it, with no particular destination, when you change your boat's direction with relation to the wind, you also will have to change the set of your sails to maintain their proper 45-degree angle to the wind.

On the other hand, if you are sailing to a specific point and the direction of the wind itself changes, you still will have to change the set of your sails to agree with the wind, even though you have not altered the boat's course at all.

The more exactly your sails are angled with relation to the wind, the faster and better the boat will sail. This comes with practice and with learning how to read the telltales that probably came mounted on your sail.

For a more intensive explanation of how to read the telltales and sail by them, read Chapter 5, "The Jib."

Right now you just want the basics of how to get the boat moving.

## *TACKING AND JIBING*

Knowing what makes a boat go forward and knowing how to angle the sails in relation to the wind direction is not enough, however. In order to get from HERE to THERE, you must also know how to perform two basic maneuvers: the tack and the jibe.

First, let's deal with the tack. Remember that this word is used in two ways. It is used to refer to the direction in which

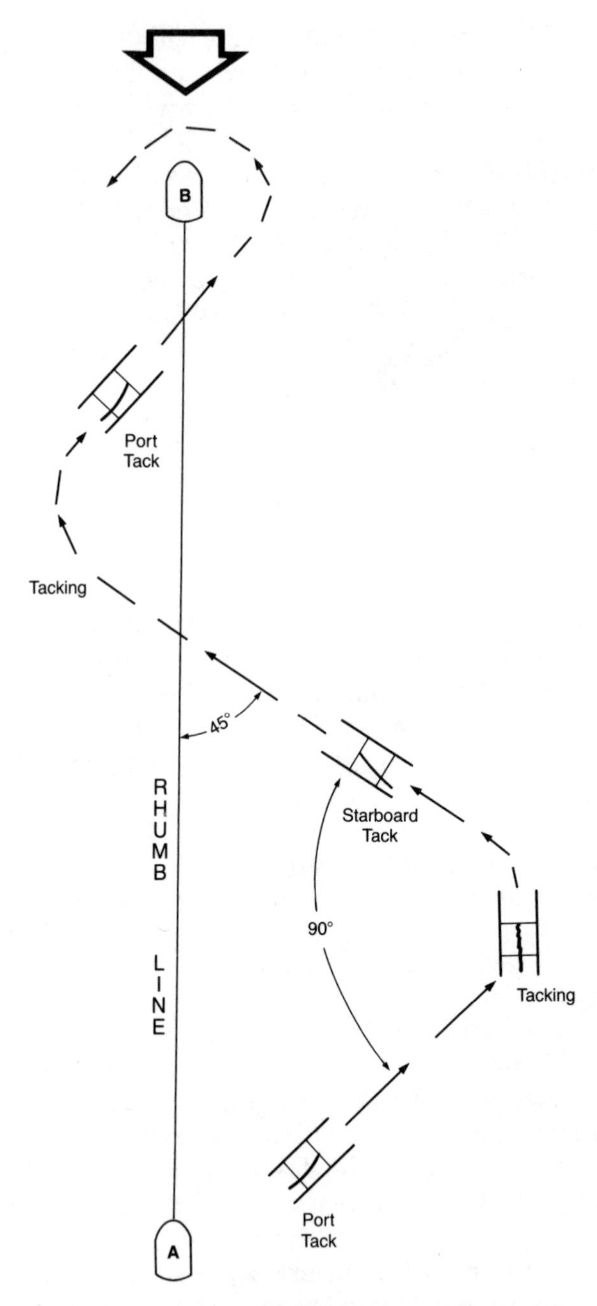


DIAGRAM 3
*Here is an example of tacking (or beating) to weather.*

you are going in relation to the wind. If the wind is coming over the starboard side of the boat, you are on starboard tack. If the wind is coming over the port side, you are on port tack. However, *tack* also is used as a verb to refer to the maneuver of changing course from one direction to the other by turning the bows through the eye of the wind.

As you already know, you cannot point higher than 45 degrees to the wind. If you want to reach a point directly upwind of you, it is necessary to zig-zag to get there, with a series of 90-degree course changes. (See diagram 3.) Diagrammed on paper, your progress would look like stairsteps across the water.

When you tack, you are turning the boat through a full 90 degrees (from 45 degrees off the wind on one tack to 45 degrees off the wind on the other tack).

To accomplish this, you must turn the bows of the boat up into the wind and across the wind until the sails fill on the other side of the boat. This is tacking.

In order to tack successfully, you must first be going to weather and close-hauled. If you are on a beam reach, for example, and decide to tack, you probably will not be able to complete the maneuver successfully. Your sails will be set out so far that when you start bringing the boat up into the wind, the wind will hit the back (leeward) side of your sails and act as a brake, stopping your momentum; and you will find yourself in irons.

First, bring the boat up to its 45-degree angle to the wind, sheet in the sails, and have good forward motion before beginning the tack.

Make sure the crew is prepared for the maneuver. He or she should uncleat the jib sheet but continue to hold the sheet tightly. At the same time the crew should get all the slack out of the sheet on the side to which the jib will be swinging, so it can be quickly pulled in on the new side.

The skipper will push the tiller to leeward, but not so hard that the rudders will turn broadside, thereby acting as a brake. You want the rudders to turn the boat through a smooth arc, so the boat's forward momentum can carry it across the eye of the wind.

As the bows cross the eye of the wind, the wind will catch the jib on the "wrong" side and start pulling it to the other side. (This is called "backwinding the jib.") At this point, the crew should release the jib sheet and pull the sheet in from the other side, at the same time moving over to what will be the new windward side to balance the boat.

The skipper should keep the tiller over until the boat has gone just a bit farther than a 90-degree turn (this will help get the speed going again), and then head it back up to a 45-degree angle from the wind.

*Voilá!* There you are, moving on the new tack.

To get to your destination, you may take a series of short tacks (zig-zags) or two or three long ones. When you reach a point where you can take just one more tack and then sail straight to your destination, this is called "laying the mark."

Ah, but what if you try to tack and the boat just doesn't want to go through the eye of the wind; it just sits there flapping its sails and not moving?

You are in irons. Here is an occasion where you will be happy to find there is more than one steering mechanism on your boat. Your rudders are useless when the boat is standing still, but your jib and mainsail are remarkably effective steering devices and very helpful in getting out of irons.

Chapter 14, "Capsize: Prevention and Cure" has a diagram and explanation of how to use sails and rudders to get out of irons. (See page 187.)

Catamarans do not tack as easily as monohulls, which can just pivot around on their centerboards. The cat has two hulls to drag through the water to make the arc. Therefore, it can help to get crew weight somewhat aft on the boat to temporarily lift the bows and thereby reduce drag in making the tack. Anyone can get into irons occasionally in light air, and especially in high winds or rough seas, when the elements counteract your momentum. (If you do get into irons in heavy wind conditions, do not keep the crew weight back. Rather make sure it is evenly distributed so the wind from directly forward cannot get under the trampoline and attempt to capsize you backward. This applies only in heavy wind conditions.)

Now let us move on to the jibe. This is the maneuver for changing from one tack to another when trying to reach a point downwind of you.

It is the opposite of tacking in that, instead of moving the bows across the eye of the wind, you are turning so that the sterns cross the eye of the wind.

Let's say you are sailing downwind with the wind coming across the aft starboard corner of your boat. Your sails are way out on the port side; therefore, you are on starboard tack. If you want to alter your course so you are heading more to the left, you probably will have to jibe over to port tack.

As you begin to turn the boat to the left in a smooth arc, at the same time begin sheeting in the main and pulling the traveler car to the center. The ideal goal is to have the main reach center as you cross the eye of the wind and then begin letting the sail and the traveler car out rapidly to the new side.

The jib has so much slack in its sheets already that it will virtually jibe itself. The crew will need to sheet in the slack from the new side and let out enough sheet from the former side to allow the jib to be as far out and forward as possible on the new tack.

When you are sailing straight downwind, a slight change in course or wind direction can cause an accidental jibe. To prevent this, try to keep the wind quartering a little more to the side away from the sail.

Most catamarans do not sail directly downwind these days if they are racing or want to get somewhere in a hurry. They tack downwind, much as they do upwind, making 90-degree zig-zags to their destination. But the jibing technique is performed in the same way. (For more detail on the jibe, refer to Chapter 14.)

In sailing, you almost always have a safety valve. If you are reaching or close-hauled and you feel overpowered by the wind—if you are nosediving or flying a hull—you can generally control these situations by letting out the sails and "dumping the wind." By easing the sails, you are releasing the pressure that creates the difficulty.

Of course, if you are sailing dead downwind with your

*Sure, catamarans have sports-car maneuverability, but most sailors prefer to leave some margin for error. (Photo courtesy of Hobie Class Assn.)*

sails already out as far as they can go and you are overpowered, there is little you can do about it. But this would be a rare situation, and one you certainly should not be subjecting yourself to on your first cruise.

## *TAKE-OFFS AND LANDINGS*

Now that you have all those mental images in your mind of just what you are supposed to do, let's go sailing.

Your boat is still sitting there at the dock or on the beach, sails flapping aimlessly in the breeze, waiting for someone to take command.

If you are already in the water and it is deep enough, put down your centerboard or daggerboards and lower and lock your rudders.

If you are launching off the beach, slide the boat into the water and walk it out into the water far enough so that you can partially lower, but not lock, your rudders to give you initial steerage.

### WITH AN ONSHORE BREEZE

Let's assume you are making this first take-off, as recommended, against the wind, with an onshore breeze.

Since you are already bow to the wind, you know you cannot get moving until you angle the boat to at least 45 degrees off the wind. Decide which tack you are going to start out on.

Have your crew get on the boat and backwind the jib on the side opposite the tack on which you want to be. This will swing your bows in the direction you want to go.

As soon as the bows begin swinging, hop on the boat and steer it toward your desired course. Have the crew sheet in the jib on the proper side. Then sheet in the main, and off you go. (Remember, your traveler should be set in the center for going to weather.)

As soon as the water is deep enough, drop the boards at

least part way to prevent sliding sideways. Then drop them the rest of the way as soon as possible and lock down your rudders.

Once you are safely away from the beach, dock, or congested areas, begin practicing the basic maneuvers just reviewed by changing course and sail set. Remember to stay substantially upwind of your departure point.

Use a gentle hand on the helm. Cats are very responsive—it's like steering a sports car as opposed to a utility van. Try sailing close-hauled, with both sails sheeted in. Ease up very gently toward the wind, and note how the jib begins to luff by caving in a little along the forestay. Fall back off a little until the luff in the sail disappears. This is where you want to keep it for sailing to weather—just at the point where it is not luffing. If you fall off any farther, you will slow down because the boat is stalling.

Try your tacking technique. Don't wait too long. If it doesn't work, you don't want to be out of sight of land. But if it doesn't work the first time, don't panic. Remember to use your sails and rudder to back yourself around. (See page 187 in Chapter 14.) And if at first you don't succeed, tack, tack again.

After sailing around, having some good, safe fun, it is time to hit the beach—only do not HIT the beach. Always sail under control when approaching a dock, beaches, other boats, or any obstacles. Near beaches, watch for swimmers and other boats.

If you are coasting downwind toward shore, a nice easy way to ride home, the wind will tend to drive you right up on the beach. But do not do this. First, prepare for your approach by raising boards and releasing the locks on the rudders. While you are still in water deep enough to navigate, steer the boat quickly and hard up into the wind by turning in the direction *opposite* the side the mainsail is on. (If you turn the other way, you will jibe at a very bad time.) Do not sheet the sails in as you round up in the direction of the wind. Leaving the sails out will help to put the brakes on, and you will stop very quickly.

You and your crew can then jump out and hold the bows into the wind. Do not hold the boat farther aft, as the wind can swing the bows and allow it to start sailing again.

With an onshore wind, you will want to back the boat up onto the beach in order to keep the sails heading into the wind.

If you must approach a dock while sailing downwind, you do best to round up into the wind before you get there. Then drop your sails and paddle to the dock.

If the dock is upwind of you, you can more easily control your stop by easing sails and rounding up into the wind just short of your destination or even right at it, making a very neat landing. But always have your paddle ready.

With any sailboat, it is usually advisable to try to come into the leeward side of a dock so that your sails will be out on the side away from the dock itself, reducing chance of damage to sails.

### WITH AN OFFSHORE BREEZE

As mentioned, we recommend that for your first sail you go with an onshore breeze so that you do not have to be concerned about how to get back. However, if you start out with an offshore wind, your departure will be somewhat simplified. Let your sails out all the way, turn the boat around stern to wind, jump on, and the wind will push you off.

When returning to the beach, you will be close-hauled and can stop the boat much more quickly by heading up into the wind and easing your sails just before reaching the beach.

Remember, just as a skier can "put on the brakes" by turning his skis uphill to stop, a sailboat can be stopped by turning it up into the wind and letting out the sails. With a little practice you will be able to stop your boat quickly and efficiently.

But remember that as soon as you are sailing farther off the wind than a beam reach, you cannot let the sail out any farther, and you have no brakes. In order to stop then, you have to round the boat up into the wind higher than a beam

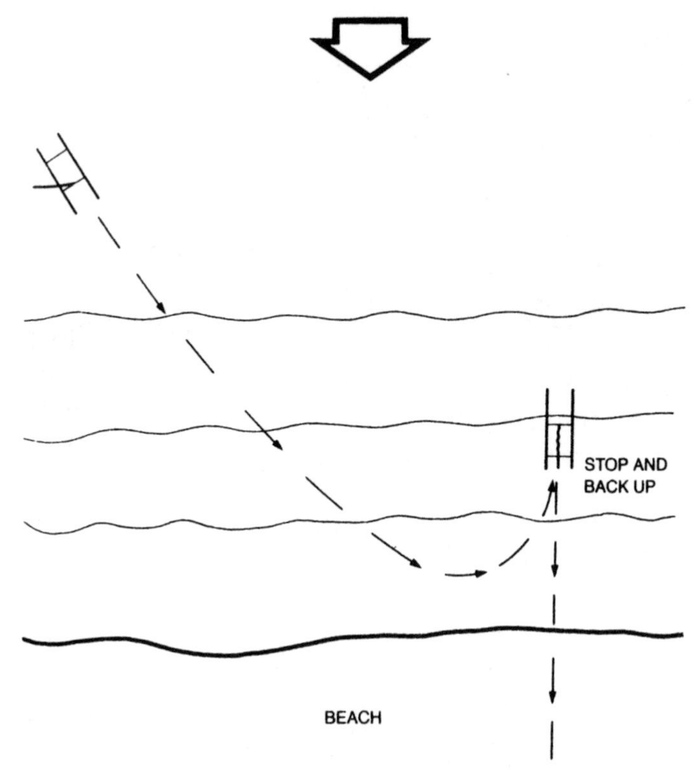


*With an on-shore wind, some just let the wind run their boat up onto the beach, risking damage to the hulls. Here is the proper way to handle the situation.*

reach. Up to that point the sail still will be thrusting you forward.

From the downwind position, you will have to turn almost 180 degrees to get the boat to stop. From close-hauled or a close reach, you will only have to turn it higher into the wind or let go of the sails.

Control is the most important thing to learn. An out-of-control sailor is as unpopular and dangerous as an out-of-control skier.

Without a skipper at the helm, a boat will drift aimlessly at the mercy of the wind and waves. It is up to you as skipper to make those elements work for you. The more you sail, the more respect you will gain for their power, both positive and negative.

| FIRST-TIME PROBLEM-SOLVING KEY | |
|---|---|
| *What's Going Wrong* | *How to Correct It* |
| You can't get the boat to go to weather—you just can't point to 45 degrees, or even 50 degrees. | Make sure your mainsheet traveler car is centered. If it is all the way out to the side, the mainsail cannot assume the proper angle to the wind, even though the sail may be sheeted tightly. If you still can't point well, slide your jib lead traveler car (if you have one) all the way back. If the clew of the jib is hooking back into the main, it is throwing air onto the leeward side of the main, destroying its effectiveness. |
| You can't get through a tack. | Make sure you have your sails in and the boat moving well before you begin your turn. Turn as quickly and smoothly as possible, but without jamming the rudders all the way over. (That would act as a brake.) Try moving weight somewhat aft so the boat will pivot more easily. Try backwinding the jib longer before releasing it. |
| If you can't tack, no matter what. | All is not lost. You can always take the long way around by jibing onto the |

| *What's Going Wrong* | *How to Correct It* |
|---|---|
| | other tack. To do this, you will have to fall back off the wind 180 degrees to straight downwind, and follow the directions for jibing. When your sails are across on the new tack, head the boat up to 45 degrees from the wind. You will be in the same position as if you had tacked. It just takes longer. |
| If the wind picks up and you can't control the boat. | Let your sails out so they are luffing a little, which will reduce the power and make the boat more controllable. |
| Your jib sheet is jammed or caught in the process of tacking. You can't get the jib across, and it is stuck in the backwind position, threatening to cause a capsize. | Head the boat up into the wind until you can correct the problem. Then back your way onto the new tack, as explained on page 187 in Chapter 14. Any time something breaks or goes wrong, head up into the wind (the neutral position) until you are ready to sail again. |
| You are having difficulty releasing the mainsheet from its cleat in order to dump air when the boat is overpowered by the wind. | You need to adjust the angle of the jaws on your mainsheet cam cleat. The jaws can be angled farther up or down. If they are set so the sheet is very easy to |

| *What's Going Wrong* | *How to Correct It* |
|---|---|
| | cleat, it probably will be difficult to uncleat. |
| Your mainsail is falling down, either because the cleat did not hold or because the halyard has broken. | If you cannot get it to cleat again as designed, tie the halyard to the forward main beam and head for shore. If the halyard is broken, drop the sail completely and sail back under jib alone. This will be easy if you have heeded the advice to stay upwind of your return point. It is nearly impossible to sail upwind on only the jib, so if you have to get upwind without your main, you had best get out your paddle and accept the first offer of a tow. |

# 3

## *THE MAINSAIL*

ALTHOUGH the butterfly-hued mainsails sported by many modern cats catch the fancy of the admiring public and help to sell boats, they are far more than just so much pretty cloth.

The big, all-purpose, ribbed mainsail of the catamaran has been developed over the years into an extremely efficient, versatile, multi-adjustable wind engine that has put the modern cat far above the pioneers in the field. It is a dream come true for the racing sailor.

It wasn't always that way, though. Back in the sixties, when cats were first catching on in this country, the sails were anything but versatile. You had a flat sail or you had a full sail, and you made the best of it.

*This bird's-eye view shows the fullness of the mainsail and the aft location of the draft. (Photo courtesy of Hobie Class Assn.)*

Needless to say, in those days many of the skippers were no more sophisticated or versatile than their sails. Increased knowledge of the boats and improvements in the sails went hand in hand over the years.

Back in the early days, the dominant skippers in most of the classes concentrated on achieving a flat sail, making their best time to the weather mark, and then holding onto what they had for the downhill legs.

They ascribed to the dogma of the day, which was that the weather leg was the glory leg—"That's where you separate the men from the boys."

I might add, they included a fair share of what might be termed "thrill seekers" as well. Many early cat sailors, as today, were not purist sailors as much as they were retired motocross racers, powerboaters, pilots, and other types of converts attracted by the speed and excitement of the boats.

These early Red Barons set their boats up to sail in heavy air. If the wind dropped, they simply did not sail. Or if they did sail, they probably did not fare well.

Sail shape did not seem to be as important to these early cat sailors as was sail size. As long as the sail was flat and cut to the maximum dimensions allowed by the class, they were happy. They wanted all the sail material possible, and if the sail had a nice shape, so much the better.

They left themselves no leeway for downhauling or outhauling the sail to improve shape, because doing so would exceed the measuring bands on the mast or boom.

Heavy air, flat sail. The combination sounds good for going to weather, and it did just that. But that was all it did. Off the wind, these pioneer boats were slow-moving tanks, John Deere tractors of the sea.

But the sailors of the sixties were confident they could hold their fuller-sailed competitors off the wind by means of luffing matches, covering, or some other defensive tactic. They often succeeded. (See diagrams 4 and 5.)

But remember, this was before the era of downwind tacking.

Downwind tacking and the full sail came into the limelight at the same time, hand in hand. The full sail did not do as well going to weather, unless one had light air and/or choppy seas. However, off the wind the full sail could easily blow by the flat sail. Add to the then-newfound tactic of tacking downwind, and the full sail became the dominant sail design in all the fleets. And suddenly the weather leg was not the only one where the men were being separated from the boys.

Still, there were times when the flat sail did not get entirely overwhelmed off the wind. In heavy air and in flat seas, for example, the flat sail could hold on much better off the wind. Those conditions were detrimental to the full sail going to weather. Many a time the flat sail had stretched out a large enough lead on the full sail so that it was impossible for the full sail to catch up.

There they were, flat versus full, in the Super Bowl of cats. And the winner? Quite frankly, no one. You might picture it as the Steelers and the Cowboys playing a seesaw battle to a 0–0 tie. How exciting!

By this time sailmakers were waking up to the needs of these new, fast and crazy boats. They began to experiment with sails that got the best of both worlds. What the winning sailor sought was a flatter sail to weather that would change to a fuller sail off the wind.

One of the first things done was to cut the sail short of the maximum bands on the mast and boom so that the sail could stretch. That stretching process provided flatness for the weather work, and with some quick, on-the-water adjustments, the sail could also develop fullness.

Undercutting the sail may have meant less sail area to some, but to others it meant a more flexible sail, one that could be shaped and molded to their liking.

Then things really began to happen to the equipment:

1. Sails became taller with less roach (high-aspect-ratio sail plans).
2. Masts became more shaped and flexible.
3. Masts were being tapered and overrotated.
4. Mainsheet blocks became more sophisticated and powerful.
5. Geared outhauls and downhauls were added.
6. Battens became more adaptable and less breakable.

All of these things combined to make your boat the speed merchant it is today.

Let's take a look at what some of these devices did.

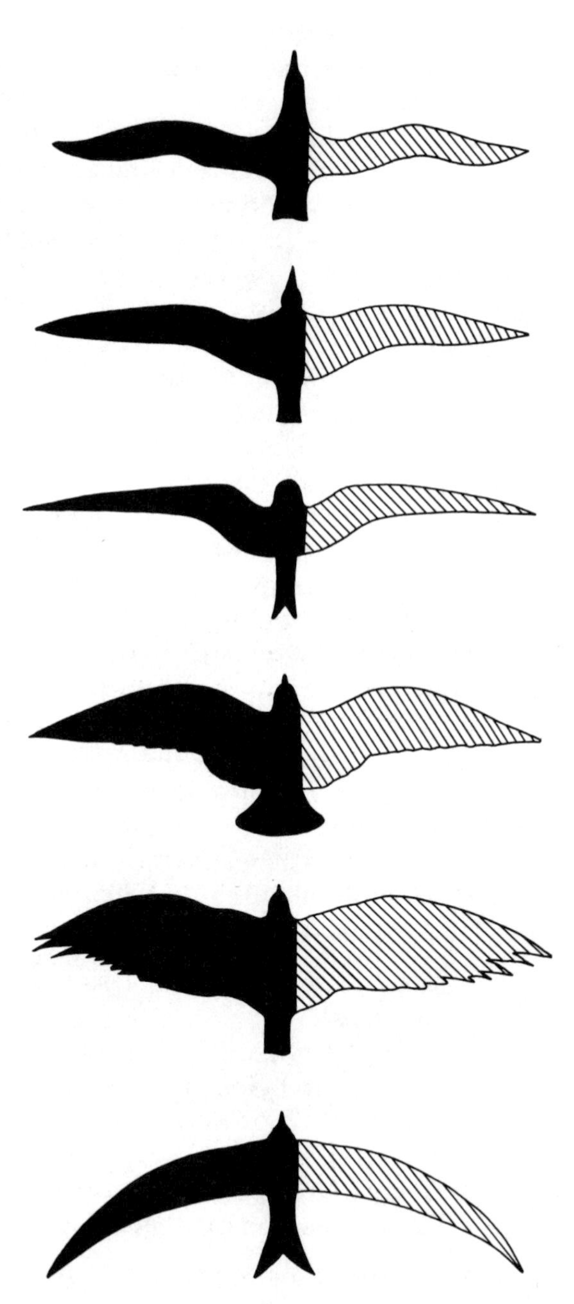

DIAGRAM 4
*Notice the variation in aspect ratio of different types of birds, based on their body size, speed and stability. For an added comparison, turn the drawings clockwise 90 degrees and note the resemblance between the blackened portion of the birds and sailboats.*

DIAGRAM 5
*Note the similarities between a bird's wing and a modern sail.*

The high-aspect-ratio sail plan was an important breakthrough over the old, large-roach, low-aspect ratio. To see why the high-aspect ratio came into being, compare wing designs of some of the best flying birds. (See diagrams 4 and 5.)

The pigeon and the buzzard both have relatively short wing spans, while the measurement from the forepart of the wing to the trailing edge is quite broad. The fore-edge of the wing also is quite thick, and the wing quite arched. These fellows have a sail plan on either side similar to the pioneer cats. These birds soar at slow speeds and have a lot of body weight.

On the other hand, the albatross has a wing span of nearly ten feet with remarkably narrow wings, yet still can carry a relatively large body. The swallow has a wide span and narrow wings. Both of these birds fly at rather high speeds. Their wings have a much greater length than breadth (high-aspect ratio).

Since the cat had already developed much higher speeds than had monohull designs, experiments began with the new, high-aspect-ratio sail plan; results were tremendous.

For example, the Tornado, before it became a one-design class, tested a number of rigs, including a wing mast. The wing was extremely high-aspect-ratio in design and far outperformed the Tornado as we know it today, with its soft rig. Wing masts, however, have thus far proven unsuitable for general use because of their poor handling characteristics while not being sailed. Therefore, the present-day Tornado carries a high-aspect-ratio rig, but a soft, battened sail.

### *THE MAST*

Obviously, a taller sail requires a taller mast. Many classes not only made the masts taller, but also tapered the mast to be smaller at the top than at the base. And the cross-section was more teardrop-shaped than the old-fashioned mast.

In essence, the mast alone is a minisail. Add to that minisail some cloth out the back, as was done to a great many near-pure wing masts, and you are developing a nice shape. It is sort of like adding feathers to the trailing edge of a bird's wing.

Because of its new cross-section and taper, this mast could also be bent at will. And bending takes the fullness out of sails. The masts that were tapered could bend more at the top than those that were not tapered. In heavy air this bend can really flatten out the top of the sail, which has less driving force than the rest of the sail but has a great deal more heeling force.

In other words, you could hold the boat down a lot easier while sacrificing very little in the way of speed.

This bending action of the mast and flattening of the sail can be enhanced by mast rotation. The closer the mast is rotated to 90 degrees, the easier the mast will bend.

People have asked me why a mast should be rotated that far, thinking that the broadside of that fat, teardrop-shaped spar would be trying to push through the wind, offering nothing but wind resistance.

But this is not so. (See diagram 6.) Lay your head right at the base of the mast with your sail rigged and sheeted the way you have had it, and look straight up. You probably will see where the mast–sail junction has an indentation. Slowly pull

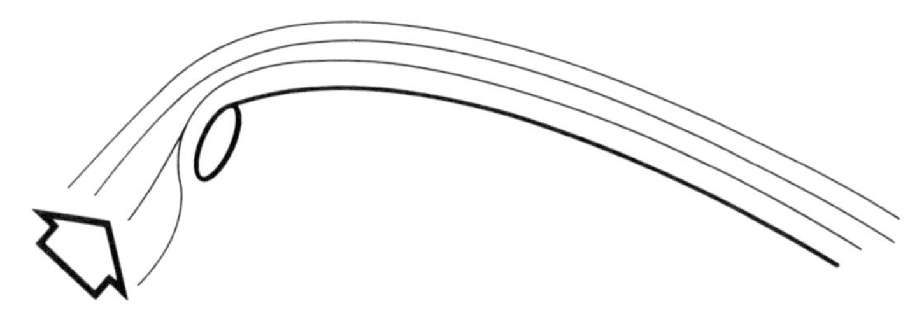

DIAGRAM 6

*In example 1 the mast is rotated almost 90 degrees, allowing a smooth entry and even flow of air on the leeward side of the sail. In example 2 the mast is underrotated, causing an indentation between mast and sail and resulting in turbulence along the leeward side.*

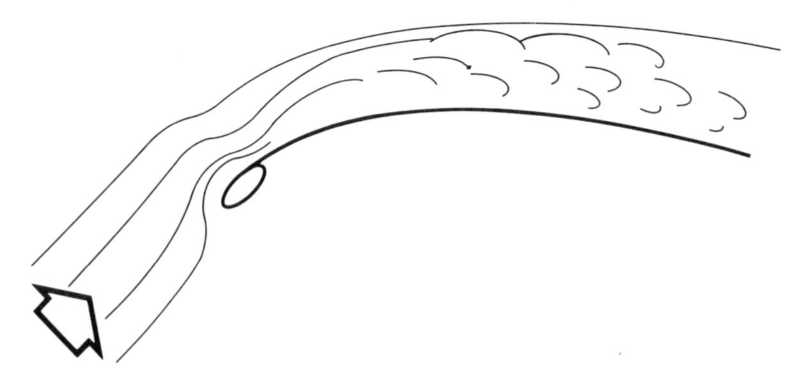

the wishbone around to 90 degrees, and you will see that indentation disappear and notice that suddenly the mast and the sail begin to look like part of one molded wing mast. It also will look like the leading wing edge of a DC-3, an old cargo plane that developed more wing lift than any other airplane.

In the Hobie 18 I just release the mast rotator, as it will not even go as far as 90 degrees, anyway.

## *BLOCKS*

Due to the high-aspect ratio, tall masts, and tall sails, it took a lot more power to pull on the mainsheet than ever before. You needed gorillas or, preferably, 7-to-1 blocks to pull the main in to where it sailed best. Blocks became more and more sophisticated, with more holding power and better cleats.

Blocks became very important also to control outhauls and downhauls. Without good equipment, there would be no way to stretch the new adjustable-type sail to gain the flatness you want to weather, or the fullness downwind.

By use of heavy downhaul procedures, one can actually bend the mast to create sail flatness. The outhaul is an extremely important piece of machinery to get the sail flat for the weather leg.

## *BATTENS*

Battens became a controversial variable at one time because of the many experimental battens on the market and the variety you could create in your own back yard. However, most classes now have settled down to a few types and allow only one maufacturer.

Battens are still an important means of shaping your stock sail. Flexible battens, when jammed in good and tight, can make a pretty full sail and, when loosened, can make a fairly flat sail.

Battens have undergone their own little evolution, and a chapter has been devoted to them later in this book.

## *FLAT-FULL, ALL ROLLED UP IN ONE*

With the birth of the high-aspect-ratio sail came the all-around, versatile sail. Wahoo! From the starting line to the "A" mark you have a flat sail. For a beam reach, just easing the mainsheet allows the top of the sail to twist off to reduce heeling moment and keep the main driving down below. Downwind, just release the outhaul and you still have a downhill screamer, ALL in our modern sail plan.

The new beach boats and catamarans of all kinds have

*With both sailors on the trapeze, the boat still wants to fly a hull, so the skippers in the foreground have eased their mainsheets, allowing a noticeable twist off the top of the sail. This technique reduces the heeling moment while keeping the driving power of the sail down low where it is most effective. (Photo courtesy of Prindle Class Assn.)*

come up to these standards. So when you buy a new catamaran, you can be fairly confident you are getting a sail with an all-purpose cut that you can adapt to your needs.

## *CHOOSING A SAIL THAT'S RIGHT FOR YOU*

If you have a choice in your sail selection, as is allowed in some classes, choose a full, flat, or medium cut, depending on such things as crew weight, waters in which you normally sail, and general wind conditions.

For example, if the combined weight of skipper and crew is heavy, choose a fuller sail; light, a flatter sail. If you will be sailing on flat inland seas, a flatter sail should do better; if a choppy sea area, you may need a fuller sail. As for wind, if you sail in an area of steady high winds, you want a flatter sail; but if yours is an area of little air, a fuller sail should do nicely.

You can use White's Three W's Formula (see Chapter 7) in selecting a sail, just as you do in determining desired sail shape for specific conditions.

Hobie sails may be purchased only from Hobie or an authorized dealer if you wish to compete, so you have no choice in that class.

Keep in mind that when I say "full" or "flat" sails, I am speaking relatively; we are seeking the truly versatile boat.

The way you sail a boat is also a determining factor in sail selection. If you are the super helmsman, never missing a shift, navigating that fine line like a tightrope walker, you may get away with a bit flatter sail than would otherwise be called for. But if you are like the rest of us and make helmsmanship errors, a bit on the full side helps to forgive some mistakes.

A flatter sail will take a little longer to get cranked back up after a tack. The flat sail is for fast sailing, but the boat needs power (full sail) to get moving to speed again. It takes good sheeting technique with a flat sail to be sure you get it going fast again after a tack. The fuller sail will get you moving considerably quicker.

## *MOLDING YOUR MAINSAIL*

You have your sail, whether custom ordered or the one that came with your boat. Now you must bend it to your will, shape it to your needs.

The first step is to determine whether you need a full or flat sail (relatively speaking) for the conditions in which you will be racing.

There is an axiom: *Flat sail going to weather and a very full sail off the wind.* But there are variables to that axiom based upon wind conditions, water conditions, and weight (with an added factor thrown in for helmsmanship, boat handling, and crew abilities). The method of determining what shape sail you want for the varying conditions is completely explained in Chapter 7 of this book.

Once you have made the decision on the sail shape needed, here are the methods for achieving that shape:

### FLATTENING A FULL SAIL

When you have a sail that is on the full side and you want it flattened, some things must be done ashore, while other measures can be completed while sailing.

To start with, you may flatten the sail ashore by using stiffer battens. (Some classes, such as Hobie, do not allow you to change to different battens during a regatta.) If you are trying to flatten the sail mainly for heavy air, just use stiff battens in the top panels.

What you are after is to get the sail very flat at the top, so that when you ease the mainsheet, only the top of the sail will spill off with a twist, allowing the lower part of the sail to continue driving you. You are reducing heeling moment, yet maintaining the powerful drive in the lower section of the sail, where there is far less heeling moment.

Keep in mind, however, that when you are sailing downwind, the battens will remain stiff and the sail flat; you could get creamed. Also, if the air lets up and your soft battens are back on the beach, consider this race your throwout. In other words, the stiff, heavy-air battens are good only for heavy-air conditions.

If you are in a class where battens may not be substituted (as in the Hobie class), easing the batten tensions will have a big effect on flattening the sail, as this allows some relief to the leech.

If it were my decision, I would much rather have a sail on the fuller side and not try to make it too flat ashore. It just becomes too irrevocable.

Still more shore duty to flatten the sail would be to ease the diamond wires. The diamond stays control the lower two-thirds of the mast's ability to bend. When the mast is

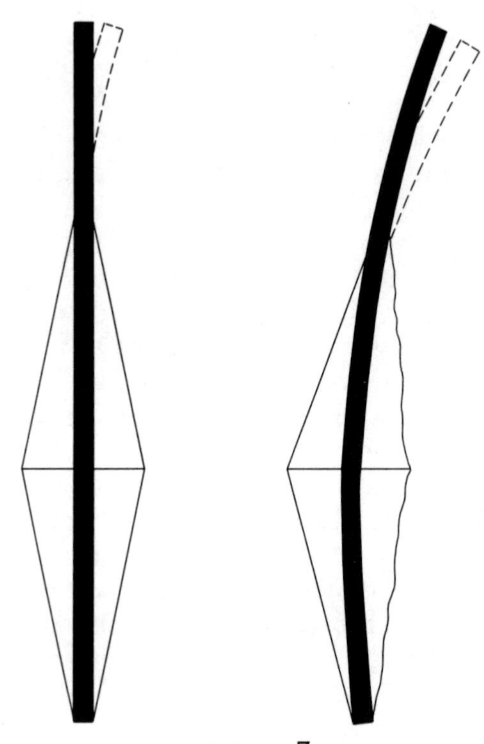

DIAGRAM 7

*In drawing 1, with tight diamond wires the lower third of the mast will stay straight, giving you a fuller sail. However, by rotating closer to 90 degrees, the top of the mast may bend, flattening the top of the sail.*
*In drawing 2, with slack diamonds, the lower third of the mast will bend, taking up the fullness from the sail material, giving you a flatter sail. By rotating the mast closer to 90 degrees, the top of the mast will also bend, flattening the top of the sail.*

rotated and the leeward staywire is tight, the mast will bend only a little, as the staywire stops it from bending.

If the stay is loose, it still allows the mast to bend only to the point where the stay will stop it, but there will be a great deal more bend than with the tight diamond stays.

Extremely loose diamond stays will permit a big mast bend.

As the mast bends out, it absorbs sail cloth from the draft of the sail and thereby makes a full sail become flatter. If the mast bends only a little, the sailcloth stays in the draft of the sail and you have a full sail.

The diamond wires should definitely be tightened or slackened equally on each side, or you will find the boat goes better on one tack than the other.

However, if you are setting up the sail specifically for sailing heavy air and choppy seas, you may find you need the power down low, as earlier mentioned; and, therefore, you do not want the diamonds loosened. You do want the top of your sail very flat.

(The last shore job is not necessarily for making the sail flatter, but can be useful in setting up for heavy air: You may want to rake the mast aft. This will be dealt with in great detail in Chapter 6, "Mast Rake.")

Now you are on the water, and you are ready for the first weather leg; you want to flatten the sail. My first thought runs toward the outhaul. Though the outhaul flattens the bottom batten probably too much, it has a definite effect on the lower two-thirds of the sail in general, and for a flat sail it should be brought out.

As mentioned before, the downhaul, when really honked down, will bend the mast and help flatten the sail. A good way to really get it tight is to have your crew jump on it while you go head to wind and really crank down on the mainsheet.

The third thing you can do on the water is to allow overrotation of the mast. The closer you rotate the mast to 90 degrees, the more it is allowed to bend. Obviously, the more it bends, the more luff and sail material will be absorbed by the bend, thereby creating a flatter sail.

### MAKING A FLAT SAIL FULLER

Let us now assume that you have a flat sail and wish to make it fuller. Again, let us first do what we must ashore.

At this point you do not want those stiff battens that we

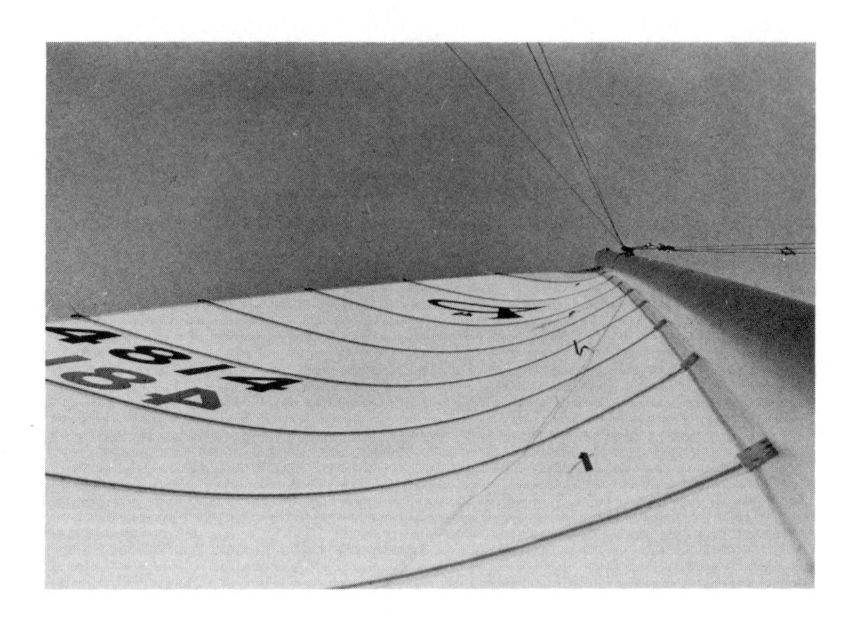

*The same sail with different sheet tension. Above, light sheet tension and a fairly straight mast result in a relatively full sail. Below, with more sheet tension, the mast is bent more and the sail becomes much flatter. (Photo by Rick White.)*

have been talking about. You want light, limber battens, and you want them shoved in fairly hard. However, be careful the battens do not poke holes through the luff of the sail. Make sure the sail is reinforced very well for this procedure. A few times I have seen a competitor with a batten mounted arrow-like across the spar, nearly ready for flight.

Take care not to tighten the battens so much that you get a scalloped effect, making your sail look like a washboard. The surface of the sail should be smooth, free of batten ridges.

The next procedure is to tighten diamond stays, giving the lower two-thirds of the spar less ability to flex, therefore allowing the fullness of the sail to stay there for your use.

The last duty ashore is not necessarily related to making the sail fuller. You may want to rake the mast more perpendicular. Again, we will deal with this in Chapter 6, "Mast Rake."

Now you are ready again for the water action. If at the last moment you decide you need a flatter sail, no problem, as the sail is inherently flat. But let us assume you still want it full. Easing the mainsail outhaul on the boom will give you a fuller sail on its lower two-thirds. Do not release it too much, however, as the fullness down below will allow the slot to be easily choked off by the jib.

Your downhaul need not be tensioned a great deal. Just make sure you take the wrinkles out of the sail.

Mast rotation could be less than on the previous sail with which we worked. The closer you turn the mast to 90 degrees, the more the mast will bend and the more the sail will flatten. Since we are trying to get a little fuller sail here, you might want to stop the rotator at around 60 degrees. Then the mast cannot bend as much, and the sail will be fuller.

However, there is controversy on mast rotation; and some sailors, myself included, always rotate to 70–90 degrees, preferring to give up a little fullness in order to keep a smooth entry into the wind, without any indentation between the mast and leeward side of the sail.

*SUMMARY*

| *For Flatter Sail* | *For Fuller Sail* |
| --- | --- |
| tighten downhaul | ease downhaul |
| tighten outhaul | ease outhaul |
| stiff battens | soft battens |
| loosen battens | tighten battens |
| loosen diamond stays | tighten diamond stays |
| rotate toward 90 degrees | rotate nearer to 60 degrees |

Any or all of the above measures may be used. There may be times when you just do not have enough time on the beach to accomplish everything that must be done, so get the major shore changes made and use on-the-water measures to correct the rest as best you can.

At this point we have gained great versatility in the sails of the modern catamaran, a versatility which is needed to exact the ultimate performance from the boat.

In my Hobie 18 I can definitely make the sail as flat or as full as I want it. Sometimes, however, I set up for a flat sail and need something else. Pilot error is still with us at all times.

The concept of getting your sail flat, full, or anything in between is now with us. We have the tools to achieve the flatness or fullness desired, but when to use each of these tools is a matter of even greater import. Consequently, Chapter 7 on my Three W's Formula becomes a very valuable one.

# 4

## *BATTENS*

TIME and experience have taught us that a sail with a full draft is superior in light air, chop, or with heavy boat weight; while a flat sail is preferred for heavy winds, flat seas, and light weight.

This again is confirmed by our feathered friends. The slow-flying, heavier birds have the fuller wings, while the swiftest-flying birds have much flatter wings.

Birds are stuck with what nature gave them, but a sailboat has no such limitation. It is for this reason that sailors in many monohull classes have a sail for every reason and every season. Thus, just before a race a major decision must be made: What sail do we use? Flat? Full? Moderate?

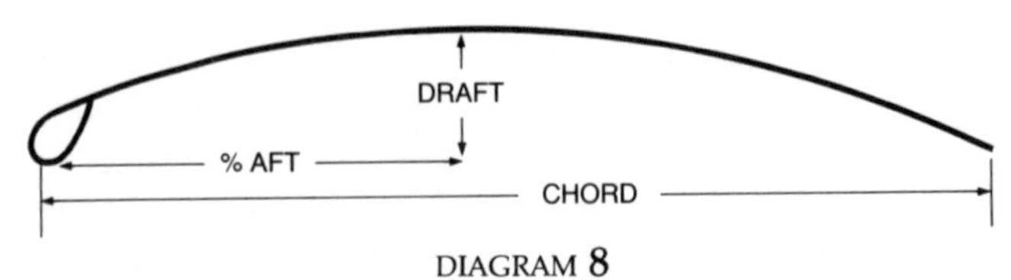


DIAGRAM 8
*A visual definition of the commonly-used terms "draft," "percentage aft," and "chord."*

In modern times it was not until the development of the catamaran that someone asked the proper question: "Why not use a sail with a changeable draft?"

The Egyptians and Chinese have been using full-length battens for centuries. They knew even back in ancient times that full-length battens give you: (1) uniform draft over the entire sail and where you want it; (2) a somewhat rigid surface, unchanged by apparent wind; and (3) the potential to change the sail at will to match the prevailing circumstances (such as outlined in White's Three W's Formula—see Chapter 7).

While the fully battened sails developed by the ancients have changed little over the centuries, it appears that catamaran sailors are the first to fully explore the potential of full-length battens and use them to get the most possible speed and power out of a sail.

Full-length battens not only improve the performance of the sail, they also make it possible to do without an arsenal of different sails for different conditions. Battens allow drafts to be moved forward or aft at will, simply by planing battens thinner at the areas you want to bend. Making your sail fuller by using light battens or flatter with stiff battens is a much cheaper manner of dealing with sail shape than changing sails.

Of course, a still cheaper, although poorer, way to deal with varying conditions is to either tighten or loosen the tie-in tension to make your sail fuller or flatter.

As for the practical side of battens in your boat, you probably will want a lighter batten for most occasions. Sailors who end up with stiff battens, either by accident or on purpose, have less variance or changeability in their sails than do sailors who have the lighter or more flexible battens.

For all-around use, flexible battens seem to work better, because they are more diverse. When you want a full sail, you simply tie them in tighter, and it is easier to acquire that fullness you desire. When you want the sail flatter, you just loosen them (making sure there are no wrinkles in the sail), and you have a flatter sail.

The stiffer batten will not allow you to get much fullness in the sail, even though you may really be cranking on the batten ties.

A good way to measure a batten's flexibility is to determine the number of pounds of pressure it takes to bend it when you are holding one end of the batten and pressing the other end against a solid object. At home the bathroom scale works nicely—just hold the batten vertically over the scale and press until the batten bends. (You may have to stand on a chair to reach the upper end of the longer battens; holding it in the middle will not give you an accurate resistance reading.) Once the batten bends, the poundage reading may even lighten up, but you are concerned with the initial resistance poundage.

Most people do not have a bathroom scale with them at the beach when they are working with their sails. My solution to this problem was to purchase a fisherman's scale for weighing fish. It is a pocket-sized gadget with a hook and weight scale. Just hook it to the top of the batten, stand the batten up straight, pull down on the scale until the batten bends, and read the poundage.

Knowing your battens' resistance poundage doesn't solve all your problems. You have to decide what is light and what is heavy; and if yours aren't what you want, you have to do something about that. At one point in my sailing history, I thought 6 pounds was light in flexibility; I now believe that 3 pounds is far better. Take into consideration that fiberglass battens grow stiffer with age. What may be a light batten this year may be a heavy batten a couple of years later.

Even if you have bought a stock boat, don't just assume your battens are like everyone else's. Always check the resistance poundage and check to make sure they are pretapered (as most are).

I noticed that in the Hobie class, where you may use only Hobie battens, the battens have not been consistently uniform in flexibility or in tapering. At one regatta we all sat around measuring batten poundages. They varied from 3 pounds to 12 pounds. Guess who had been doing the worst in the regatta. You win if you guessed the 12-pound battens.

Hobies are now delivered with tapered battens. They taper the second, third, fourth, and fifth battens from the top. The rest are left untapered. The tapering begins at a distance back from the mast about equal to the length of the top batten, and from that point the batten tapers down to a smaller thickness at the mast.

There is probably nothing significantly wrong with the way Hobie sails are delivered. In the class, you do have the privilege of changing the taper of your battens if you so desire. The reason the lower part of the sail's battens are not tapered is to keep that portion of the sail a bit flatter where the jib overlaps, so there is less possibility of backwinding the mainsail.

If you wish to do tapering yourself, the cheapest, easiest way is to use an old, who-cares knife. Hold it perpendicular to the batten and shave. The knife will dull quickly, so just keep one of those quick kitchen sharpeners handy and hit the blade with it whenever needed.

When tapering battens, keep in mind that you may want the draft in your battens a little closer to the mast than where you want the draft in your sail. No matter where you taper for maximum draft, the draft probably will move aft from that position when the mainsail is sheeted in.

A great many battens have been and still are being made that, because of the way they are constructed, cannot be tapered; or else they are already tapered for you and modifications cannot be made. The laminated, foam-filled type cannot be modified. They are excellent for some sails because they are lightweight, flexible, and not easily broken.

The location of the draft has been a controversial subject

for years. In birds, 33 percent is normal, but in boats the draft may vary to as far back as 50 percent. Remember that while your boat is on shore, not performing, a draft may be at 35 percent, but when sheeted in with the wind in the sails, the draft may be blown 5 to 10 percent farther back.

The advancement in battens over the last twenty years has been phenomenal, and it is difficult to believe there will be much more improvement. Right now, in our science of sailing, we would be hard pressed to ask for more from the battens.

# 5

## *THE JIB*

THOSE of us who have been in sailboat racing for a while know the proper term for the foresail is "the damn jib." It has perhaps acquired this undeserved nickname because it is the more challenging of the two sails to control.

While it is not the most important and powerful, the jib can either tremendously aid the performance of the main or render it ineffective.

Just as behind every great man there is a great woman, in front of every great main there is a great jib. And the jib has a much more important function than just filling up that empty space between the mast and the forestay.

In the development of the modern-day jib, man took a tip

*This Nacra 5.2 needs to have the jib barberhauled to a position farther away from the mainsail. While the top of the jib is twisting off nicely to conform to the main, the foot of the jib appears to be pinching back into the main. (Photo courtesy of NACRA)*

*Looking from aft and leeward, you can see this boat's slot is open and the top of the jib has a slight twist off the top, as does the mainsail. (Photo courtesy of the Prindle Class Assn.)*

from Mother Nature. She has donated to us a great deal of knowledge that can be applied to sailing, just as it is to flying. We have simply to observe birds and insects with their varieties of wing styles and flying techniques. Sailing, after all, is merely flying on a vertical plane rather than a horizontal plane.

So what does this have to do with the jib? Birds possess on their forewings a small, narrow leading wing, more fully developed on some than on others. Birds of prey generally have much larger leading wings. A great many insects also have this overlapping leading wing.

The most obvious example is the eagle, whose leading wing is quite well developed and thereby easy to study. At closer look, this leading, conducting wing could be compared easily to the thumb of your hand. Man must have observed this wing section for years, not knowing quite what it was or what it did. But since the eagle is a near-perfect wind utilizer, this leading wing section had to serve some purpose. Man's observation of this characteristic has had an important impact on both sailing and flying. (See diagram 9.)

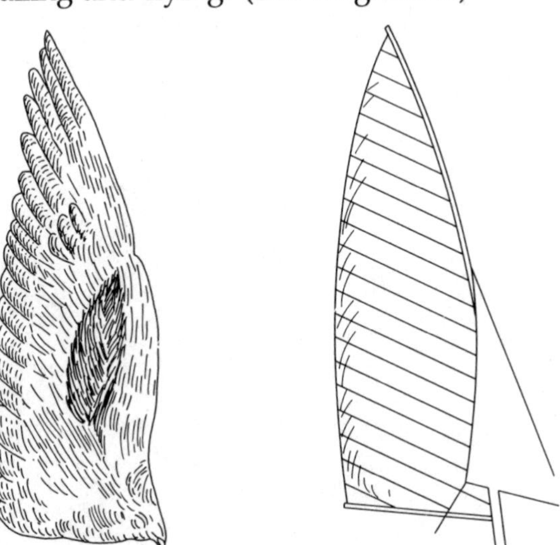

DIAGRAM 9

*There is amazing similarity between a bird wing and the modern sail plan.*

DIAGRAM 10
*This is a wing cross-section of a Handley-Page biplane.*

Aircraft have been using the leading wing effect for nearly as long as planes have flown. In the 1920s such airplanes as the Handley-Page and the Lachmann both had pre-wing sections. (See diagram 10.) In the modern STOL craft (short takeoff and landing) and in modern jet airliners, a preceding wing is cranked out for takeoffs and landings. The mechanical birds that now fill the skies are all in effect using a jib.

The purpose of this leading wing is the same, whether it

DIAGRAM 11
*Drawing 1 shows a cat-rigged boat, and drawing 2 is the same boat with a jib added. Note the difference in the air circulation patterns on the two sails, as indicated by the arrows. The even, aft flow across the mainsail in drawing 2 is caused by the slot effect of the jib.*

is on a bird, an insect, an airplane, or a sailboat. In all cases, it is acting as a jib.

The purpose of the jib on a sailboat is to create an accelerated flow of air across the leeward side of the mainsail. (See diagram 11.) That appears to be its only job. It is a complementary sail to the main and is never to be treated as a primary. The bird cannot fly on its small leading wing, nor could a Boeing or Douglass take off on its leading wing. The jib is there only to make the mainsail more efficient.

Just as the leading wing gives a bird or an airplane more lift, so it gives a sailboat more "lift," which in this case translates into motion forward rather than upward.

## *HOW THE JIB HELPS*

Most of you know why a sailboat is able to go forward through the water. In simple terms, the wind flows more rapidly across the convex curve of the leeward side of the sail than it does over the windward side. This difference in airspeed causes a lower or negative atmospheric pressure on the leeward side of the mainsail. The sail is sucked into this negative pressure area. But because its hull shape or its daggerboards prevent the boat from sliding sideways, it is instead "sucked" forward through the water.

The jib's function is to increase the velocity of the air across the leeward side of the main, thereby increasing suction and the consequent forward speed of the boat.

This increased velocity of air is achieved through a valve effect. Wind striking the concave side of the jib is forced to compress and thereby speed up as it forces its way through the comparatively narrow slot between the jib and the mainsail.

Some might argue that the jib-slot flow would eliminate or blow away the negative pressure developed on the leeward side of the main and thereby reduce the suction that pulls the boat along.

To better understand the situation, look at drawings A and B in diagram 12. Figure A, a cat-rigged sail plan, shows

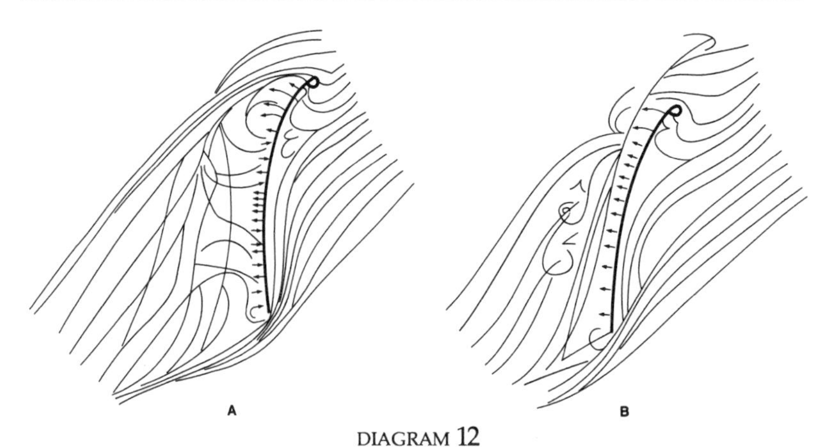


DIAGRAM 12
*Diagram A shows a cat-rigged boat and the wind's actions upon its sail. Diagram B shows the same sail with a jib added.*

the action of wind eddies on the leeward side of the mainsail, which involves two sets of forces: One is the negative pressure or suction (indicated by the arrows pointing to the left); the other, the retarding forces or returning eddies of air (the arrows pointing to the right) on the leeward side of the main.

Drawing B is the same sail with a jib added. Now the air currents take on a totally different pattern. In this drawing the return eddies (arrows pointing to the right) are nearly nonexistent, and the wind flows through the slot, down the leeward side of the mainsail, toward the leech.

What is happening is that the retarding flow of returning eddies is stopped from reaching the leeward side of the mainsail by the current of air off the windward side of the jib and across the leeward side of the mainsail. However, the negative pressure forces that are coming off the main are not at all influenced by the air flow off the jib. Only the hindering return eddies are blown away.

The funnel, or slot, has contracted or jetted the air between the two sails and increased the velocity between them; so actually, the negative forces are even greater; and the main will be sucked into the vacuum with even greater force. In other words, the greater the velocity of this current of air

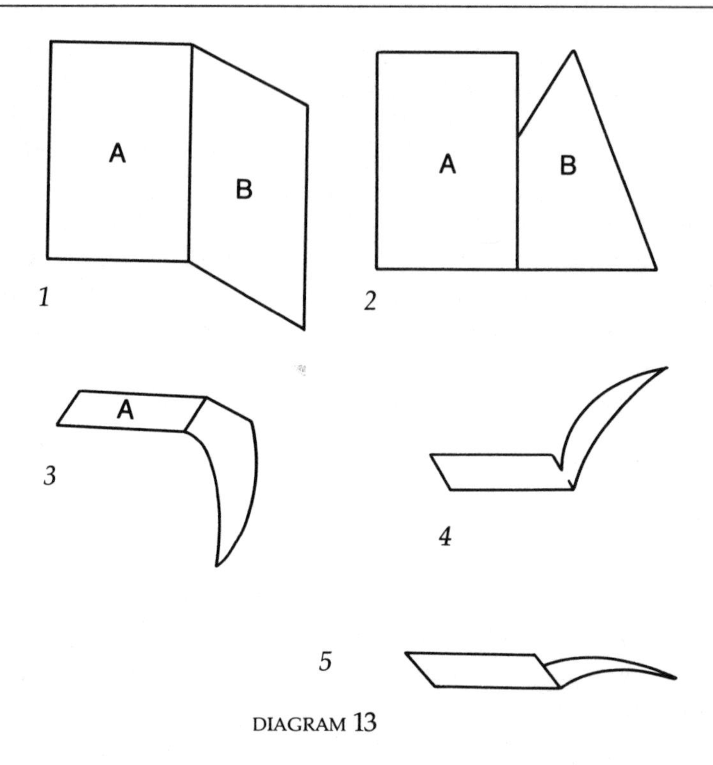


DIAGRAM 13

between the sails, the less atmospheric pressure and thus the greater the negative pressure.

For proof of the suction theory, try this very simple, easy-to-do experiment. (See diagram 13.)

Take a piece of heavy writing paper and fold it in the middle (drawing 1). Cut one side in the form of a sail (drawing 2). Bend the sail side around your finger until it is shaped somewhat like your catamaran sail, arched with a nice draft. Now, so that it will swing easier, with the tip of the scissors, perforate along the fold by punching small holes (drawing 3).

Hold paper part I directly in front of your lips horizontally and blow along its upper side. You will see that part 2 (the sail) moves upward dramatically, toward the air current (drawing 4).

If you wish, you may hold the paper vertically as it would be on your boat, but holding it horizontally proves even stronger the forces of negative pressure or "suck" that lifted the paper.

In this experiment you have been creating an air current across the leeward side of your sail. Now, if you blow on the *under* side of part 1, or the windward size of the sail, it will only lift up to the horizontal plane, not beyond (drawing 5).

This simple demonstration, designed by Dr. Manfred Curry, should prove to you:

1. The correctness of the theory of suction.
2. The tremendous effect of the wind off the jib (simulated by your blowing across the upper side of part I or across the leeward side of the sail), which accelerates the air current over the lee side of the main, thereby increasing the lift of the mainsail.

Understanding this jib-and-main relationship is not all that difficult, but the practical application of it may be elusive and difficult.

Again, you are trying to form a valve action: a wide opening in the front and a small opening in the back, creating a jet stream of air. The problem here is that the valve can easily be adjusted incorrectly. If the setting for the small aft opening (the slot) is too loose or too tight, the phenomenon is hindered or even destroyed.

If the jib is set too tight in relation to the mainsail, it will throw a stream of air directly into the leeward side of the main, causing tremendous backwinding and turbulence, totally choking off the main. If the setting is too loose, you are not gaining the maximum pressure available across the leeward side of the mainsail.

Keep in mind that whatever the main does, so should the jib, to complement the power of the main. Although the jib is out front all the time, it definitely is not the leader in determining sail shape. It must always be the faithful copycat of the mainsail. To get maximum benefit from the jib and the slot

*Even off the wind the two sails should take on a similar configuration. As the main twists off, so should the jib. If the jib were to be brought in tighter, it would choke off the efficiency of the mainsail. (Photo courtesy of Hobie Class Assn.)*

effect, wherever goeth the main, so goeth the jib.

If the main should be twisting off at the top, so should the jib. Whether it is a beat to windward, a beam reach, or even a broad reach, if the main is set at a given angle to the wind, the jib should be set at the same angle and conform to the main's shape.

The jib is a complementary sail and, if not set the same, will hinder the power of the main, destroying what the mainsail is trying to provide.

If you were to look at the leech of the jib in its perfectly trimmed position, you would see it taking the same shape as the mainsail at the point where the jib leech overlaps the main. Obviously, if the belly of the main is very full at the point where the two sails overlap, then the jib should be very full at that point. If the main is flat, the jib should be, too.

## JIB LEAD PLACEMENT

Tension on the jib sheet is obviously part of the mechanism for achieving proper jib shape. But equally important is placement of your jib leads (the points on the boat from which you loosen or tighten the sail from its clew point by means of the jib sheet).

There are some age-old theories on jib lead placements. And there are some "ironclad" rules. I would suggest, however, that these are not so much rules as they are starting points to find where indeed you must set your lead to get the most power from your jib and the best contour to complement the main.

One rule is to take one half the angle at the clew (see diagram 14) and extend a line down through the clew to the deck. That setting should give you equal pull on both the foot and the leech.

But that may not be what we want. A good deal of our sailing demands us to have the leech fall off or have the top twist off. To do this we must sheet on the foot more than the leech. Therefore, that particular rule does not quite answer all the questions.

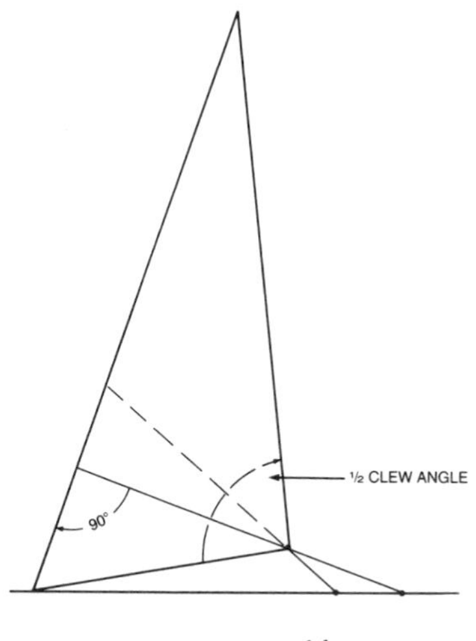


DIAGRAM 14

*The jib lead is attached to the cable slightly inboard. The barber hauler is not tensioned and so the pull on the jib is directly from the ratchet block. (Photo by Rick White)*

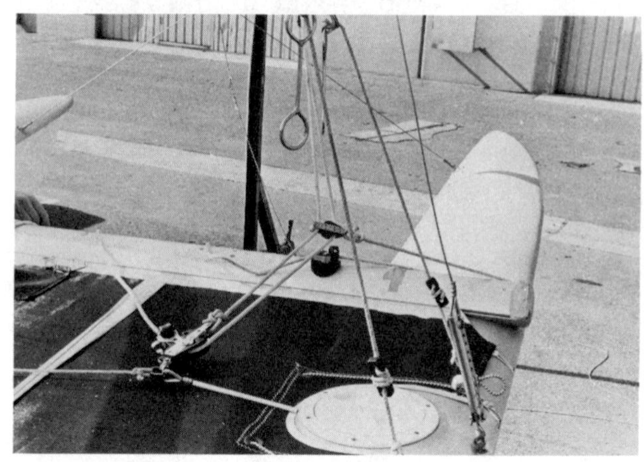

*The barberhauler is partially tensioned, making the effective pull on the jib somewhat outboard from the ratchet block. (Photo by Rick White)*

*The barberhauler is fully tensioned, pulling on the jib from the gunwale of the boat, rather than the ratchet block. (Photo by Rick White)*

The second rule is to measure a line at a 90-degree angle from the luff wire, draw a line from there through the clew, and the extension of that line is where the jib lead should be placed. (This may not be possible if the sail has a radical cut or the forestay has a radical angle.) With this rule you should be pulling harder on the foot of the sail, allowing the leech to be looser and thereby falling off more.

Of the two rules, I would lean toward the latter, preferring to err on the side of the leech that is too loose rather than have one that is too tight. A backwinded mainsail will perform very poorly, and a tight leech will cause just that.

The bad and sad thing about backwinding is that you do not always know it is happening until it is too late—as your competitors who are not being backwinded disappear over the horizon. You simply will not go as fast, but there will be no apparent reason.

You probably have read or heard that you can tell you are backwinding the main if the cloth section near the mast is luffing or the mast is counterrotating. But by the time you have noticed these symptoms of backwinding, you are already disastrously backwinded.

Even the slightest backwinding can slow your boat, and slight backwinding gives no clue. The mainsail telltales will be streaming back because there is still the flow of air across its leeward side. The sailcloth along the mast will not show signs of luffing, and your mast will not radically counterrotate. If your backwinding is so severe as to give visible signs, you are far beyond being in trouble—you are in the tank.

Sometimes understanding a theory can make the practical application easier. Perhaps it is now more obvious why the jib block or sheeting point on the boat can be so critical.

## RESTRICTED CAT CLASSES

In a good many classes, including the Hobies, you are restricted by the factory-installed travelers, with class rules that outlaw any modifications for inhauling, barberhauling, or "trash hauling" (which I have seen in some cases back in the experimental days of the Tornado).

First let's talk about the restricted cat classes. The setting of the jib lead should be directed by the presented theory: Do not choke off the slot, and do not slow down the power of the jet stream by allowing the sail to fall off away from the lee of the mainsail too much.

For example, on the Hobie 18 the jib leads should rarely be set forward in beating to the weather mark. The only time you need to place them forward is off the wind in heavy air (when you do not want your crew weight on the leeward side, where the crew would normally be holding the jib by hand).

In my opinion, the Hobie 18 travelers are not far enough aft to give much of a variable in jib lead placement. You are really restricted on this boat. In heavy air the placement should be far back, allowing the leech as much of an opening as possible, because in heavier air it is much easier to backwind the mainsail than in light air. As the air lightens, you may move the lead forward, but not past the halfway mark on the traveler track.

Off the wind, you want your jib leads forward and outboard, far beyond the limits of most travelers. On some boats this is done with the help of barberhaulers. On other boats, such as the Hobie 18, barberhaulers are not allowed.

The best substitute is your crew, who, while hand-holding the jib clew, is usually sitting in just the proper position (forward and on the leeward side of the boat) to view the entire leech and its complementary relationship to the mainsail.

*Note:* Make sure your crew does not sit right in the slot, as this simply acts as a wind brake right smack in the middle of your slot's jet stream.

The Hobie 16 has an inboard-outboard traveler but no fore-aft adjustment per se for the jib leads. The same effect can be achieved, however, depending on which of several holes the jib sheet is attached to on the clew plate. Again, the same theories apply when determining the best setting.

While going to weather sometime, have your crew take the helm. Lie with your head in the middle of the trampoline and look at how the leech configuration fits the mainsail.

Move the lead around with your hand and play with different settings. You may come up with some ideas to allow the jib to better complement the mainsail.

Many of the hot Hobie 16 sailors recommend the jib traveler be set all the way inboard for weather work, with a slight easing of the sheet to be sure there is no backwinding, and perhaps allowing a little twist off the top of the sail when necessary.

### NONRESTRICTED CLASSES

On to the boats with no restriction on the jib settings. Try the same thing as with the Hobie 16, lying down on the trampoline or deck and hand-holding the jib while going to weather. See where it best complements the mainsail, and then simply rig your boat to place your jib lead in that position.

And "simply" should be the word to remember. What is not advisable is a bunch of inhaul, outhaul, and barberhaul lines running all over the decks. The simple way is the best way. As the inverse of Murphy's Law might dictate, "The less that can go wrong, the less that will go wrong."

Rigging a simple jib lead setting can be quite creative. Since most boats have trampoline decks in this day and age, you cannot merely bolt something to a deck. But plastic-covered cable is available that can be strung from hull to hull in any position you desire.

Another form of placement is a plastic or noncorrosive metal reinforcement, sewn under the trampoline, onto which you can bolt your jib lead. You would actually be sheeting right from the trampoline.

For the most part, you will find that the different wind conditions create different lead placement requirements. So you will want to allow for some type of traveler or movement for your jib lead setting.

You probably will find that when the leads are set aft for going to weather, you also will want them to come more inboard. As the leads go forward when you are sailing more off the wind, you will tend to want them also to go outboard.

You can rig up a nice traveler to do this trick, and you will find it pays big dividends on a beam reach, as you can run it forward and outboard at the same time. Just the ticket!

### *LUFF CONTROL*

Luff control is the most obvious adjustment of the jib and certainly must not be overlooked. The tension on the luff along the forestay, when tightened, causes the draft of the jib to move forward, with a somewhat flattening effect. When the luff tension is loosened, the draft is allowed to move aft, giving the sail a somewhat fuller effect.

The degree of tension required can be related directly to White's Three W's Formula, as discussed in Chapter 7. Therefore, in heavy air (flat sail), flat seas (flat sail), and lightweight crew (flat sail), you should have a tight luff control. For those same conditions, jib leads should be set aft.

If the case calls for a fuller sail, the luff tension should be eased and the jib leads may move forward, as long as they do not cause a backwinding situation.

Ideally, the luff tension should be changed as you go around the race course. Off the wind, the luff should be let off to the point just before it wrinkles; then, upon approaching the "C" mark, tightened to give better weather performance.

However, in most classes changes of this nature are next to impossible. For example, on the Hobie 18 you must be an acrobat with a death wish to climb out on that thin, slippery bow to make such an adjustment, even while just sitting still. Picture yourself doing that in race conditions. Therefore, most of us set the luff control basically for going to weather and just live with it downwind.

Set your luff tight enough so that when sheeted and going to weather in a given wind condition there are no scallops along the luff, but so that at the same time, when you are sailing downwind, the luff is still allowed to fall off and be free without an uncooperative bend or vertical wrinkle.

For you lucky souls who have the availability of adjust-

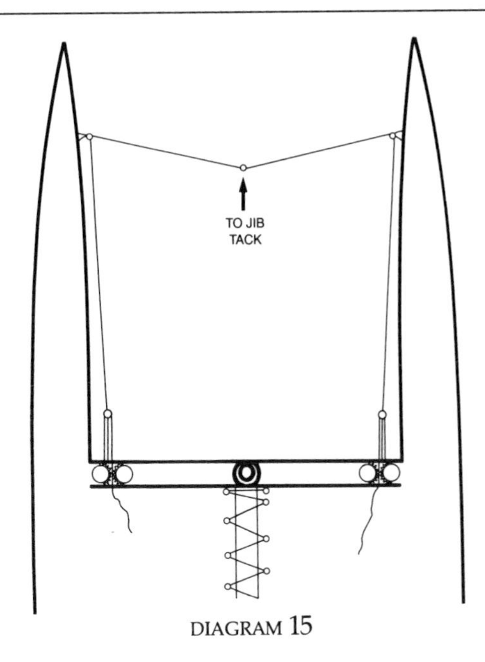


DIAGRAM 15

ment on the race course, use it if you can. If you presently do not have a cockpit-operated luff tensioner in your boat and your class allows it, then by all means install one.

There are two basic types: halyard and downhaul. The halyard type allows the sail to be set permanently at its lowest position and then tensioned off the top of the jib pulley and controlled from one spot on the mast.

The downhaul-type tensioner can usually be set up to control from both sides of the boat (making it easier to get to) but will change the sail set. That is, it will lower the entire sail, including the clew, thereby changing your jib lead setting.

A good way to set up the latter system is to run a cable forward from the main beam on each side of the boat. You should have a three-to-one purchase line to the cable, and a cleat on each side. The cable then should run through a pulley located on the bow at the attachment point for the forestay bridle. From there the cable should come up to the jib tack attachment point and be attached in such a way that it will downhaul the jib. (See diagram 15.)

*SHEETING*

Although we have talked on and off about sheeting, just to be sure, let's go over it as a subject in itself.

Going to weather is where you are most likely to find problems with sheeting. Or you may have problems and never find out what they are unless you understand the crucial difference that can be made by one click on the ratchet block.

Here is what happens. The more aft you set your jib leads (tensioning the foot more than the leech), the more radical the effect of your trimming will be upon the leech. Ease off the sheet a notch or two, and that may loosen the foot of the sail by an inch, but it may at the same time loosen the leech by several inches.

And much worse, tighten the foot a notch and suddenly your leech is inches tighter; you are badly overtrimmed, closing your slot dramatically and horribly backwinding the mainsail.

Again, maybe the cloth on the main won't luff, and I am sure the mast will not counterrotate, but you nonetheless will be backwinding the main.

So next you ease it. Ease it too much and you will have lost your pointing ability and power.

If you must be overzealous in sheeting, make sure it's the mainsheet, not the jib sheet. If anything, you want the main oversheeted and the jib undersheeted. The last time I told that to someone, he increased his boat speed by 20 percent.

In summary, remember that the jib is the sail that complements the mainsail—sort of an Abbott to a Costello, a Martin to a Lewis, a Laurel to a Hardy. Its only purpose is to let the mainsail excel, to create between itself and the mainsail a perfect air valve that jets a winning stream of air through a perfect slot to accelerate the suction of the mainsail.

Use every device at your disposal to mold this little guy to the image of his big brother.

On your jib handling ability may rest your racing success.

# 6

## MAST RAKE

THE concept of mast rake was once a very simple one . . . but catamarans have changed all that. Now the theory of mast rake is probably the most controversial of all subjects in this era of sailing.

Traditionally, there had always been only one reason to rake your mast forward or aft or perpendicular: to balance the boat. Too much weather helm could be corrected by raking the mast forward, and lee helm could be reduced by raking the mast aft.

But the catamaran has already shattered many sailing myths and traditions, and mast rake is definitely on that list.

Now it has been discovered that mast rake also can have

*This Nacra 5.2 sailor has his mast raked radically aft. The mast position allows the bows to more easily ride out of the water in unstable conditions. (Courtesy of NACRA)*

an effect on the boat's power, stability, speed, leeway, and/or pointing ability.

The popular theory in recent years has been that if you rake your mast back, you will point better and go faster to weather, even if you have a weather helm.

How did this idea get started? More important, does it really work?

## THE ASYMMETRIC PHENOMENON

The mast rake theory came into being shortly after the arrival on the scene of the Hobies and Prindles, with their asymmetrical hulls, and as other boats of similar design followed.

Presumably, the original intent of the asymmetrical design was to create a boat without the nuisance of daggerboards or centerboards—one that could be beached easily and yet sail very nicely.

Whether by accident, ignorance, or intent, some sailors began raking their masts back farther than the directions called for on this type of boat. They found their boats going faster and pointing better to weather, even though they had increased their weather helm.

This seems against the laws of physics, and indeed it *is* on centerboard or daggerboard boats such as the Hobie 18, Nacra, Tornado, etc. Normally, if you sail with your rudder at an angle to correct for weather helm, you create drag and slow down the boat. But the asymmetric-hull catamaran, as we will explain, is another kind of animal, with its own special laws of physics.

These suddenly "hot" skippers knew that what they were doing worked, but they didn't know why it worked.

The concept involved is actually nothing particularly new. It is a logical extension of a theory that was developed back in 1922 by Dr. Manfred Curry and C. A. Bembe of Germany.

They conducted experiments with arced-surface center-

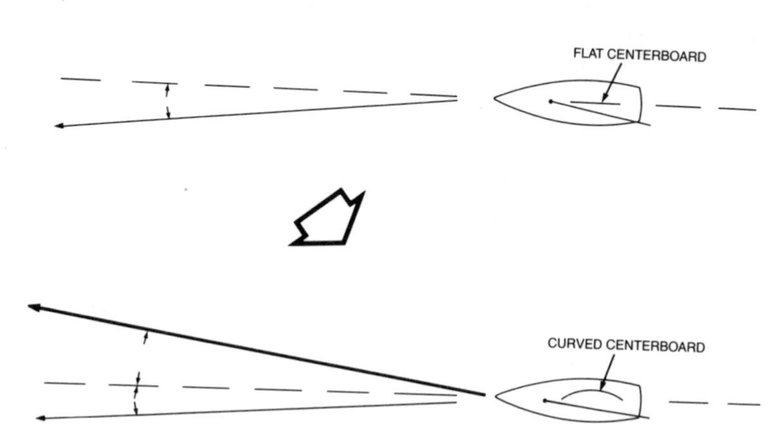


DIAGRAM 16

*The boat with the flat centerboard has a 5-degree drift to leeward (solid line) below its axis (dotted line).*
*The boat with the board arched to windward lifts 10 degrees higher (dark solid line) than its axis (dotted line), and 15 degrees higher than the course with the flat board (light solid line).*

boards, that is, concave on one side and convex on the other (the same idea as the asymmetrical hull). (See diagram 16.) They discovered that a traditional centerboard, flat on both sides, would allow a drift to leeward. The drift was not as great as with no board at all, but certainly significant.

Their arced board, however, with the humped or arced side toward the weather quadrant, created lift in that direction. When its angle of attack was straight through the water, the arced board created a lift toward its arced side. Surprisingly, they discovered also that this board presented very little water resistance or friction in its forward movement.

It is much the same as the wing of a bird, sailing against the wind with motionless wing: The lift is upward, or in the direction of the arc.

These old experiments probably were instrumental in the

development of the modern asymmetric hulls. And they indicate that what keeps these boats from drifting sideways without centerboards is partially that the outer flat side of the hull inhibits sideways motion to leeward, but, more significantly, that the curved side of the hull promotes lift to windward. (This is true, of course, primarily when the leeward hull is depressed in the water more than the windward hull.)

Curry and Bembe also found that it helps the lift if you can elongate the curve by attaching the rudder immediately behind the centerboard or keel and accentuating the curve somewhat by sailing with a bit of weather helm. This has been proven by the weather performance of certain designs of fin-keel racing yachts with the rudder attached directly behind the keel.

In an asymmetrical hull we have, in effect, an elongated version of Curry and Bembe's experimental centerboard, flat on one side and arced on the other. (See diagram 17.) And attached directly behind it is the rudder.

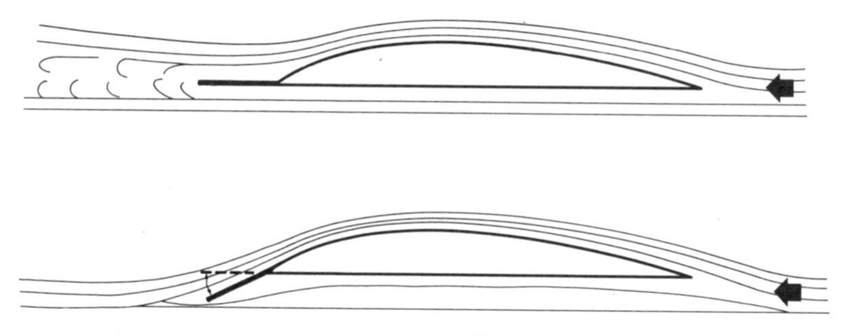

DIAGRAM 17

*With neutral helm (rudder straight aft), it actually causes more drag or exit turbulence.*
*With the rudder corrected for weather helm, the arc of the asymmetrical lifting hull is elongated, allowing for a smoother exit as well as more lift.*

When we rake the mast aft on such a boat, we accomplish three things:

1. We bring the power of the boat back so that the aft portion of the hull is somewhat more depressed in the

water closer to the rudders, so the rudders can also act as centerboards in resisting leeway.

2. We also create a weather helm. This makes us angle our rudder in such a way that it continues the curve on the arced side of the hull, smoothing the water flow along that side and thereby actually reducing drag, increasing speed, and increasing lift to weather.
3. It also gives the boat more fore-and-aft stability, which is a very helpful feature for Hobies, Prindles, and other boardless boats of similar design.

With all these benefits, it's no wonder those aft-mast-rakers were cleaning up on the race course.

And naturally a lot of sailors jumped on the bandwagon and started raking their masts back, regardless of the type of catamaran they had. An apparent axiom discovered!

Ah, but the only thing you can count on these days is death and taxes. Raking your mast aft may work for the boardless, asymmetric-hull cats, but the axiom does not necessarily hold true for catamarans that have daggerboards or centerboards.

The cats with boards do not have the underwater hydrodynamic lift created by asymmetric hulls. In addition, their boards and rudders are widely separated, and the rudder cannot operate in a way to add to that curving lift effect. On the contrary, in these boats weather helm will result in underwater drag and slow down the boat.

Therefore, the underwater lift theory, a major reason for raking a mast back on the asymmetrical hulls, is not a major factor on a boat with boards (even though boards and rudders do create some lift, if they have leeway).

This leaves us with only two main reasons for raking a mast aft on boats with boards: fore-and-aft stability; and bringing more load back over the rudders so they can help add some lift and prevent leeway. However, as we shall explain, these advantages may be outweighed by resulting disadvantages.

Thus, the controversy rages on.

*Two Prindles battle it out, giving a good demonstration of variations in mast rake. No. 501's mast is raked much farther aft than that of No. 172. (Photo courtesy of the Prindle Class Assn.)*

## *STABILITY VERSUS POWER*

Raking the mast aft can indeed improve the boat's fore-and-aft stability in heavy air. But by the same token, it can somewhat reduce its power. Raking the mast perpendicular or forward, on the other hand, can increase the boat's power.

The principle of stability is illustrated again by our best teachers, the birds. To quote from Curry:

> We notice that Nature gives most wings a backward slope; swallows' wings are an extreme in this point. But the more the bird tends toward a quiet soarer, like the gull, the more the wings are placed at right angles to the body. We came to the conclusion in our former observations on birds that no advantage was gained with regard to power by a backward slope of the wing, but that this property of the bird's wings served only to ensure the stability of the flyer.

Evidence of the power principle was garnered in the early 1900s by Professor Prantdl of Gottingen, Germany. (See diagram 18.) He set up a wind tunnel to measure the lift of two wings. "A" had its wings set at right angles, while "B" was set with wings raked aft 23 degrees. His results showed the lift developed by the right-angle wing to be 11 percent greater than the raked wings.

Mother Nature knows best; and so fast-flying or acrobatic birds tend to have their wings angled back for stability, while birds that have a great deal of power in their wings are more likely to have their wings perpendicular to their bodies, or even a little forward.

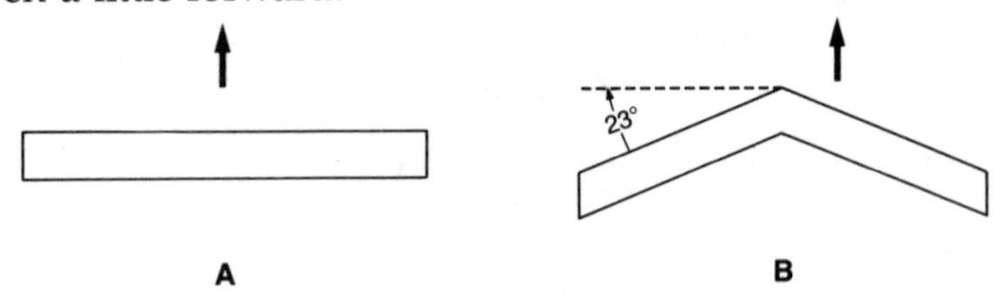


DIAGRAM 18

*Professor Prandtl's wing tests showed that wings angled back (B) developed 11 percent less lift than the wings at right angles (A).*

And the same rule applies to aircraft. Those with high lift and power have nearly perpendicular wings, while those with less lift have their wings angled aft, such as jet aircraft.

All this evidence relates directly to the mast on your boat. You will definitely find more power with your mast perpendicular, as opposed to aft.

Here is one explanation for the lessening of sail power with the mast raked aft.

If you sail with your mast perpendicular, the leading edge of your sail plan strikes the wind at a right angle, and the wind then proceeds back through the sail plan on a fairly horizontal plane; whereas, the aft-raked mast is struck by the wind at its base first and on up to the top of the mast in a staggered progression.

In addition, the wind usually comes off the water and strikes the sail in an upward direction in the first place; with the sail tipped back, the wind will tend to skip diagonally across the sail and battens rather than flowing parallel to the battens.

With an aft-raked mast, the boom section, or lower aft portion of the sail, is lower toward the deck than with a perpendicular mast. This can cause that lower, aft section of the sail to be blanketed from any wind effects by the hull and trampoline itself. Add to that the possibility that the boat is heeled, and you may be blanketing the sail a third of the way up.

Thus, you are reducing the power in your main by raking the mast aft.

In downwind sailing it still holds true that the perpendicular mast will have more power.

## *THE HELM CONTROVERSY*

With a perpendicular mast you probably also will find that your helm is much better balanced, generally, although this may be dependent on many other circumstances as well.

In essence, on the cat with boards, you are striving to keep the boat as well balanced as possible and, at the same time, to get as much power as you can safely, efficiently, and fully use.

The boat's balance depends on several factors. A number of pressures are at work on your boat. In the sails, you have pressure developed in the pocket of both the jib and the mainsail, while below the waterline, you have resistant pressures upon the centerboards, the rudders, and quite often the bow entry.

Somewhere is an axis, an absolute center point for all these pressures, and when all are balanced perfectly on either side of this axis, you will have neutral helm.

The mast is a major factor in neutralizing helm. Weather helm can be increased by raking the mast farther aft and decreased by raking the mast farther forward or perpendicular.

Weather helm is recommended by a great many sailors, with the term modified by the word "slight." A truly slight weather helm is fine. But at times a fellow sailor may tell you he has a slight weather helm, and upon sailing the boat, with feet braced, arms and back straining, you can hardly keep her from rounding up head to wind.

Helm of any kind is detrimental to boat speed on the centerboard boats (with the rare exception of some designs that can take advantage of the underwater lift theory). It is a sea brake that is constantly flapping away at the stern, while you are trying to make a clean entry and no-wake exit through the water. It is fighting you all the way. You should try to neutralize your helm, but if you need to have it, helm should be to the weather.

Just briefly, there are other ways to change helm: (1) by moving the draft in the sail either forward (reducing weather helm) or aft (increasing weather helm); (2) by putting your crew weight forward (reducing weather helm) or aft (increasing weather helm); or (3) by raking your rudders forward and under (reducing weather helm) or aft and out (increasing weather helm).

Despite the fact that weather helm is generally considered to be undesirable because of the drag it creates, there are two schools of thought on the subject. This brings us to that other main reason some sailors give for raking their masts back: Bringing the center of effort farther back puts more load on the rudders so they can be more effective in preventing leeway. It divides the job more evenly between the boards and the rudders.

So we have one school of racers raking their masts as far forward as necessary to create neutral helm and eliminate drag; and we have the other school raking their masts aft, creating some weather helm, but at the same time reducing leeway.

Both theories have very successful proponents: winning racers who are using opposing ideas. It would appear that neither school is right or wrong; neither has discovered a great "truth." Each theory has advantages, and each has to make tradeoffs.

Those of you who have weighed the pros and cons and decide you would prefer your mast raked aft but do not want to increase weather helm may find that the best solution is to rake your rudders forward, thus eliminating one of the major drawbacks to the aft rake.

## *THE TRADEOFFS*

Now let us try to analyze the advantages and disadvantages of sailing with a perpendicular mast:

| *Possible advantages* | *Possible disadvantages* |
|---|---|
| more mainsail power | may have more power than can be handled in heavy air |
| less drag through helm | closes the jib slot, possibly reducing power, particularly in heavy air. |
| | possibly more leeway |
| | less stability in heavy air |

The advantages here seem outweighed by the disadvantages, but most of the negatives deal mainly with heavy air. It could be, then, that the perpendicular mast is very effective in light-to-moderate air.

Now let us compare the advantages and disadvantages of an aft-raked mast:

| *Possible advantages* | *Possible disadvantages* |
| --- | --- |
| opens slot for more power in heavy air | reduces power in mainsail |
| less leeway by loading rudders and boards | increases drag from rudder helm |
| more stability in heavy air | |

It appears that the aft-raked mast has a good many more advantages than disadvantages, but again, these mostly seem operative in heavier air.

Comparing the two schools of thought on paper, it appears the perpendicular mast is more productive in lighter air, while the aft-raked mast excels in the heavier air.

Before making your decision on mast rake, keep in mind that, as mentioned earlier in this chapter, you are striving *to get as much power as you can safely, efficiently, and fully use* while keeping the boat as well balanced as possible.

But before conditions get to the point where you cannot hold the boat down, the bows are diving constantly, and your crew weight is as far back as it can efficiently be, then, much like the swallow or the jet airplane, you seek stability and reduced lifting power.

For each increment aft you rake the mast to gain stability, one increment of power is lost. In a "stink" situation, as Jack Sammons points out in his book *Welcome to A-Fleet,* you may forget all about retaining much power. In that case you need stability. There are times when simply finishing a race can win you a regatta.

So in summary, aft mast rake on asymmetrical hulls is very desirable, despite the fact it does create weather helm. That very weather helm is also adding to your underwater lift to weather.

As for boats with symmetrical hulls and boards, no one has yet made a hard-and-fast case for either the perpendicular or the aft-raked mast. Both have their advantages and disadvantages. But overall, it appears that in light air the perpendicular mast has an edge; while at the heavier end of the weather scale, an aft-raked mast is most advantageous.

However, extremes of any kind will produce poor results, so do not overdo your mast setting in either direction.

# 7

## WHITE'S THREE W'S FORMULA

WHILE working on my last book, I searched for a simple way to analyze the kind of sail (or sail shape) needed for any of the infinite combinations of racing conditions.

Drawing on my own years of experience, at that time I came up with a great solution. Coining the term "Three W's," I described a method for determining the best sail shape for beating to weather, based on the three conditions that affect sail shape: wind, water, and weight conditions.

Since my introduction of the concept of the Three W's in 1974, in *The Complete Manual of Catamaran Racing,* I have seen numerous articles and books using the Three W's. Apparently, it helped everyone to best describe when and where to use what sail.

But everything involved with sailing has become more precise, and therefore I have devised a new version of this aid: White's Three W's Formula for desired sail shape going to weather.

In the original version we determined what shape of sail was needed for each of the three influencing conditions and then sort of averaged out how the sail should be to best accommodate all three conditions. If two conditions called for a flat sail and the third called for a full sail, you would come up with something like "pretty flat," or "moderately flat."

My new formula is designed to get away from those vague, abstract descriptions. In a sport as infinitely filled with variables and abstracts as sailboat racing, the more things we can pinpoint, the better.

Therefore, I have now assigned numerical values to sail shape, ranging from a low of 10 for a flat sail to a high of 30 for a full sail, and covering all the moderations in between.

The numbers are assigned as follows:

| | |
|---|---|
| *Flat sail* | *10* |
| *Moderately flat* | *15* |
| *Moderate* | *20* |
| *Moderately full* | *25* |
| *Full* | *30* |

Then we may use White's Three W's Formula for desired sail shape:

$$\frac{\text{wind} + \text{water} + \text{weight}}{3} = \text{desired sail shape}$$

In place of wind and water and weight, we insert the appropriate numerical value of the sail shape required for each condition (independent of the others). Adding the three figures and then dividing by 3 will give you the average shape that should work best for this particular combination of conditions.

The sail-shape values that are to be assigned for each of the conditions are premised on the following basic theories:

√ For light wind a full sail; for heavy wind a flat sail.
√ For heavy waves or chop, a full sail; for flat seas, a flat sail.
√ For heavy crew weight, a full sail; for a light crew, a flat sail.

Nothing can replace experience for knowing whether your sail should be set full, flat, moderately, or whatever. But what we all need, no matter what our degree of experience, is a basic rule of thumb, and that is what the formula is all about.

Now let us study the basic rules that tell us what sail shape we need for the three W conditions.

### *WIND*

Take the first of these conditions, which is wind. When the air is very light, it is pretty well established that a relatively full sail propels the boat easier than would a flat sail. Some theories try to negate this basic principle, but the age-old, proven fact is that it takes less wind to drive a full sail than to drive a flat sail.

A slight digression is in order here to present briefly the case for the flat sail in light air. Advocates of this theory claim that the full sail will not be able to bend the wind quickly enough, nor allow the wind to attach all the way along the sail, to provide power. They claim further that the full sail offers too much friction, while the flat sail offers less resistance to what little air is stirring.

Obviously, the theory goes much deeper than that, but my vote for the full sail is based on much older and more reliable evidence.

Take a look at birds in general. Nature herself shows us that slow-flying birds (light air) have a great deal more arch or camber in their wings than do the fast-flying birds (heavy air).

Another good comparison would be the contrast in wind configurations of such slow-flying aircraft as the Ford

Trimotor or the DC-3, whose landing speeds are below 50 mph (light air), with their tremendous wing arch, as opposed to the high speed jet aircraft with flat wings that cannot land at speeds less than 150 mph (heavy air).

In other words, the lighter the wind, the more need for power to get the boat moving.

Another argument for the full sail in light air is in the basic theory of what makes a sailboat go forward.

You see, there are two pressures on the sail. On the lee side of the sail is a negative pressure or a suction effect. That negative pressure can amount to three to four times the positive pressure, which is on the windward side of the sail.

To quote a turn-of-the-century sailor, Dr. Manfred Curry, "We yachtsmen sail, properly speaking, not by means of the pressure which arises from the impact of the wind on the sail, but chiefly by means of the 'suck' which acts on the leeward side of it. A sailboat is sucked, not driven, forward." The deeper the draft or arch in the sail, the more "suck" (and, therefore, power) is created.

Of course, if you set your sail up too radically full, you will reach a point where the shape becomes inefficient.

In light air I usually start with the mainsheet not very tight. Once the boat begins to move forward at a desirable speed, you can slowly sheet in, flattening the sail, creating your own apparent wind.

Yet, even though I am using sheeting to have a full sail and then flatten it, overall the sail is set relatively full compared to the way I would set it for a heavy air race.

So the rule is: *A full sail in light air.*

On the other hand, when the air is heavy, you need a flat sail. It is obvious that when you have a lot of wind, you will be overpowered if you have a full sail. You would have way too much "suck" for the boat to handle. Therefore, since you do not need or cannot use the power, you flatten the sail, reducing the negative pressure in relation to the positive pressure.

Between light air and heavy are a vast number of different wind strengths and, therefore, as many different sail settings. If 2 mph of wind is light (a full, 30-point sail), and 20 mph is heavy (a flat, 10-point sail), for example, then 11 mph would be exactly moderate (20 points). Too bad it can't be that easy, but moderate can run from lightly moderate (a 25-point sail) to heavily moderate (a 15-point sail). Here we have to make a judgment call.

So our basic rule of thumb for wind conditions looks like this:

| *Wind Condition* | *Sail Description* | *Numerical Value* |
|---|---|---|
| light wind | full sail | 30 |
| moderately light | moderately full | 25 |
| moderate wind | moderate sail | 20 |
| moderately heavy | moderately flat | 15 |
| heavy wind | flat sail | 10 |

## *WATER*

The second condition that affects sail shape is water. A lot of judgment and guesswork will be needed for this one, since it is often difficult to determine in advance what the conditions are.

We all know what a flat sea is. If you can comb your hair and shave using it for a mirror, that is flat.

For flat seas you want a flat sail (one of those perfect 10 sails). The reason should be obvious. The water is offering less resistance to the forward motion of your boat, therefore you need less power to get you through it. Take advantage of this lower resistance to go for speed with the flat sail rather than power with the full sail.

At times you may run into large ground swell waves; and, although they may seem huge, particularly as you watch them crash on the shoreline, the surface of the water is smooth. In other words, if the troughs are long and the tops are not breaking, you could be dealing with flat water in your judgment of the wave condition.

On the other end of the wave spectrum is the extremely choppy, turbulent sea. This condition requires a full sail (a definite 30-pointer), to drive through extreme resistance offered by the rough water. In short, due to the fact that wave action is attempting to slow you down and knock you around, you need more power to blast through the tough going.

Again, between these two extremes are many other wave configurations which leave you still another judgment call. Let us say the waves are choppy, but not really hurting boat speed much; or say that the water is somewhat on the flat side but with a lot of powerboat chop. Then you could refer to the wave condition as being moderate (a 20-point sail).

In summation, our formula ingredient concerning wave condition is determined as follows:

| *Water Condition* | *Sail Description* | *Numerical Value* |
|---|---|---|
| heavy waves | full sail | 30 |
| moderately heavy | moderately full | 25 |
| moderate waves | moderate sail | 20 |
| moderately flat | moderately flat | 15 |
| flat water | flat sail | 10 |

## *WEIGHT*

Our third and final condition affecting desired sail shape is weight. In the case of one-design racing, where all boats are equal, this condition refers to crew weight and extra equipment you may carry aboard.*

*Inasmuch as the Three W's Formula is not restricted to catamarans, if you ever find yourself sailing on one of the big racers, you want to consider boat displacement as well as crew weight.

AXIOM: *A heavy crew needs a full sail; a light crew needs a flat sail.*

A heavy crew will be depressing the boat more deeply into the water, creating more wetted surface and, therefore, more friction and drag. They will need the additional power provided by a fuller sail to counteract that weight and drag.

A light crew, not needing the power, can go with a flatter sail (which is also a more efficient and faster sail).

Let us assume that you and your crew total up to the minimum weight for your class. It would seem, then, that you have a light weight condition and therefore require a flat sail (the perfect 10).

On the other end of this scale we may have "team beef," running 100 pounds over class minimum weight. These folks will definitely need more power for their weight condition: a full sail (the nice round 30).

The weight condition is somewhat easier to judge than the other two. Everyone knows what he weighs, whereas we usually have to estimate wind velocity and wave height. Light weight, obviously, is close to the class's minimum weight, and sailors in each class generally have a consensus of what "heavy" is. You have merely to figure out where your weight falls between those two figures.

Hence, our point scale for determining the best sail shape based on the weight condition:

| *Weight Condition* | *Sail Description* | *Numerical Value* |
|---|---|---|
| heavy weight | full sail | 30 |
| moderately heavy | moderately full | 25 |
| moderate weight | moderate sail | 20 |
| moderately light | moderately flat | 15 |
| light weight | flat sail | 10 |

Now we have discussed how to find the appropriate sail

shape for each of the three conditions that affect it.

Remember, each condition is to be considered entirely on its own merits, without regard to the other two conditions.

Just rate the desired sail shape at somewhere between flat and full (between 10 and 30) for the wind condition, then for the wave condition and then for your weight condition.

Add the three numbers and divide by 3. The result will be the best sail shape for all three conditions together.

Here are some examples to try out the formula:

Boat A has a crew weight of only 5 pounds above the class minimum. Today they are sailing in Sandusky Bay, Ohio. As usual, it is choppy, but the air has dropped off to under 5 mph. What sail shape does he use? Let us apply White's Three W's Formula:

| | |
|---|---|
| *Wind is light, requiring a full sail* | *30* |
| *Water is choppy, requiring a full sail* | *30* |
| *Weight is light, requiring a flat sail* | *30* |

Using the formula:

$$\frac{\text{wind} + \text{water} + \text{weight}}{3} = \text{desired sail shape}$$

We have:

$$\frac{30 + 30 + 10}{3} = \frac{70}{3} = 23.33$$

Therefore, the desired sail shape would be 23.33, which on our numeric scale makes the sail almost a moderately full sail.

Another particular example could be offered by David Rodgers and Mike Christiansen when they competed in the Hobie 18 Nationals in Key Biscayne, Florida, in the summer of 1982. Dave and crew are pretty light. Although I have no exact knowledge of their weight, I would say they are close to minimum. The seas for most of the races were choppy and turbulent, and the wind was 20 knots on this particular day. Using our formula, then:

| | | |
|---|---|---|
| *Wind, heavy* | *flat sail* | *10* |
| *Waves, choppy* | *full sail* | *30* |
| *Weight, light* | *flat sail* | *10* |

$$\frac{\text{wind} + \text{water} + \text{weight}}{3} = \text{desired sail shape}$$

$$\frac{10 + 30 + 10}{3} = \frac{50}{3} = 16.67$$

Therefore, the desired sail shape for them in that particular race was 16.67, almost halfway between flat and moderate, so a moderately flat sail.

And another example: The air has just died, the waves are still choppy, and you and your crew have been getting chubby by overdoing pizza lately. All the W's require full sails (30's), so you just add them up and divide by 3 and you have 30, which means a full sail.

Okay. Now that you have the basics of our math session down pat, how about a tricky one?

PROBLEM

The wind is blowing 10–15; the sea is large swells, but flat; you and your crew weigh 315 (minimum weight is 285).

ANSWER

*Wind—Let's assign it an 18 sail.*

(The mean wind speed may be considered blowing slightly above moderate by our earlier description, although it is important to remember that all these numbers are simply relative figures.)

| *Water—Let's use a number 12 sail.* |
|---|

(Although the sea is still flat, we have added a couple points to cover the swells.)

| *Weight—Let's assign an 18 sail shape.* |
|---|

(Thirty pounds over minimum weight, for the sake of this example, is a little lighter than moderate.)

$$\frac{\text{wind} + \text{water} + \text{weight}}{3} = \text{desired sail shape}$$

We have:

$$\frac{18 + 12 + 18}{3} = \frac{48}{3} = 16$$

Therefore, the desirable sail shape is numerically a 16, or about moderately flat.

As you can see, you can try to make it easy on your brain by assigning the nice round numbers for flat, moderate, and full—10, 15, 20, 25, or 30—or you can make your formula as precise as you wish. If the wind is 10 knots, maybe that's a 13-point sail instead of a simple 10-pointer.

I must keep repeating that all these findings are relative. Who really knows what "moderate" means? How flat is "flat"? Or how full is "full"? Each person's use of the formula and assignment of numbers may vary slightly depending on what that person considers to be the upper and lower ranges of wind, wave action, and weight. My "heavy air" could be your "moderate."

Alongside other boats, either in or out of race conditions, is the place to figure some of these things out in your mind, when you have a ready measure of boat speed.

White's Three W's Formula simply provides a rule of thumb, a foundation on which to build your sail shape. Use of the formula also will help increase your awareness that every race is unique and conditions are seldom identical; it will get you thinking about what you may really need in sail shape.

This overall formula is to be used basically for going to weather. Off the wind you want a full sail in nearly all conditions. For a close reach, all you need is what you had going to the weather mark, and then just ease the sheet a bit. This will allow the sail to become relatively full for close reaches.

Even on beam reaches in any air at all you probably won't have to worry about getting the sail any fuller than what you can create by using a soft main sheeting, as your apparent wind goes so far forward you certainly don't want to be overly full in the mainsail.

Try using White's Three W's Formula before each race for a while, and you will notice an overall improvement from your normal standings.

# 8

## WEIGHT DISTRIBUTION

A KEEL boat has thousands of pounds of fixed ballast below the water to keep it well balanced. But a catamaran has no such comforting stability. Instead, it has movable ballast above-board, in the form of you and your crew.

Where you place your crew weight aboard your catamaran (or any other light displacement boat you happen to sail) is as important as how you trim your sails. If the craft is dragging her sterns, is heeled to windward, or has her bows under water, she obviously will sail poorly.

Those are extremes. But getting the boat at a perfect attitude (position in relation to the water) is not an extreme; it is a necessity.

*In a drifter, keeping the weight extremely forward, thus depressing the bows and keeping the sterns out of the water, will greatly help your forward motion. (Photo courtesy of NACRA)*

*This is good boat position, with the bows nearly as deep as they can possibly be, the windward hull just kissing the water. (Photo courtesy of NACRA)*

*Here is excellent boat attitude: The burdened hull is deeper at the bow than at the stern, while the windward hull is just skimming the water, stern clear of the water. (Courtesy of the Prindle Class Assn.)*

Your boat has one ideal attitude for maximum performance. This attitude is basically the same for all points of sail and all weather conditions.

First, you must gain an understanding and have a mental picture of what this perfect attitude is for your type of boat, and then you must strive to maintain it at all times. Yes, at *all* times!

The variable conditions outlined in the preceding chapter, "White's Three W's Formula," do not change the attitude of the boat. Rather, they change your positions on the boat to achieve the exact same attitude for all conditions.

As depicted in accompanying photographs, the proper attitude for most catamarans is leeward bow slightly down or depressed in the water, windward bow just kissing the water, both sterns out of the water. The importance of proper attitude is extreme in the case of the asymmetrical hull—you do not want the windward hull creating opposing lift to the labored leeward hull.

Keep this picture in your mind at all times, and move your crew weight fore or aft or leeward—whatever the condi-

*A good example of how to keep crew weight grouped closely together. With only one person needed on the trapeze, the crew stands behind the helmsman, allowing him to lean back into the lap of the trapezer. This concentrates the weight to reduce hobbyhorsing and allows more weight outboard. (Photo courtesy of NACRA)*

tions call for—to keep the boat in the ideal attitude.

One important general rule is to treat the weight of yourself and your crew as though the two of you are one chunk of balance. Don't spread the weight out at opposite ends of the boat.

When on the same side of the boat, you should be side by side. If one is on the trapeze, the ideal would be for the trapezer to be positioned with feet on either side of the person sitting on the hull, or at least as close as possible.

When sitting on opposite sides of the boat, crew and skipper should be placed directly opposite each other and move forward or backward in unison to maintain proper boat balance.

The reason for this Siamese-twin act is that your boat can become a bit of a seesaw out there, and while that is a fun game for children, as a sailor you will find the game intolerable. Waves or boat chop can set off the seesaw game; and if you and your crew are at opposing ends of the seesaw, the fulcrum being located somewhere near amidships, you will continue the game for a considerable amount of time.

If you are both sitting together, as near as possible to the fulcrum point, you will find that after one or two seesaws, the game is over and your seesaw board is back at its original attitude.

To repeat, you must keep the boat at the ideal attitude at all times—no games. Remember: United we're stable, divided we seesaw.

*Never allow the hull to fly this high while racing. Although it looks very showy, this position kills speed. (Photo courtesy of NACRA)*

*This particular trapezing technique is not recommended under racing conditions. Although the young lady looks very picturesque, she is going to get very tired. She is not wearing a trapeze belt. (Photo courtesy of the Hobie Class Assn.)*

To further clarify how weight distribution relates to the Three W's, let us take some examples.

### Example 1

The wind is light, the water is flat, and your weight is light. These conditions only dictate where you are to sit on the boat; they do not dictate the attitude of the boat, as the attitude must remain a constant.

For the above conditions, the crew will be on the leeward side, as far forward as practical, and the skipper probably will be sitting on the windward side as far forward as practical. With the weight in these positions, the boat will maintain our desirable attitude.

### EXAMPLE 2

The wind is heavy, the water is flat, and your crew weight is moderate. Under these conditions, your weight distribution must be totally different from that dictated in Example 1, but with the same goal of keeping your boat in that perfect attitude.

In this case you and your crew will need to get your weight outboard and aft on the windward side. (How far aft will depend on how heavy the wind is.)

The reason for the weight positioning in Example 2 is that heavy air will tend to cause the leeward bow to drive down under the water.

This phenomenon is explained through a theory of friction. The hulls have much more friction with the water than does the sail with the air. Since the sail is generating a lot of power and has relatively little friction to hinder it, it can and does go much faster than the hulls.

Down below the boat tries to keep up with the sails but cannot because of the greater friction it has in its contact with the water. Therefore, it drags behind the sail. (See diagram 19.)

The sail now is being tripped by the hulls and wants to fall flat on its face; and all that power in the sail is trying to help it do just that.

It reminds me of the football player who has had his feet partially kicked out from under him, but keeps stumbling and falling forward into the end zone, his torso continuing on much faster than his feet.

So, you see, the power of the sails drives the bow down, thereby tripping the boat. Your job in getting your weight out and aft is to counteract the tripping effect and still keep the boat balanced in its ideal attitude.

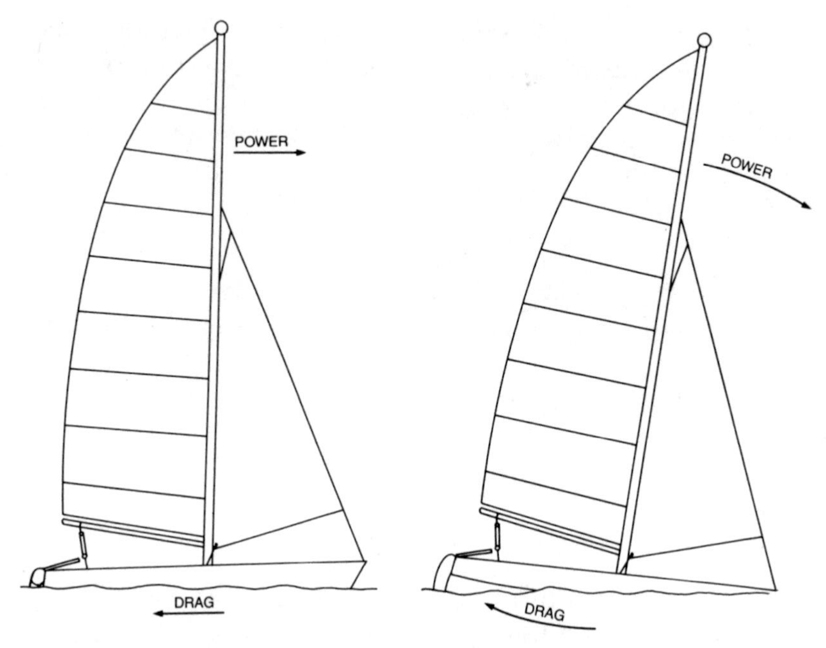


DIAGRAM 19

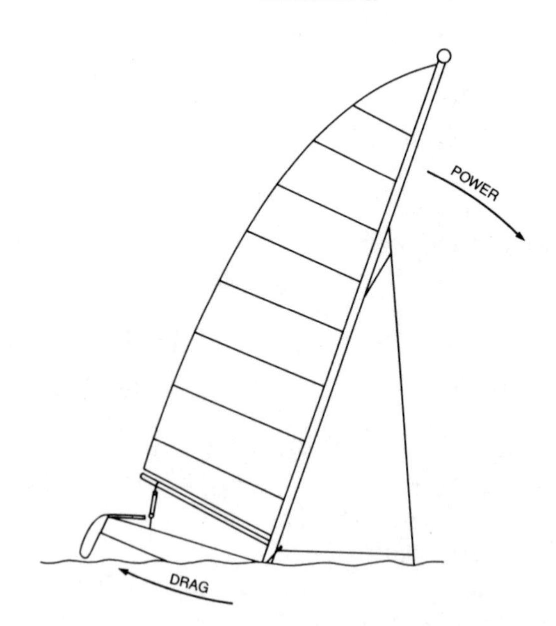

If the water is still flat, it is easy to decide how deep the leeward hull should be—keep it as deep as you can safely get it without risking a pitchpole.

If the seas are choppy, it may be necessary to let the bows ride slightly higher in the water—enough so that the decking on the tops of your bows is not striking the waves and slowing the boat down, as well as increasing danger of a pitchpole.

In downwind sailing there is a mild exception. Rather than heeling the boat slightly to leeward, with the windward hull kissing the water, it can be somewhat beneficial to sail the boat flat, with the windward hull in the water. Using the buoyance of both hulls can give the boat more stability on this point of sail. In fact, in heavy air, having both feet under you, so to speak, can be a deciding factor in preventing a pitchpole.

A word on helmsmanship, along this same line of thought: When you are quartering downwind and a large puff hits, heading down in a cat offers more stability, as you are using the buoyancy of both bows. Heading up presents the possibility of flying the windward hull and simultaneously tripping over the leeward hull if weight cannot be shifted fast enough to compensate.

Maintaining the proper boat attitude is often most difficult on those screaming reaches that have helped make catamarans so popular. The sail tends to develop the most speed and power on this point of sail. In order to harness and use power and prevent tripping (pitchpoling), crew weight must be as far aft and outboard as possible.

When you have done all you can as far as weight distribution and the leeward bow still dives, most sailors recommend easing the jib quickly and also easing the main a little, if necessary, and then snapping the sails back in. It only takes a few seconds for the boat to correct itself to the proper attitude.

A lightweight crew in heavy air may find it necessary to sacrifice a little sail power and leave the jib in a luff to avoid constant nosediving and keep the boat in its proper attitude.

Being conservative and going a little slower can sometimes pay off in the long run, when you consider how much time you would lose righting your boat after a capsize.

## *TOO HEAVY—TOO LIGHT?*

The way in which you distribute your weight to balance the boat will vary somewhat, but only in degree, according to how much weight you have to distribute. When weight is relatively heavy, the crew may not have to move as far aft in heavy air or as far forward in light air to achieve proper attitude as would a light crew.

If the skipper weighs 200 pounds and his crew only 100, he may want the crew on the low side, holding out the jib to improve shape for broad reaches and downwind tacking.

On the other hand, if the skipper is 100 pounds and the crew 200, he will have to decide whether getting better jib shape is worth having the boat in a less than perfect attitude.

Because of the importance of keeping the sterns from dragging, there has been much debate over the years whether it is better to have the lesser amount of weight in the skipper position and the heavier person in the crew position. Many, including myself, have experimented very successfully with putting a lightweight crew on the helm.

However, careful attention to the principles of weight distribution should help to overcome any such ballast imbalance.

There also is a question as to how important the overall crew weight is in affecting the boat's general performance.

Obviously, all other things being equal, a light crew will have some advantage over a heavy crew in light air. The boat weight won't be as heavy, and it won't have as much wetted surface to cause drag.

However, in heavy air a heavy crew will have a much easier time holding down the boat and preventing the nose from diving, without easing sails and sacrificing speed and power.

The disadvantages either way can be diminished greatly by compensating with sail adjustments using White's Three W's Formula.

If you want to really get into it, you can do as has been done in some monohull classes for years: Have a light-air crew and a heavy-air crew. But beware: If the weather conditions change during a regatta, you can't change crew—you must finish with the crew you start with.

I personally tend to opt for the lightweight crew. We shoot for the class's minimum weight (even if we have to diet all spring), and try to be no more than 15 pounds over, at maximum.

Light weight seems to me to have a slight edge overall. You can do better on all points of sail in very light air than the heavyweights (all else being equal). In heavy air you sacrifice some going to weather, but light weight is not a disadvantage going downwind. And you have less wetted surface (therefore, less friction) on all points of sail.

It's generally known that when you want a catamaran to go faster, you just build it lighter. Of course, then they start to fall apart. I'd rather have a heavier-built cat and go with the lightest possible crew.

In summary, the principles of weight distribution call for you (and your crew) to move anywhere you have to on the boat to keep it in the proper attitude.

You should try to keep all movable ballast (skipper and crew) together as much as possible, or at least laterally equal in position, to prevent seesawing.

Don't worry if you have to move around a lot, as long as it is aiding the proper attitude. But this movement must not disturb sails or create seesawing. In heavy air you sometimes find yourself scurrying around like a monkey. But in light air, it's the smooth easy movement of a soft-pawed cat. The inches you gain in boat attitude may be lost in yards by shaking that elusive zephyr out of your sail.

Keeping in mind there are wind puffs, differences in waves, and any number of variations in conditions, you must adjust your crew weight to maintain the proper attitude.

To quote Wayne Schafer from Jack Grubb's book *Hobie Cat Sailing,* "Weight trim is elusive; you must constantly shift your position on board to accommodate the conditions. Doing this well is a sensitive art."

# 9

## *THE START*

STARTING a sailboat race is sort of like being on the line of scrimmage in a football game.

Every football player knows what he is supposed to do when the ball is snapped; every sailboat racer knows what he "wants" to do when the gun goes off.

Just as the ball carrier is looking for a hole to break through for a clean green run down the field, so the racer is looking for the perfect spot that will let him break out of the pack in front and with clear air.

If things went as planned, we'd see a lot more touchdowns and a lot more perfect starts. Unfortunately, what looks great on the blackboard too often looks like chaos at the moment of truth.

*In large championship fleets, starts can be exciting and challenging. (Photo courtesy of the Hobie Class Assn.)*

*Three competitors jockey for position in pursuit of the elusive, "perfect" start. (Photo courtesy of the Hobie Class Assn.)*

The race start can be one of the most important parts of the race, but unfortunately it is the one part at which you get the least practice. You can work at sailing to weather and downwind and reaching, jibing, tacking, stopping, and backing. But it seems as though the only time we get to practice starts is when it isn't practice—it's the real thing.

For the benefit of the beginning racer, to help make some sense out of the confusion on the starting line, here's a review of basic starting preparations and techniques.

## THE TEN COMMANDMENTS OF PRERACE PREPPING

1. Have the course information handy on the boat. There is nothing worse than getting the best start, being first at the weather mark, only to discover you don't know where to go next.

The Hobie class association has stick-on course decals outlining all the courses that are to be used in any of their sanctioned races and assigning each course a number. The race committee needs only to display the course number; you check your decal for the description of that course; and you know where to go.

In other fleets, the course may be announced at the skipper's meeting prior to the race. Or if a printed sheet of course designations is given out, try to enclose it in a waterproof, see-through plastic bag to take on the boat with you, unless you have a photographic memory.

2. A pennant and flag information decal also should be aboard the boat. Again, these are stick-ons, available at your favorite dealer, giving you ready reference to the various pennants that may be flown by the race committee. Pennants are often the race committee's only means of communicating to the racers—that life jackets are required, there is a postponement, the course is shortened, the race is being abandoned, etc.

3. A starting watch is a must. There was a time when such a device was extremely expensive and did not hold up

for any length of time. But the age of electronics has brought us a wide variety of inexpensive watches, many of which will give you a ten-minute or five-minute countdown feature. It sure beats having your crew count "one thousand one, one thousand two . . ."

4. Be sure to take along a protest flag. You should not look upon it as meaning you have a chip on your shoulder and are ready to protest all who cross your path. Most people don't like having to air out their flag during a race. But on the other hand, if you are flagrantly fouled and you have no protest flag, 90 percent of the time your protest will not be acknowledged, let alone heard.

And if you don't protest, someone else may protest you for not protesting.

Make sure your protest flag measures in and qualifies according to your class requirements. In the Hobie class a red and white paisley bandana won't do. It has to be solid red, and it must measure 10 inches square.

5. Be sure the jib luff tension is as close to where you want it as possible. Obviously, if you have a jib luff that is adjustable from your boat's cockpit, you may wait until you are sure of the winds. If it is similar to the luff control on the Hobie 18, you had better adjust it as best you can ashore. It may require another adjustment on the water, but at least you will be close to what you need.

6. The jib leads should be set for your first weather leg. Prevailing conditions should dictate where the leads are set.

7. The draft of the mainsail should be set either full or flat, forward or aft, depending on the prevailing conditions. Use White's Three W's Formula to determine degree of fullness or flatness.

8. The luff of the mainsail should be tensioned for the prevailing conditions.

9. The outhaul should be set for the first weather leg, again depending upon the prevailing conditions.

10. The mast rotation should be set at whatever angle you feel is best for the prevailing conditions.

A good way to keep track of what to do before going out

on the water and finding out you forgot a major item: Get a laundry pen (waterproof ink) and write out a checklist on your throwable cushion. Then your throwable cushion is tied right on your trampoline with all the information you need. Simply use it as a checklist, and it takes some of the burden off your brain, especially just before a big race, when your head is spinning and your stomach churning. Then all you have to remember is not to forget your throwable.

And before you leave the beach, remember the old sailor's proverb: "The speed of your boat increases with your own confidence."

Before getting deeply into starting techniques, you may want to review some very simple, basic boat handling. While approaching the starting line you may be required to maneuver your boat with precision in very close quarters, and it is imperative to have total control over your boat and have close teamwork between skipper and crew.

Maneuvers you need to master are sudden stops, rapid acceleration, slowing down, speeding up, reaching off, turning in a full circle through a tack and jibe, feathering up, and sometimes all of the above in quick succession. In other words, you should be prepared to put your boat through any paces called for by the circumstances, without having to think about it much.

The mechanics of executing these basic maneuvers are explained at the end of this chapter. (See pages 126–30.)

## *DEVISING YOUR STARTING PLAN*

We have completed our checklist and, if necessary, reviewed basic boat handling. Now let's head out for the race course—EARLY (despite the fact that the modern beach cat sailor has the dubious distinction of always being late getting off the beach for the race; also despite the fact that catamaran race committees have the equally dubious distinction of always starting races late).

Getting out to the race course early is a good idea, and it may give you an edge over the beach-clingers. It is helpful to sail up the first weather leg to feel out the shifts, trying to note the wind patterns—which is a lift, which is a header—and above all, get your tacks smoothed out; get loose.

Watch carefully for the ten-minute warning signal (a white shape). Some start the countdown on their watches at ten minutes and others at five minutes. Remember that the shape is the official signal, not the gun or the horn. The five-minute signal is a blue shape, and the start signal is a red shape.

And be sure you get the course number, displayed on the committee boat. You may well have the finest start known to the civilized world, but if you do not know the course, you are lost after rounding the weather mark. Most competitors will be glad to tell you what the course number is if you miss it; but a few cutthroat types will do anything to win, including being unsportsmanlike.

As soon as the starting line has been set by the race committee, try to determine which is the "favored" end of the line. The favored end is that closest to the direction from which the wind is blowing. And that is the end of the line where you want to start. If you start at the favored end, you will already be ahead of the boats starting at the other end, giving you an advantage right off the line.

You probably will see quite a few sailors parking head-to-wind on the line (see diagram 20) and looking each way to see which end is favored, a very easy way to read the line. However, a caution: If you are not directly head-to-wind, you may be getting a bad reading.

Another way is to sight perpendicularly off a telltale, either on your boat or on the race committee boat. You may also simply sail to weather over either or both ends of the line (see diagram 21), while at the same time watching the angles being taken by boats on the opposite tack doing similar testing.

In any case, determine if the favored end of the line is toward starboard, where the committee boat usually is lo-

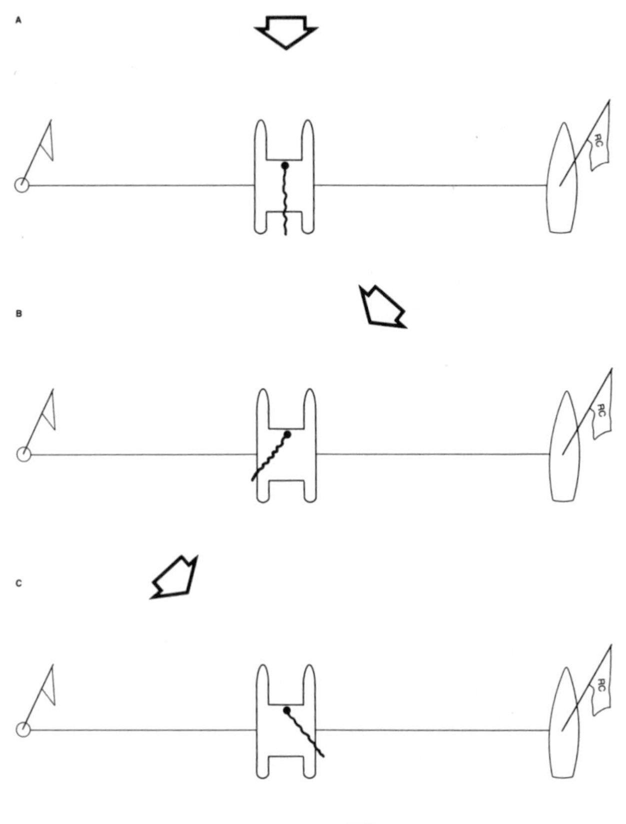


DIAGRAM 20

cated, or port, where the starting mark is located.

If other classes are starting ahead of you, you know that you are not allowed near the starting area until the fleet immediately ahead of you has started. Their starting signal will be your five-minute preparatory signal.

In some regattas you will be unconditionally disqualified for being in the start area before your start, and rightly so, as you have no business interfering with another fleet's start.

After that preceding fleet is gone, you then will have only five minutes to test the line, hardly enough time to do all that and still make a proper start on time. But you can learn a great deal by watching the fleet ahead of you. Observe which is the favored end. Notice which end seems to have the advantage, which end gets congested the most, etc.; and use all this

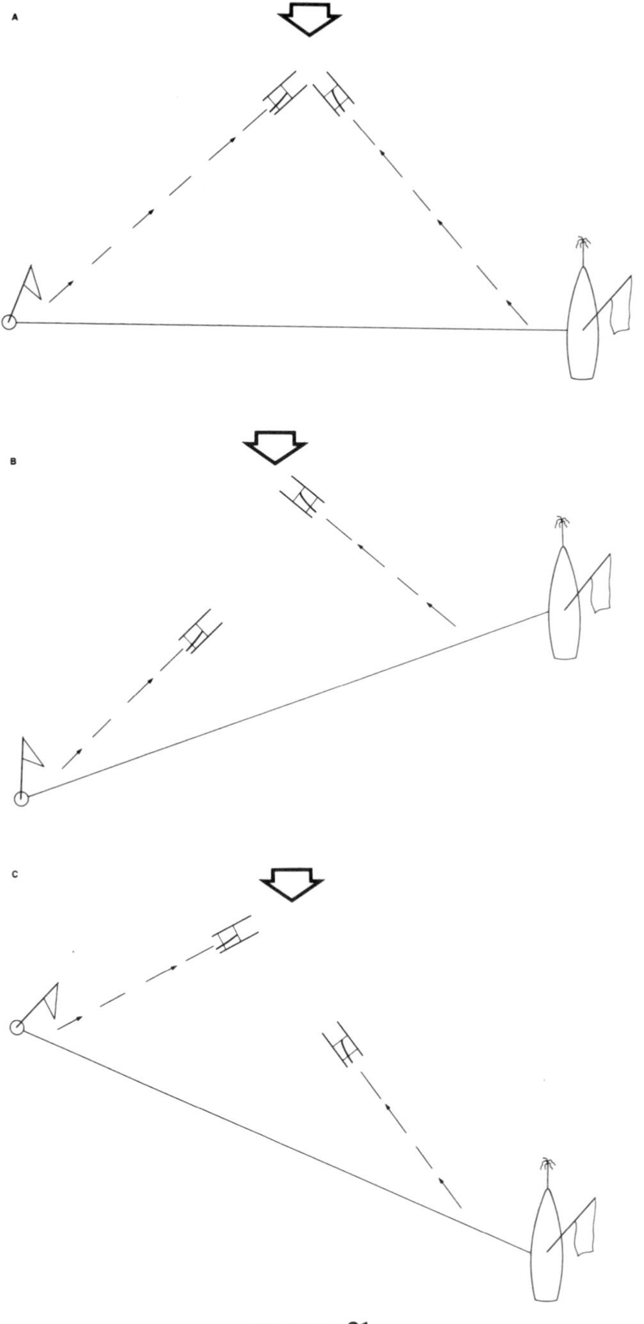


DIAGRAM 21

information in formulating your starting plan and maybe some alternative strategies. It's a rare start that works out exactly as planned.

Your starting plan should primarily be determined by where you wish to be after the start. You may want to go off immediately to the right side of the course or to the left, maybe up the middle.

Another factor that has bearing on where you want to be is your competition. You may have to cover a certain boat or boats (see the section on tactics in "The Weather Leg," Chapter 10, pages 138–57). That is another important input to your decision on where and how to start.

Nonetheless, it is all part of the same question: Where do you want to be after the start?

The best way to discuss starting is to take a few examples.

## *THE EVEN LINE*

We have an even line (that is, neither the port nor the starboard pin is favored); it is a big fleet with excellent competition. Here you have the entire line to use, as all positions will be equal after the starting gun goes off. You may have noticed that there was a header a half mile out on the left side of the course, so you want to be on the left side of the course, anyway.

Normally, boats on an even line (as well as a starboard-favored line) will try to be the most starboard boat. That creates a jam-up at the race committee boat end of the line.

If you want to be on the left side of the course, you will get there faster if you start at the port end of the line; and at the same time you will avoid the traffic jam at the starboard end of the line, where you could be covered, backwinded, or both by other boats.

On the other hand, if you had a tremendous desire to be on the right side of the course, you would have to fight for a good spot at the starboard end of the line. If you started at the port end, you would never get a chance to tack out to the right side of the course.

A good trick that can be used, if you have to get out to the right side, is a delayed start. This takes a good deal of patience. The situation normally occurs when the line is starboard-favored as well, and all the boats will be perched right upon the race committee boat, getting nervous, "upping" one another, and doing lots of shouting.

Meanwhile, just park in a position a bit above the lay line at the RC boat and wait. Do not get impatient, because if you start too early, you will find that somebody has fouled or stalled or is going backward right at the race committee boat, creating a roadblock on the line.

When the gun goes off, be ready to dive into a good hole coming in off a reach. Carry the reach up and above the boats that will be five to ten lengths ahead of you by now; then tack off immediately into clear air.

You really are not sacrificing as much as you think with this start, for it is getting you to the side of the course you think will "pay," and though you are five to ten boatlengths behind, you are off in clear air, while the rest are backwinding each other terribly.

Let us say you just want to be in the middle, as neither side appeals to you, and you see no obvious advantage. The middle offers a bit of security, for if a big shift comes, you are closer to whichever side of the course has become favored, and you can quickly get into the thick of things.

If you want the middle of the course, you can either be at the starboard end or any position down to the middle of the starting line. The closer you get to the starboard end, the less restricted you will be to tack off to the right side of the course whenever you want. But keep in mind also that you want clear air, and the jam-up at the starboard end may dictate getting on down the line into clear air.

## *THE STARBOARD-FAVORED LINE*

The second example is with the starting line favored toward the starboard end. This is a line poorly set by the race

*On this starboard-favored line, the Prindle #3 has a great start and has immediately established himself in the lead. The entire fleet is below him, although the boat just below him has a slim chance of working into a safe leeward position. (Photo courtesy of the Prindle Class Assn.)*

committee in nearly all cases. The race committee is asking for damage to their boat, for every competitor wants to be at the starboard end with a big lead over the entire fleet. However, only one boat can be there, and all of them are going to be fighting for just such a position.

One boat will win that berth. All the others (which could be as many as eighty boats) will lose it. This may be a good place to use the delayed start, as explained earlier. The delay would give that top position to one boat, maybe two or three; but you will still be right in there and not far behind.

However, if you want or need to hold onto the starboard tack, you must work up and out of the wake and backwinding of the leading boat's safe leeward position. (See the tactics section of Chapter 10, "The Weather Leg.")

Another possibility is to give the one boat his position

and get on down the line and into clear air where you can drive the boat well and keep moving. The boats jammed up near the starboard end are going to play havoc with each other's air. Meanwhile, you are trucking along without any disturbed air. You could continue to drive until such time as a header comes along, and you could easily be right back amongst the leaders.

## *THE PORT-FAVORED LINE*

The third line you will have to deal with is the port-favored line. If the line is not set at too extreme an angle, this usually is an excellent line, as it disperses most of the boats

*In an obvious port tack favored line, Boat #40029 has jumped off to a good lead, blanketing #40013, and with a safe leeward position on 40023. #40028 also is off to a good start on a chancy port tack start. (Photo courtesy of Hobie Class Assn.)*

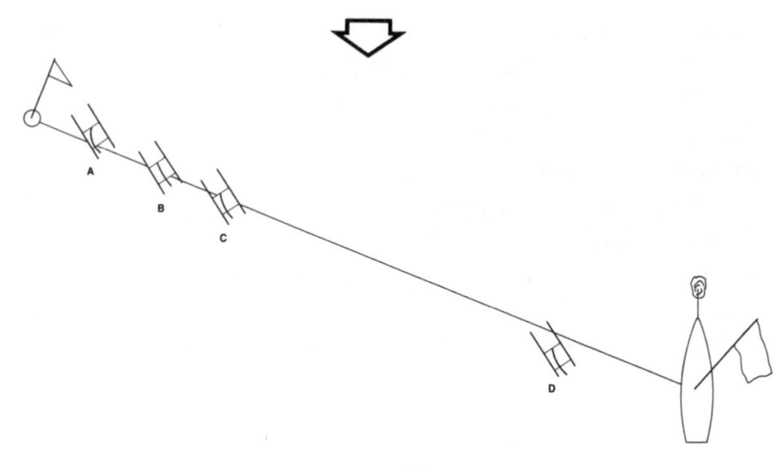


DIAGRAM 22

pretty evenly all the way down the line from the race committee boat to the port pin. The most advantageous place to be in this case is the port end, for it automatically puts you ahead. (See diagram 22.)

Assume you want the left side of the course; then you want to be the most port boat on the line and on starboard tack. That puts you ahead and also has you heading for the side you think will do the best for you.

If you desire the middle of the course, you will want to be at the port end, but you do not have to be number one boat at the pin. In fact, the closer you are to the pin, the worse your chance of staying in the middle of the course; you may not be able to tack for the weather pin at all until the lay line, when everybody else decides to go for it.

By starting up the line a ways, you are less likely to be trapped over on the left side of the course; however, you are giving the boats to leeward a head start. It is a decision that must be made.

If you want to get to the right side of the course, there are two ways: Stay up the line more and tack off quickly; or try a port-tack start.

You know you want to tack off to the right side of the course quickly and, chances are, so do all the boats toward the starboard end of the line. You can probably be as far as halfway down the line and still be able to get to the right side.

Most of the boats will tack to port fairly quickly; and for those that don't, you will just have to duck their sterns, although there probably will be only a few.

We all know the port tack start is very risky business. The bigger the fleet and the better the competition, the worse are the odds you will be able to pull it off. If you are going to give the port-tack start a try, do not tip everyone off beforehand. Be sure you definitely have a port-favored line, however. Make sure you can indeed beat the starboard boats, if all is equal.

Then make a timed start. For example, reach out from the

*In another port tack favored start the boat farthest away and to the right has the immediate lead. He also has achieved the position of blanketing everyone below him, and everyone to windward will be backwinded. In this case #4606 should tack to port immediately to try to find some good air and get out of the backwinded position. (Photo courtesy of the Prindle Class Assn.)*

port pin with one minute fifteen seconds remaining to the starting signal. Sail for thirty seconds, jibe, using up no more and no less than fifteen seconds, and reach back to the pin. You must hit the pin on a reach and then, upon rounding the mark, head up and sheet in quickly; the speed of the reach will shoot you way up to windward and have you really moving. Keep it there; you must maintain speed.

If on your approach back to the line you see a good many boats heading for the pin on starboard, be prepared to duck their sterns. This probably will not hurt you unless there is a steady wall of starboard boats. Then you have blown it. If there are only a few starboard boats, then a hole, dive for the hole, head up and sheet in, again gaining and keeping that speed.

## *THE OSCILLATING LINE*

In the next case we have what appears to be a port-favored line, but you are aware of a good deal of oscillation in the wind. If you commit early to the port end of the line and the wind clocks, you will be in the tank.

In this case it would be a good idea to time the distance of the starting line for the present condition, thus knowing exactly how long it takes to get from the starboard end of the line to the port. Let us assume it takes a minute to cover that distance. Make your approach to the starting line from the starboard end by at least two minutes until the start. Be prepared to make a dash for the favored port end of the line; or if the wind clocks, be ready to park and wait for a starboard end start.

If the line goes back to port-favored with only a little time left, head on down as far as you can go and, with as much speed as possible, hit the line at the signal. If the wind is still holding to port, tack quickly, as you are sailing a header. With wind oscillating this much, you probably will want to take it up the middle, anyway. If you think the wind is going to continue to clock to the right, you probably will want to get to the right side of the course.

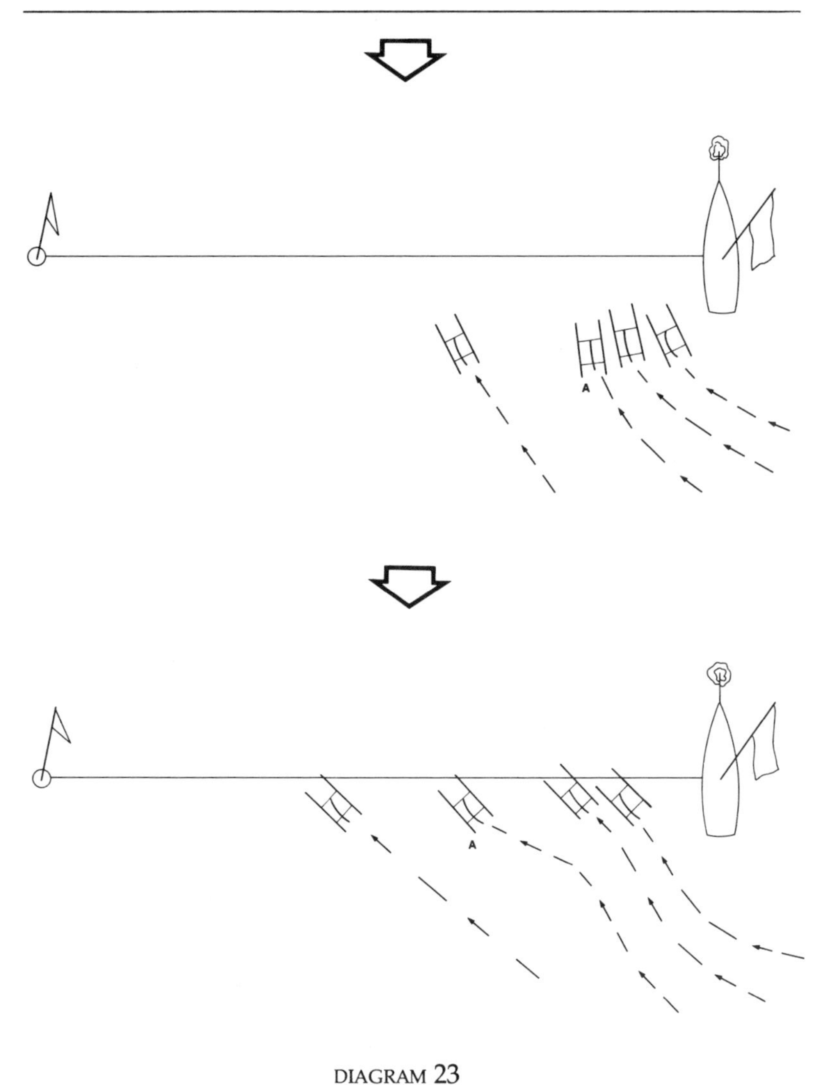


DIAGRAM 23

The safe place is the middle: You can tack out easily and are near the rhumb line if there are any major shifts.

A couple of general principles should be applied at all times. As you are approaching the lay line, very near starting time, keep luffing up the boat above you, without allowing the boat below you to do the same thing to you. (See diagram

23.) What you are trying to accomplish is to provide a hole (save an empty parking space) below you.

Thus, when there are five to fifteen seconds left—or whatever it takes to get to the line—you quit luffing, bear off into the hole, and drive out into clear air, leaving the chap above you in a backwinded position.

If it is light and fluky air, be sure you do not get too far from the starting line. If you get too far away, you may not make it back in time to race with your fleet.

There are as many ways to start a race as there are starters. No single technique always works. You should show as much aggression as you dare, mixed with a bit of prudence, a dash of logic, a cup of planning, and a grain of luck.

If a particular technique of starting does not work for you, try another; be inventive. A good start can win races for you; and even if you finish dead last, there is something about a good start that is rewarding.

## *BASIC BOAT MANEUVERS*

A boat out of control on the starting line is as bad as an out-of-control skier on a crowded slope. If you cannot control your boat in all circumstances and conditions, if you cannot put it through its paces with instinctive reactions, you will be doing a lot of 720s, or worse, causing damage to your boat and others.

### STARTING-LINE CONTROL

The starting line is the place where you will find yourself in the closest proximity to the most boats, although the following maneuvers may also be useful at marks where many boats are converging at the same time.

While the cat has the ability to really scream along, it also has the ability to stop almost immediately, due to its light weight and therefore low inertia, or momentum.

When you jam over the rudder to head up, you throw out

a good-sized brake off your stern. At the same time you ease the sails and head the machine up almost directly into the wind. All this braking action stops the light weight of the cat very quickly. That is why it is easy for a cat to go into irons; it has so little momentum from weight to help carry it across the eye of the wind in tacking.

But for our purposes on the starting line, you would be stopping the boat just where you want to stop it.

Doing it again, you are moving swiftly along on a close reach and decide to stop. You jam the rudders hard over and bring it up almost directly into the wind, at the same time easing the sails to a full luff. If you still are not stopping fast enough, push the boom of the mainsail out to the leeward side of the boat. This adds a tremendous amount of wind resistance to slow the boat even faster. You also could have the crew backwind the jib on the windward side of the boat as well, for additional braking power.

You probably do not want to tack in the above situation, so be sure not to carry the helm over too far. If the boat goes completely head to wind and starts to tack or go into irons, backwind the jib on what had been your windward side, and the bow will swing back to the original tack.

Once you have brought the boat up into the wind enough to stop it or slow it to the desired speed, and if you want to "park" it, fall back off to about a 45-degree angle to the wind and leave your sails out so you do not move forward. You will then be sitting still with the wind quartering your bow. Any time you feel like moving, it is a matter of simply sheeting—first the jib and then the main—and off you go again. By controlling the sheeting, you can either crawl forward very slowly or take off at maximum speed.

Backing up is a useful trick to learn, and catamarans do it very well. This maneuver can be used to get out of tricky docking areas or narrow channels, and it is a technique you may need sometimes on the starting line.

To back up, you steer the boat head to wind; then push the boom out on whatever you want to be the leeward side when you stop going backward. Backwind the jib on the side opposite the one the main is on.

When the boat begins to move backward, it will start moving quite fast. As it begins to back up, the rudders will want to flop to either one side or the other, so you must hold the tiller very firmly and guide the boat so it does not fall off to either tack.

## STEERING

Many people first getting on a sailboat of any kind do not realize that the rudder is only one of three major steering devices on the boat.

The boat's three steering devices are the rudders, the mainsail, and the jib. They can be used to help one another in steering the boat, or they can counteract and fight each other. They can become useless when working in opposition to each other.

The function of the rudders is the most obvious. Assume you are sitting on the windward side of the boat. If you pull on the tiller, the nose of the boat goes away from you (or down). When you push, the bows come your way (or up). That is simple enough, but the sails can overpower simple rudder control.

Also remember that rudders do not work at all if the boat is static. There must be movement through the water in order for the rudders to have any effect.

The mainsail and jib act to balance the boat's power and steering. Given neutral helm (steering of the rudder straight ahead without pull either up or down), if the jib is in (sheeted) and the mainsail is out (slack sheets), there will be more force in the jib than in the mainsail, tending to drive the bow away from the wind.

On the other hand, if the mainsail is in (sheeted) and the jib is out (slack), the predominant power is in the main, overburdening the stern of the boat, which brings the bows up into the wind.

The power in these sails can easily overpower any rudder steerage you may apply. If the sails are not trimmed properly for the steerage you are applying, the rudders will be overpowered and simply stall, having little or no effect on the direction of the boat.

By the same token, the sails can be a tremendous asset to steerage. As a matter of fact, the sails can steer a boat by themselves, without any aid from the rudders. Someday while out playing off the beach, try going in a straight course with just the sails. Pull up the rudders and sail the boat with sheet tension alone. It can be done very easily (unless your sail plan is really out of whack), and it is a good way to appreciate both the balance of a boat's sail plan and the steering powers of the sails.

The jib makes a wonderful forward wind rudder. If you are head to wind (in irons) and wish to get out of the position, you simply pull the jib to the opposite side of the tack onto which you want to be. The wind hits the arch, creating negative pressure on the leeward side and positive pressure on the windward side of the sail. Since there is no forward movement, there is lateral movement in the direction of the negative pressure (leeward side) and the bows swing in that direction.

As soon as the bows are across a point between 20 and 30 degrees angle to the wind, snap the jib through to the leeward side and sheet, bringing the bows the rest of the way through the wind and off on a beat or close reach.

Going a step further, this same procedure can help you complete a tack in adverse conditions where it is difficult to get the bows to come all the way around. This bit of extra side thrust by the jib ensures your not having a bad tack.

The jib also serves as a good way to get a boat moving from a dead stop. Picture yourself sitting dead in the water, with the wind quartering your bow. You are not in irons, but actually in a position to beat to weather, except that your sails are out and flapping. Now you want to go forward.

If the main is brought in alone, there is a good chance the boat will be overpowered by the main and just round up head to wind. However, if you bring in the jib first, it keeps the bow off the wind, and then the main can be brought in to begin accelerating. This maneuver can be done with the main alone, but it takes a bit of finesse. It is simply safer using the jib.

You probably will have to approach the starting line with moderate, controlled speed, not stopping and not going all out. Cruising primarily on the jib with the mainsheet slack is not a bad idea, as it ensures your not going into irons on the starting line.

However, it is best to approach with more main than jib, as it takes the skipper more time to sheet the mainsail than it does for the crew to sheet the jib.

It will take a bit more concentration on the helm to be sure you do not go into irons, but when you need to get the boat moving quickly, you can do so.

# 10

## THE WEATHER LEG

THAT uphill battle to the weather mark is a true test of your boat's tuning and balance, as well as of your ability to use the boat's potential to its fullest. The beat to the "A" mark is almost always the first leg of the race, and that is where you want to establish yourself as a top contender in this particular race.

You want to get to that mark first, or as close to first as possible. That requires a combination of two abilities: helmsmanship and use of tactics.

### *HELMSMANSHIP*

While many races can be won on tactics, it first takes helmsmanship and boat handling to acquire adequate speed

*Rounding the leeward pin and heading back to weather can be a real Chinese fire drill. (Photo courtesy of Hobie Class Assn.)*

in order to use tactics. If you are extremely slow; if the entire fleet appears as tiny objects on the horizon in front of you; if you begin feeling very lonely; chances are tactics will not do a thing for you.

The first thing you must do is get the boat moving with adequate, if not super, speed.

We have spent a great deal of time discussing boat speed—how to acquire it through proper rigging, sail shape, and weight distribution and when and how to use these "tools." But now we must talk about a mechanical part that is a crucial factor in winning or losing a race: the loose "nut" on the tiller bar. That loose nut is you, the skipper.

This is a good time to review White's Three W's Formula and make sure you have the boat set up the way you want it for the conditions of the upcoming weather leg. Once you have the boat set, it is up to you and your crew to do your jobs.

Before we get into how to sail in a variety of conditions, there are a couple of things you may want to try overall to help you get the boat to that first mark.

USING THE JIB

The jib is a really helpful telltale for steering the boat to weather. In my first book, I observed that the jib should be the exclusive guide for sailing to the weather mark. I now think it is more accurate to say it should be used as the most obvious telltale on the boat.

The jib, trimmed properly, will quickly indicate a luff or a stall. The luff is created by the wind coming across the sail at an angle too far forward; the stall, by the wind hitting the sail from an angle too far aft. The main cannot pick up on these improper angles. This is because the main is a fully battened, fixed-camber type of sail, and you have the jib creating a flow across its leeward side all the time so that it appears never to stall.

Therefore, it is easier to read the jib. Both sails should be read all the time to ensure proper trim and complementary shapes, but use the jib to tell how high or low you are going on the wind.

Most classes have telltales on the jib when they are delivered. If yours does not, put some on the sail at points marking each vertical third of the sail, 12 to 20 inches back from the luff.

The telltale on the windward side will be streaming aft if you are not luffing. If you are luffing, it will begin to make radical actions. If the telltale on the leeward side of the sail is streaming, it means you are not stalling. If it acts radically, then you are stalling. In order to tell what is happening, you must read the telltales on both sides of the sail constantly.

A small, finite line between luffing and stalling is where your boat will go its fastest and highest to weather. You are seeking that sweet spot. That is where concentration comes in.

At times you may want to sail high on the wind. When doing so, the telltales on the windward side of the jib may indicate a luff. In some conditions this is not a bad situation. We will deal with that later in this chapter. However, a stall is unforgivable. There's quite a contrast: A slight luff can sometimes be helpful; a slight stall, disastrous.

### POSITIONING THE TRAVELER

One general rule of thumb should be kept in mind: *Going to weather your traveler should be set in the center in nearly all cases.* (The Hobie 14 seems to be an exception to the rule.)

In light air you probably will be trying to sail as high on the wind as possible, and so the traveler needs to be centered to gain as much pointing ability as possible. On the other end of the range, in heavy air you will want power to go to weather, but you want it located in the lower portion of the sail. Therefore, you ease the sheet to let the top of the sail twist off while allowing the bottom to stay in the middle with lots of power. The twist-off reduces power at the top of the sail to nothing but at the same time reduces its heeling moment.

If you run the traveler out and flatten the sail in a heavy air condition, you are reducing the power of the sail at the bottom as well as at the top, and the reduction at the top will not be enough to significantly reduce your heeling moment. Then when you are overpowered by a gust, you will be bleeding it off by luffing the entire sail plan, slowing the boat and losing power at the same time—not desirable.

### ADJUSTING FOR WIND, WAVE, AND WEIGHT CONDITIONS

Different wind, wave, and weight conditions generally make for different sailing styles.

*Light air and flat seas.* As we discussed in "Weight Distribution," you will have the bows very deep, with the leeward hull deeper. The main should be sheeted fairly tight. According to White's Three W's Formula, you know you should have a full sail for light air, and so you do.

However, on the weather leg you use that full sail to get speed going in the catamaran; then as the speed begins to increase, you may sheet tighter, flattening the sail. If the boat starts to slow up a bit, ease the main again to gain the power you need to keep moving.

Meanwhile, the jib should still be complementing the

main. It is preferable to have the jib cleated (in all but heavy air, where there is danger of capsize) so you can steer by it.

Again, let us say the boat begins to gain a bit of speed. When you sheet in the main, you will notice that the jib may be brought in a bit as well. But as soon as the boat begins to slow a little, and when you ease the mainsheet, also ease the jib. You are looking for power, and you do not want the jib backwinding the power right off the leeward side of your main.

As for the actual steering of the boat, in the centerboard-type boats, with deep bow entries, it is better to pinch to weather a bit. As in all weather conditions, you never pinch too much or for too long a time. You gain speed by driving off a bit; then head up and let the speed carry for a while; then back off the wind; then up; and so on, carrying yourself upwind as far as possible, yet without losing any of the speed.

If you sail too close to the wind for too long a time, the boat will lose a great deal of speed, which will be hard to regenerate in light air. If you fall off the wind too much or for too long, you will be losing valuable ground in sailing toward the weather mark. You will be going fast, but so will the sailor who drives it off and then works it up.

*Extremely light air conditions.* In extremely light air conditions, where there may be a wisp of air once in a while, do not worry about sheeting tight. You want your sail full. If a little puff comes your way, you want to use as much of it as possible. If you are sheeted in, the flatter sail will do little to get you moving. The fuller sail, with its power, will begin moving you easier, and you may then begin sheeting in a little tighter.

In other words, the only time you can start to flatten a sail in light air is when you are actually moving forward, helping create some apparent wind forces. If you are dead in the water, as you probably will be in the extreme situation described here, you need all the power you can get to start moving.

In this airless condition, you probably will also notice that your telltales are nearly worthless. The plastic vane-type telltales cannot pick up shifts in air this light, nor can ribbon or cassette tape. Very light feathers may pick up some of the wind, but the best telltale for this condition is cigarette smoke. I quit smoking in 1967 and refuse to sacrifice my lungs to catch a wind shift, but if you or your crew have not yet kicked the habit, by all means use it as a tool. Smoke will show you any little bit of air there may be.

In this condition you also will be required to have a great deal of patience. The race may be abandoned, but do not count on it. You must capture and use what little air there is, so do not be crawling, bouncing, and jumping around on the boat, as that knocks all possible wind right out of the sails. You must be as still and patient as that log in the water that turns out to be an alligator waiting to catch his dinner.

*Light air with choppy waters.* You will not be able to pinch at all. You must not worry about the weather mark; keep the boat driving through the waves and chop, no matter what. The pincher may appear to be outpointing you, and that may be worrisome; but he will be pushed leeward by the waves down to where you are, despite the fact that his bows appear to be pointing higher. In other words, his leeway will overcome his pointing; and on a course from A to B, you will both arrive at B, but you will be there before him. It's a sailracer's version of "You take the high road, and I'll take the low road, and I'll be to Scotland before you."

*Moderate air, flat seas.* Your need for a flatter sail is obvious, and you should be sheeted fairly tight as well. Do not, however, kill off too much power. This condition may require one or both of you on the wire to keep the boat attitude in the proper place, as outlined in Chapter 8, "Weight Distribution."

Steering the boat must be a constant oscillation between footing and heading high. You should be constantly concerned with the speed of the boat, driving it off to build speed, then converting the speed to advance the boat toward the weather mark, but without dropping off too much speed.

If you drain off much of that speed, you have to start all over again (that takes time and tremendous distance) to redevelop that speed. If you spill off a little speed and gain some good footage to weather and then fall off again while the speed and control are still there, you are starting to find that fine line that walks a boat to weather.

*Moderate air and choppy seas.* You will find a fuller sail in order, and you should not sail as high as before. Anytime there is a chop, you must power through it. By heading high, you are spilling off power. Do not reduce power in wave action.

*Heavy air and flat seas.* It's rare to have a flat sea along with heavy air. When you do, you are shooting for a flat sail, one that can twist off at the top when you need it. There are no waves to stop progress, so you can steer the boat considerably higher than you would if the seas were rolling.

The relatively flat sail will allow you to sail very high on the wind with a considerable amount of speed. There is really no big need to sail off and foot the boat until the chop picks up.

Even though you have little water resistance, you may get puffs that want to put you on your ear. Ease the mainsheet and the jib together, if possible. By easing the main, you should be letting the top of the sail twist off; the bottom will fill out slightly and continue to propel the boat to weather.

The twist-off relieves the heeling moment while diverting the power to the lower section of the mainsail to allow you to keep driving forward.

With the mainsail getting somewhat fuller, the jib must be eased some to accommodate that fullness. Otherwise, the jib, trimmed to complement a flat sail, will now be backwinding the somewhat fuller sail. Upon easing sails, you want to steer off the wind a degree or so to keep the drive. When the puff has passed over, sheet the sails in again and resume a higher course.

*Heavy air and choppy seas.* As the chop builds up with the

heavy air, you begin to steer more off the wind, easing the mainsheet, thereby keeping the drive in the lower part of the sail with the top twisting off. The jib should be set rather loose. You must power your way through when the wind and waves are up. Your object is to keep the weather hull just kissing the water but the boat blowing through waves without a stutter.

*Long, smooth swells.* Here it is best to set up your boat and sail pretty much as you would for flat seas, but use the waves to work your way to weather. Sail high on the front of the swell, and fall off down the back side. You are using the speed from the long back side of the wave, coupled with your driving her off, to head higher on the short front side of the swell.

## *TACTICS*

Overall, your ability to be first to the weather mark depends on a combination of correct sail shape (based on wind, water, and crew weight conditions), and well-coordinated steering and sheeting to go as high and as fast as you can.

But ability alone will not suffice. On the mental side of the game are certain strategic maneuvers that can ensure victory or dictate certain defeat. So now we move on to a discussion of tactics.

### BASIC FACTORS

Before examining actual situations, here are some basic factors that will influence your tactical decisions:

*The "mess" behind you.* First of all, you should realize that your boat does not simply go through the water without leaving a devastating "debris" of mixed-up air and water behind it. As you can see by diagram 24, the wind to the leeward and aft of your boat leaves a mess of eddies and areas of simply no air.

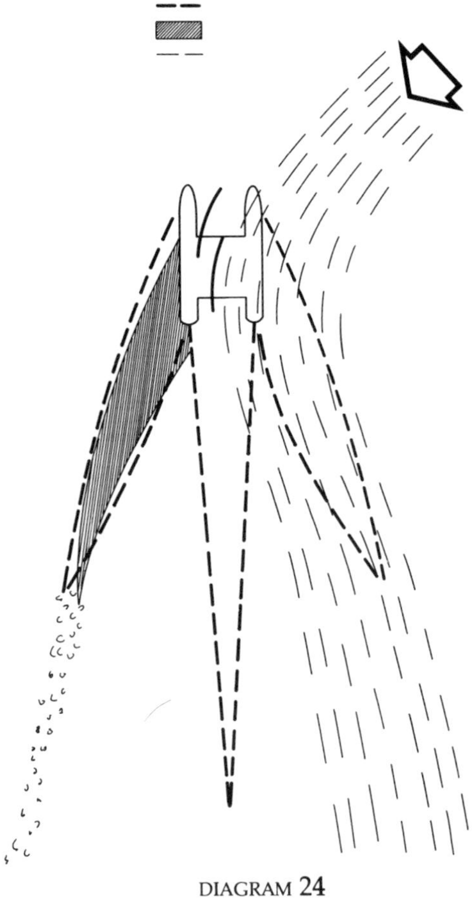

DIAGRAM 24

To the windward side it leaves behind an area of backwinding. Backwinded air is air that has hit the windward side of your sails and then rebounded back and aft and to weather a bit, shifting the wind for any sailor above, aft, and to windward of you.

As for the water, your boat also leaves a wake behind it. Although the sleek hulls of the catamaran leave much less wave action than do the broader, deeper monohulls, they do still leave some.

This mess you leave behind you should be used in your tactical calls during a race. Others will certainly use it against you.

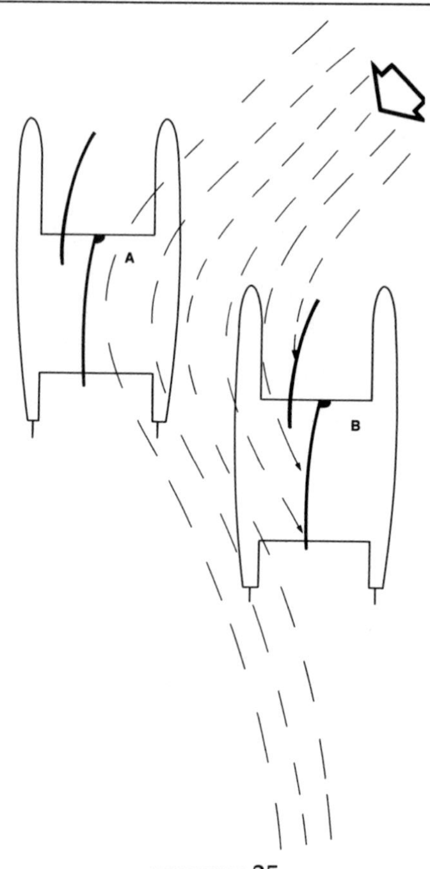


DIAGRAM 25
*Boat B is being backwinded and consequently impeded by boat A.*

*Wind shift.* This is another factor that can work for or against you tactically.

The wind never blows from the same direction at all times and in all places. On a given race course the wind can vary tremendously, not only in direction but in velocity as well. You have probably heard frustrated skippers lamenting a day's racing with comments like "Would you believe Sam and I were going to weather on identical headings, and we were on opposite tacks?"

The variable velocities of the wind will often make one side of the course faster than the other. Sometimes the wind

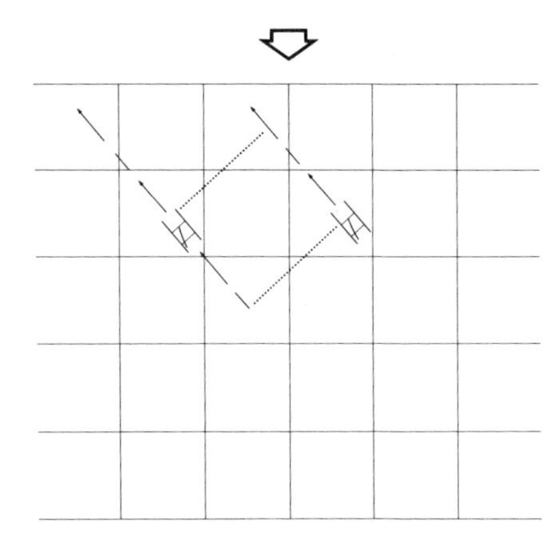

DIAGRAM 26

*With the wind straight on to the grid (in diagram A), neither of these boats has an advantage in position over the other.*

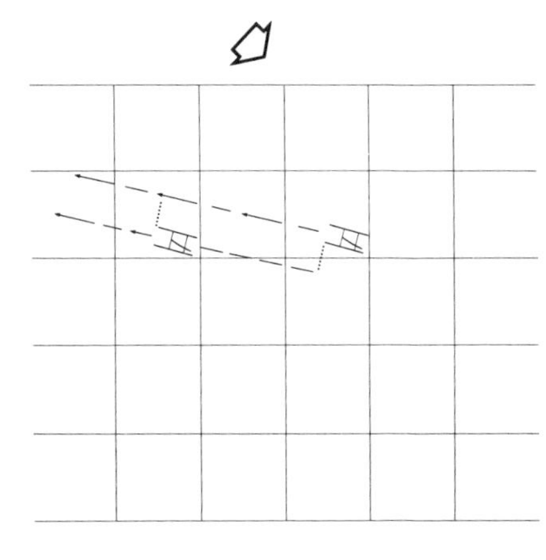

*In diagram B the wind has shifted to the left on the grid, (A header) giving the boat on the left a decided advantage and a sizeable lead.*

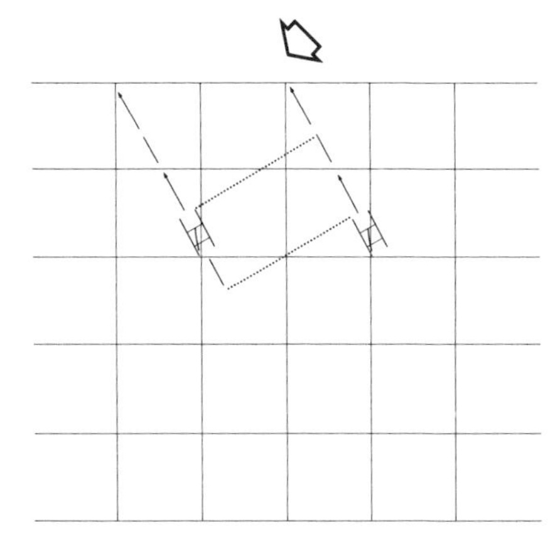

*The wind has shifted to the right-hand side a decided advantage and lead.*

will seemingly pick out one boat and give it lots of push, while the others just sit bobbing in the water.

However, the wind variables with which we deal the most are the simple header and lift. These flaws in the wind are pretty constant and are everywhere on every race course. There is seldom if ever a "steady wind."

A lift will allow the boat that is beating to weather to sail a course closer to its destination (the mark). A header, on the other hand, will make you steer a course farther away from your weather destination. On a lift you can sail higher; on a header you must sail lower.

Some sailors have a difficult time ascertaining whether they are on a lift or a header. One of the best ways I know is to relate yourself to other boats. A grid is the easiest way to show this. (See diagram 26.)

## BASIC TACTICS

Before getting into offensive and defensive tactics, let's review those basic sailing rules that you should always keep in mind regardless of whether you are sparring with opponents or are pretty much alone on the race course.

- √ Sail toward the side of the course having the best air and sea conditions.
- √ Tack on headers, hold on lifts.
- √ Tack as little as possible, but tack when you should.
- √ Always take the tack that brings you more directly to the mark.
- √ Stay in clear air.

When you are dealing with an offensive or defensive tactical situation, it is often necessary to take action that is contrary to these basic sailing rules. But use them whenever possible, and always take them into consideration when making decisions.

If you are all by yourself on the course, either in the lead, in the back, or even mid-pack, use the basic sailing rules and sail consistently until you are in a position where you begin confronting other boats.

*You don't want to overshoot the mark; but then again, some marks deserve a wider berth than others. (Photo courtesy of the Hobie Class Assn.)*

DEFENSIVE/OFFENSIVE TACTICS

There are basically only four situations requiring defense or offense; however, they make up all of racing.

1. You are being overtaken from behind for reasons you do not yet know. *(Use defense.)*
2. You are leading and being challenged by one competitor. *(Use defense.)*
3. You are leading and being challenged by several competitors. *(Use defense.)*
4. You are behind. *(Use offense.)*

Let's look at each case step by step.

*1. You are being overtaken from behind.* (See diagram 27.) Let us say you have just rounded the leeward pin and start off close-hauled for the weather mark. The next boat around hardens up as well, but points 5 degrees higher. He seemingly has a lift that you did not get in rounding. It is not unusual for a boat to *appear* to be pointing higher after first rounding the

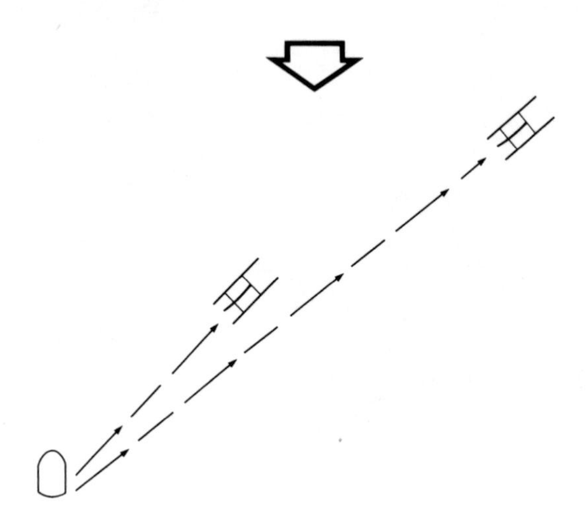

DIAGRAM 27

*PROBLEM: You are being overtaken from behind for reasons you do not yet know.*

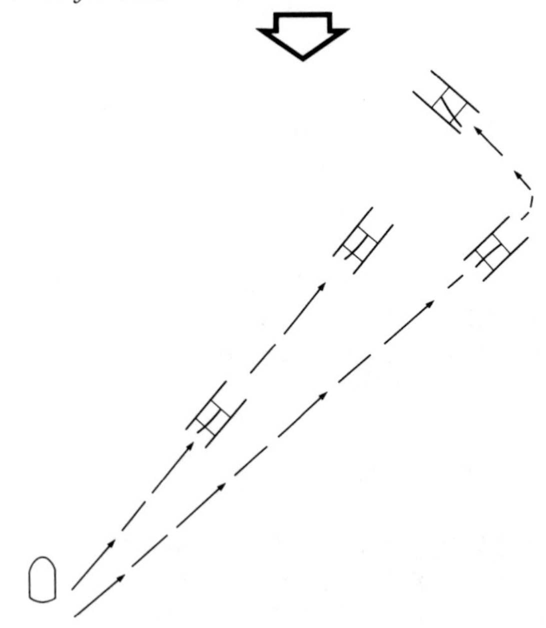

*SOLUTION 1: Tack immediately, losing some ground, yet still remaining ahead.*

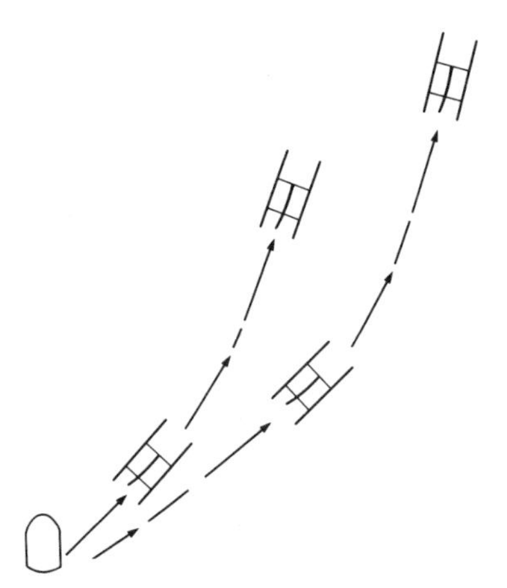

*SOLUTION 2: Hold port tack and possibly get into same wind pattern as the overtaking boat.*

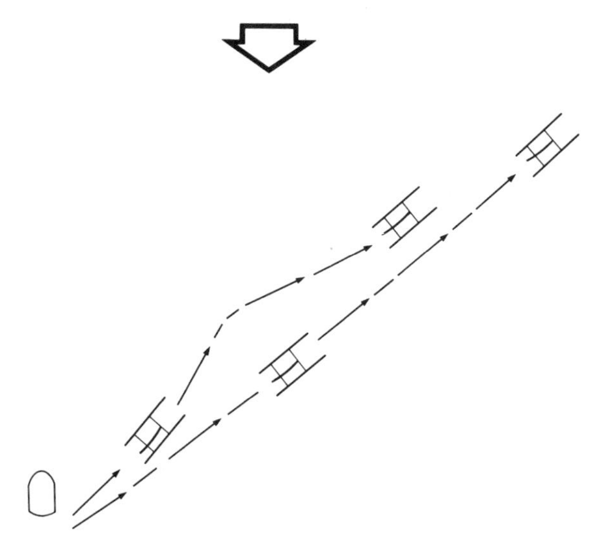

*SOLUTION 3: Hold port tack and possibly the overtaking boat will get into your wind pattern.*

mark. However, if the competitor continues on a lift, you must make a decision, and quickly.

If you hold on to see whether his lift will continue and it does, then you will soon be in a situation where, if you tack, you will be astern. Since that would serve no purpose, you probably should hold onto the tack with the expectation that you both will soon be in the same wind pattern.

Had you tacked upon first seeing that the competitor had a lift, you would have lost a lot of ground to him, but you would still be ahead. This probably would have been a good decision.

2. *You are leading but being challenged by only one competitor.* Even though you may be sailing near the back of the pack or mid-fleet or in the top, you will notice that somehow you are always racing someone. There almost always will be a boat near you, and you usually choose your course and tacks with reference to that boat.

Suppose in this situation that you are on port tack and ahead; approaching is a competitor on starboard tack, but behind. (See diagram 28.) You may simply clear his bows; you may instead tack to a safe leeward position.

In the safe leeward position, the wind bouncing off your sails is backwinding the boat that is windward and aft. The wind he is getting is a few degrees more of a header and it is somewhat disturbed air. Also, he must contend with your wake.

So the safe leeward position will allow you to pull out ahead faster and to point higher, while he will go slower and head down until soon you will be blanketing him with your eddying air shadow on the leeward side.

If you have enough room to go above the starboard boat, tack and blanket him—that would be even better. But beware! Inherent in the catamaran is an inability to tack very fast. If your tack is not completed and you are not off and moving on starboard tack in time, the competitor will have broken through your lee, and he then will establish a safe leeward position on you.

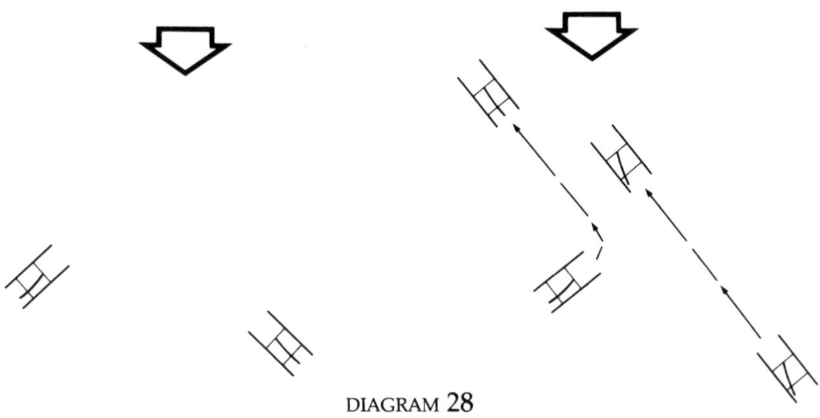

DIAGRAM 28
*PROBLEM: You are on port tack and ahead.*
*SOLUTION 1: Tack to safe leeward position.*

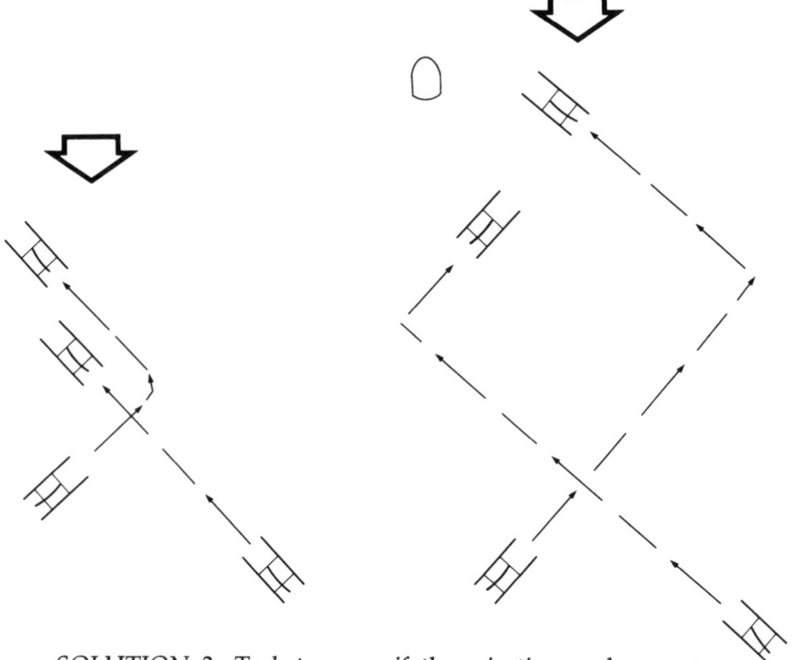

*SOLUTION 2: Tack to cover if there is time and room to complete the tack.*

*SOLUTION 3: Hold port tack until reaching the lay line and then tack to starboard.*

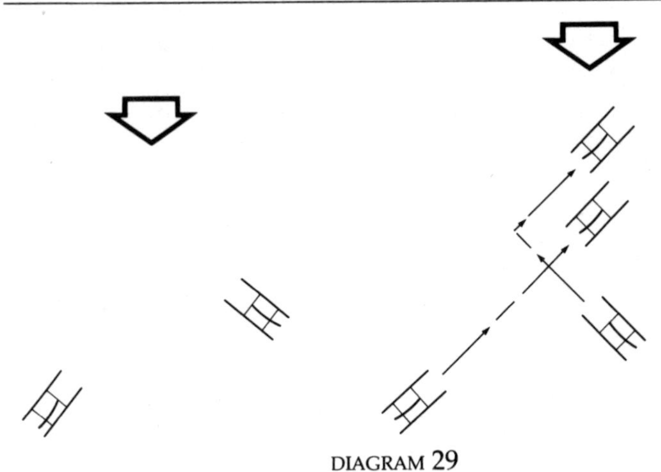

DIAGRAM 29

*PROBLEM: You are on starboard and ahead.*

*SOLUTION 1: Tack and cover the port boat if you can complete the tack in time to remain windward and ahead.*

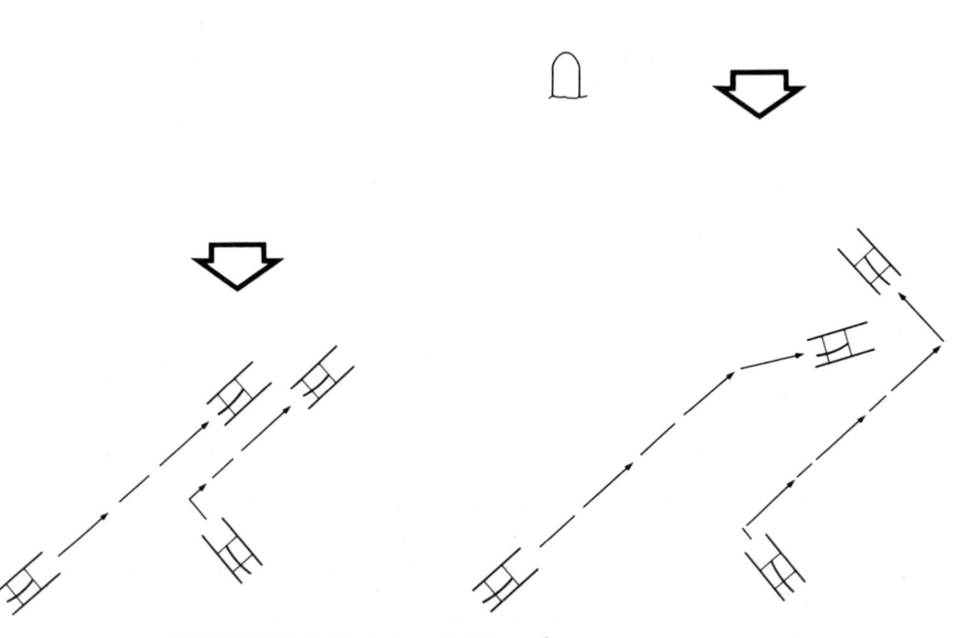

*SOLUTION 2: Tack to safe leeward.*

*SOLUTION 3: When the weather mark is near, tack to port and then on the lay line you will have starboard rights.*

Now let us assume you are on starboard and ahead, while the other boat is on port, not far behind. (See diagram 29.) You can obviously use your starboard rights to remain ahead, but what of the next meeting with the same boat?

If you know that the next encounter will be at the windward pin, you will be wise to tack to port, below and ahead of the port-tack competitor, thereby establishing a safe leeward position. He will not have the drive or the pointing ability that you do, and you should soon be able to lift up from under that position and on up to a position blanketing him.

Had you tried to tack on top of the port tacker, you would still have been in the process of regaining speed, allowing him to break through your lee and into the safe leeward position.

Should you be a bit more in the lead and have enough room, the best thing to do would be to go slightly above the port-tack boat and tack. But in doing so, remember that you must be able to get through the tack and get moving before he is able to get through your lee-blanketing effect to establish a safe leeward position.

In this circumstance, a good time to throw over the helm is when you get to your competitor's weather hull. By the time you make the arc to port, you will be above him by a boat length or two, and in getting your boat under way again, you will be throwing that competitor a lot of "bad gas." (Your wind shadow, by the way, goes as far aft as the apparent wind goes forward.)

Your one other decision could be to exercise the starboard rights and not tack to port until you reach the lay line to the mark. However, then on your next encounter with that boat, speeds being equal, he will be on starboard, with you on port, and it could be marginal as to whether or not you can clear his bows. You will have to be prudent and dive behind his stern and then tack, a maneuver that will lose you a great deal of distance.

To give another Situation 2 example, suppose you have the lead and are to windward on the same tack.

You should stay between the competitor and the next

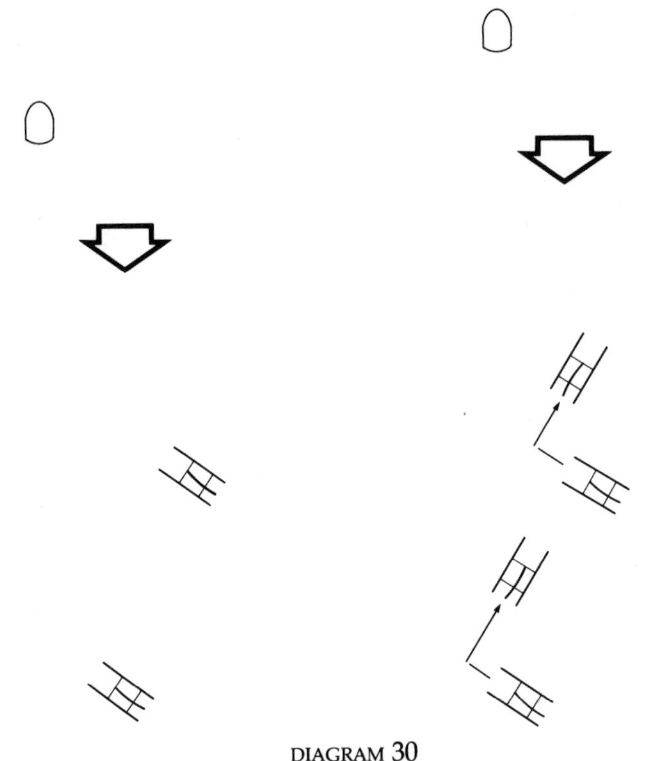

DIAGRAM 30
*PROBLEM: You are ahead on the same tack.*
*SOLUTION: When he tacks, you should tack to cover.*

mark. (See diagram 30.) That is, if he tacks, you should tack as soon as he is directly behind your sterns, or sooner. You will then still be to windward and still ahead. You are then covering his every tack.

You may not be feeding him "gas" the entire time, but you are in the ideal position of getting the same air he does. If you don't cover him, he may get some unexpected big wind shift that you may not, and suddenly the roles will be reversed.

3. *You are leading but being challenged by several competitors.* Your defense in this situation is quite tricky. Visualize your-

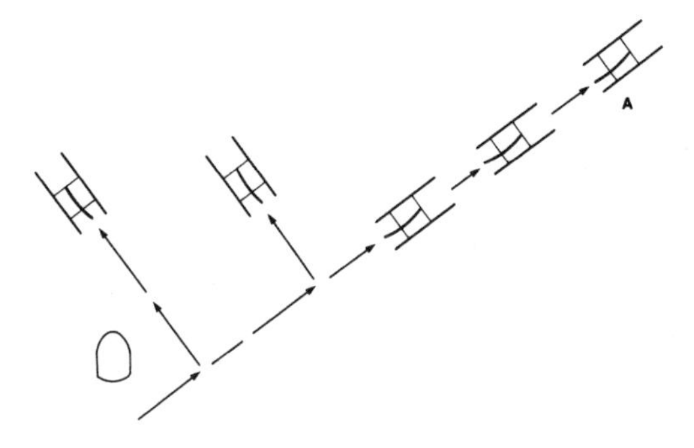


DIAGRAM 31

*PROBLEM: You are leading and being challenged by several competitors. Half the fleet splits tacks.*

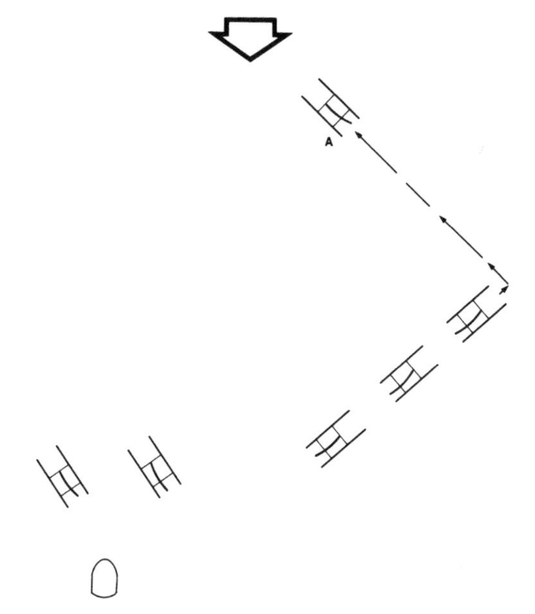


*SOLUTION: Tack to middle of course and cover the most threatening side, dependent upon which particular competitors are the most formidable.*

self rounding the leeward pin and heading out on a port tack. As you continue to sail on that tack, you notice that all your competitors are staying on the same tack as well. That is just great, for if they continue to parade along behind you, you have it made.

However, watch for those who take the other tack. Once they have split tacks, see who they are. In many races your job is simply to beat a few key boats to preserve your place in the standings. If it is the first race of a regatta, you have no idea who you are going to have to beat, so you must judge who you think will give you the most competition before the regatta is over. At any rate, if the tough competition has split tacks with you, you should tack to starboard and cover them.

In a variation of the above situation, half the fleet is on the right side of the course, while the other half is on the left. (See diagram 31.) You should be working a bit closer to the middle, watching to see who appears to be gaining an advantage. If the left side looks as though they have gotten a particularly nice shift, it is in your best interest to head for that side of the course to cover. That decision could easily be wrong, however, and you might lose all the boats to the right side.

In making that decision, you should definitely weigh the competition in each group as well. If your most formidable foe is on the right, you might be wise to head for the right side of the course!

4. *You are behind.* The best rule in this case is always to do exactly the reverse of what the boats ahead of you are doing. (See diagram 32.) You must take the offensive. If you simply do the same thing as the boat or boats ahead of you, you will just be joining their parade. Then you are being very cooperative by allowing yourself to be covered.

If you split tacks after rounding the leeward pin, the lead boat should, according to our previously laid-out defenses, tack to cover you. You should then tack again to get out from under the cover.

Keep in mind that if there are a number of other boats in the race and two of you have a tacking battle, you both will be

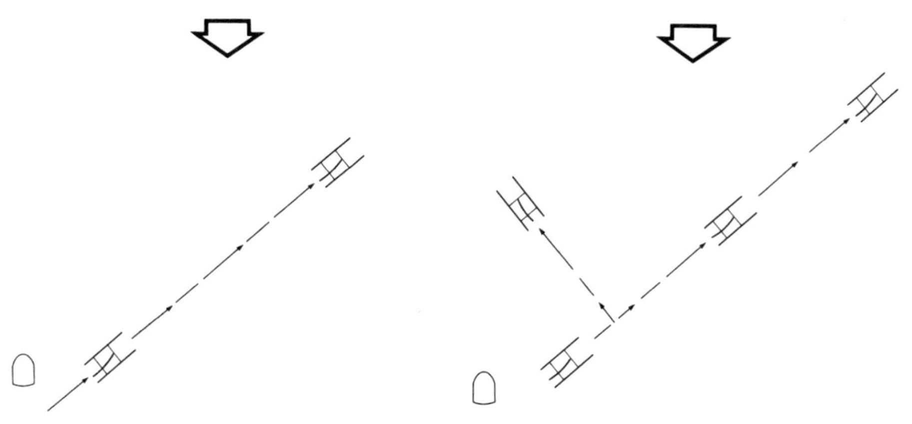

DIAGRAM 32

*PROBLEM: You are behind.*
*SOLUTION 1: Split tacks; try to get into different wind patterns.*

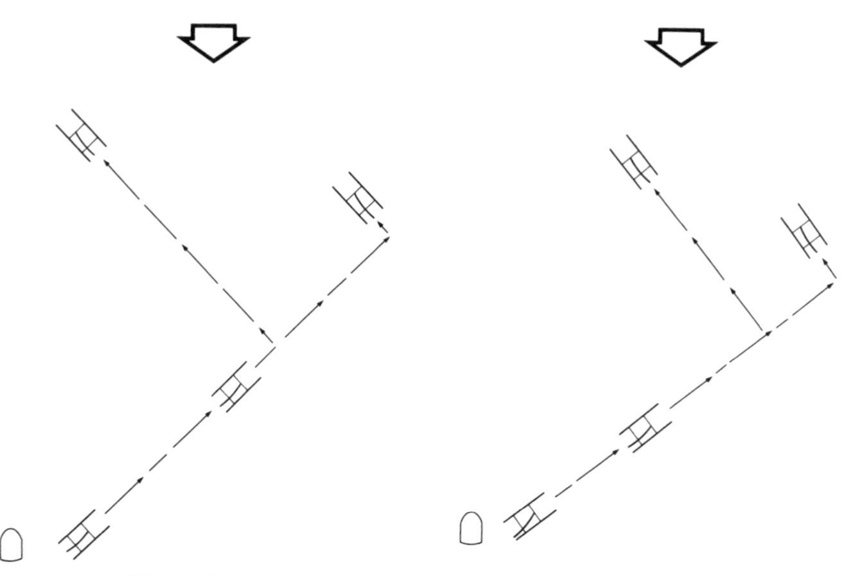

*SOLUTION 2: If lead boat 'Y' tacks, sail at least 100 yards above him and tack.*
*SOLUTION 3: When lead boat tacks on lay line, sail somewhat above him before tacking.*

in the tubes with reference to the other boats. So decide carefully: Are you trying to duck the cover of just one boat or many?

But let us assume the boat ahead has covered you but is not affecting your air. You have clear air and are moving well.

You may elect to hold onto that port tack and sail as efficiently as possible. And he may be so worried and anticipatory of your next tack to get out from under cover that he will not be sailing quite as efficiently. Consequently, you may be able to move out ahead and maybe up toward him more to weather. Then in the case of a header of any kind, you should tack immediately—you will find you have gained substantially on him.

When you are approaching the lay line, there is another especially good maneuver. After the boat ahead of you has tacked, sail a hundred yards above the line where he tacks, and come about. This allows you to stay in similar air. If you both get a lift, you will close the distance on him. If you both get a header, you are still behind but have not lost that much ground.

In addition, if there is a header, you might make the mark, while he must tack two more times. Again, you will gain. On a lift you will be able to drive the boat harder to the mark and should not lose much ground.

Going on to still another situation, the boat leading is starboard and ahead; you are port and behind. (See diagram 33.) If he does not tack to safe leeward on you or tack to blanket you and simply sails on by, exercising his starboard rights, you have nothing to worry about, particularly if you are nearing the "A" mark. Simply keep sailing efficiently; and, with a good clean tack to starboard at the lay line, you may either have him on starboard or at least be worrying him sick.

Had that starboard boat tacked to either a blanket position or a safe leeward, then you would most likely have had to tack back out to starboard to get into clear air.

Suppose in another situation that you are on starboard

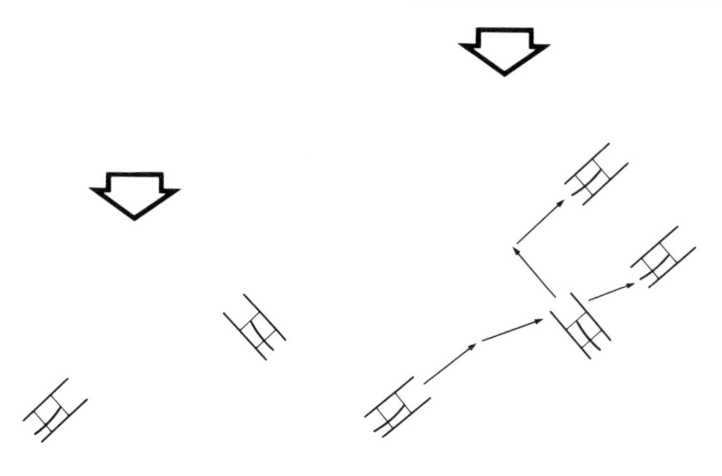

DIAGRAM 33
*PROBLEM: The lead boat is starboard and ahead; you are port and behind.*
*SOLUTION 1: If the lead boat tacks to cover, drive off and through his wind shadow into clear air.*

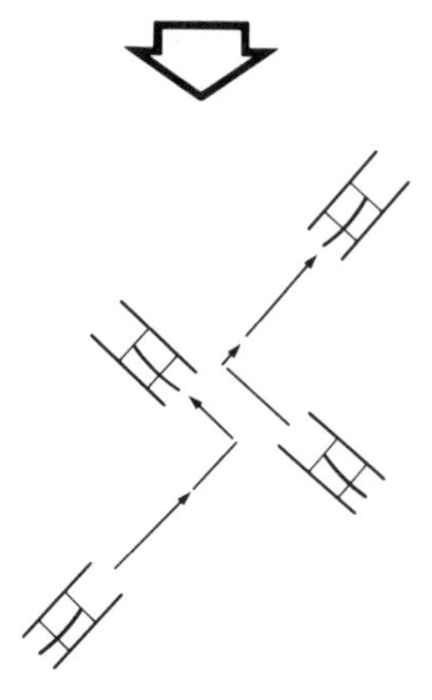

*SOLUTION 2: If the lead boat tacks to cover, tack to starboard and into clear air.*

and behind; and here comes the competitor on port and ahead. (See diagram 34.) If you are fairly far behind, you may sail on beyond him and under his sterns for a short way—perhaps 50 to 100 yards—tack, and be in clear air.

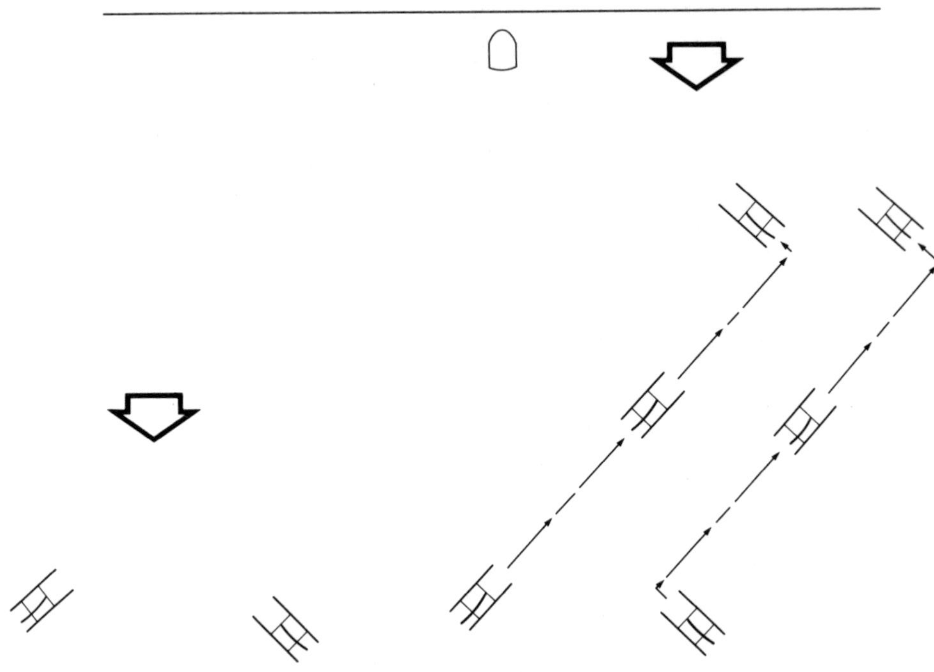

DIAGRAM 34

*PROBLEM: The lead boat is port and ahead; you are starboard and behind.*

*SOLUTION 1: Tack to port and at the lay line you will again have starboard rights.*

Or you could tack below him at a distance where you will not be blanketed by his sails, and concentrate on driving forward and as high as possible, with the hope of working into a safe leeward position.

If your distance behind is not too great, your best bet would be to tack under and work toward a safe leeward position.

In racing, as in chess, you usually are involved in several tactical decisions at a time. Unless you are the lone boat in the lead and concerned entirely with defense, you probably are going to be balancing offensive moves against boats ahead of you with defensive moves against those behind you.

Defense will help keep you in the same position; but if you want to move up through the fleet, you need to be aggressive and offensive as well.

Once your helmsmanship and boat handling skills become instinctive, your mind is free to tackle the endless tactical decisions on the mental side of racing.

# 11

## *THE DOWNWIND LEG*

AFTER rounding that weather mark and heading into the downwind leg, you may think this is the time to relax and have a beer. WRONG. This is the leg of the course that changes a great many positions. You have not won the race by being first to the weather mark—not at all. Now is when the race really begins.

To make things easier to discuss, let's divide this into three parts: first, setting the boat up for downwind sailing; second, helmsmanship; and third, tactics.

## *SETTING UP FOR DOWNWIND SAILING*

Going to weather, you were sailing with a relatively flat sail compared to what you need for the downhill ride. So now think "full."

As discussed in the chapters on the sails, when you begin the downhill leg, you want to loosen your sails and make them full. Ease the outhaul and possibly the luff tension; run the main and jib travelers to the point where they make the sail the fullest. If your boat has boards, pull them up.

You are trying to get the sail full to develop as much power as the boat can generate. Also, you want to reduce as much wetted surface as possible.

A small caution here. Sometimes in a choppy, troubled sea, you may want a board down to make the steering easier. You will have an axis upon which to turn the boat quickly with the board down; and if the sea is slapping you back and forth, to and fro, you can control the yawing of the craft easier with a board down.

The Hobie 18 does not have daggerboard gaskets underwater, and the only thing that keeps the water from gushing up like Old Faithful is the fit of the board itself in the trunk. That also helps the underwater flow of water around the trunk to slip on by without too much turbulence. However, if you pull the board up too high, you will create a cavity in the trunk underwater, which will indeed cause a great deal of turbulence. So, pull the board up only about halfway.

## *HELMSMANSHIP*

In the old days when catamarans were going wing-and-wing on the downhill leg like monohulls, this was indeed the time to relax a little and watch the water go by.

But these days, all high-performance cats tack downwind, sailing at approximately 45-degree angles to the wind (or actually 135 degrees off the wind direction), just as they do in going to weather. (See diagram 35.)

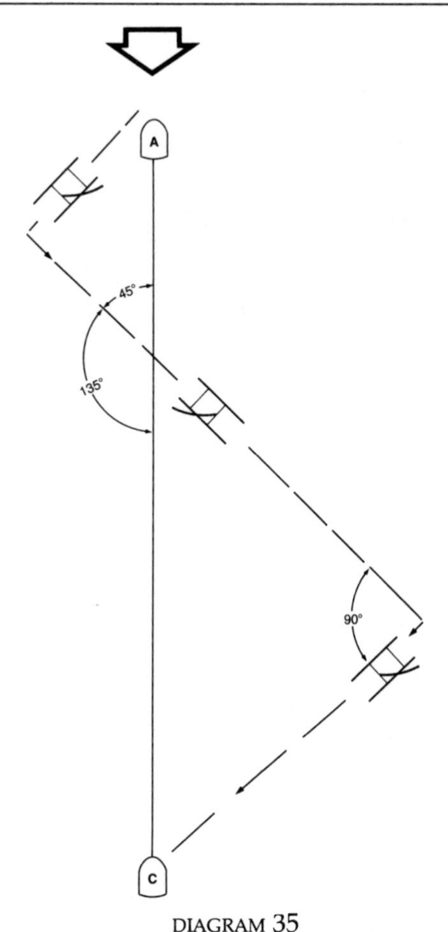


DIAGRAM 35
*Here is an example of tacking downwind to get from mark A to mark C.*

By tacking downwind, you are using the cat's tremendous speed to create a forward-moving apparent wind. The additional speed is more than enough to compensate for the additional distance covered. A straight line may be the shortest distance between two points, but it is not always the fastest.*

*Note that the Hobie 14 sails straight down. And some Hobie 16 sailors will use the wing-and-wing technique occasionally in extremely light air.

Just as on the weather leg, when tacking downwind you must have some way to tell you how deep or high you want to steer the boat.

Some folks use a telltale, which can be located in any number of places. The most popular is the bridle fly, a feather or plastic wind vane mounted between the bridle stays and beneath the forestay. The telltale should be pointing at about a 90-degree angle to the boat.

Another good place for the telltale is on the side stay. In this location you basically are looking for the same thing: The telltale should be streaming perpendicular to the boat, or a little aft.

While these techniques are good for a rough idea of the direction in which you should be steering, they do not allow for that "sweet spot," similar to what we had in going to weather.

There definitely is a "sweet spot" in tacking downwind. If you head too high, you will certainly be going fast, but you will be covering too much additional distance by not sailing deep enough toward the mark. If you head too low, your sails will stall (the opposite of luffing on the weather leg), and you will lose a tremendous amount of speed. You will be taking a shorter line to the mark, but much too slowly.

There is a small, finite line between heading too high and heading too low that makes your boat go fast and, at the same time, deep and toward the mark.

For the most part, finding that spot is a seat-of-the-pants feel, but there is a way to get that feel. Try using the jib as a telltale.

The crew should hold the jib in a set position, complementing the mainsail, and should keep that shape in a constant position, whether hand-held or barberhauled. The helmsman may then steer his course much as he did going to weather, using the jib as a telltale. When the jib luffs, fall off the wind, and when the jib stalls, head up.

Try NEVER to let the jib stall, as it is harder to get the boat moving fast again from this situation. If it is too hard to walk that thin line I just mentioned, stay toward the side of a small luff. The luff is not nearly as damaging to your speed on the downwind leg as is a stall.

You can read the luffs and stalls with the telltales on the jib. If the windward telltale acts radically and is not streaming relatively aft, then you are luffing. If the leeward-side telltale acts radically and is not streaming aft, you are stalling.

The skipper must really concentrate on reading these signs in order to get the boat to perform well, sailing both deep and fast.

Another bonus to this technique of sailing downwind is the ability to pick out wind shifts easily. Since you are walking a thin line, you will immediately notice overall changes in your direction. Despite the oscillation of waves and the fact that you should be heading up for a bit of speed and falling off to drive it as deeply as possible, the overall direction will be noticeable.

### WINDS AND WAVES

The variety of winds and waves will make some difference to you in the manner and direction in which you steer the boat.

In light air and flat seas you have little helping you get toward the leeward pin. There is nothing stopping you, but there is also nothing helping you. You are best advised to head a bit higher than normal in these conditions.

However, when you have seas and heavy air, you should head somewhat deeper. Here you have the sea trying to push you down to the "C" mark anyway, so let it help you. Ride what waves you can, surf the boat when you can, and keep her driving deeply as much as possible—never to the point of stalling, however.

When you catch the back side of a wave, the boat will speed up in its descent, and the jib telltales will show a luff. That is a great time to get a whole bunch deeper, by falling off until the jib is no longer luffing. But when you run out of wave and start trying to head up the next wave, the boat will slow down considerably, and your telltale will show a drastic stall.

Before reaching that point on the next wave, anticipate

what is going to happen and begin heading up at the slightest trace of a stall. Then the faster the boat slows and stalls, the faster you want to head the boat back upwind. Do not let it slow down; keep it out of a stall. A stall will kill you!

If the air is extremely heavy and you cannot hand-hold the jib on the leeward side, bring the crew to windward and aft, but still try to get the jib complementing the main as best you can, and endeavor to steer by the jib telltales. To get the jib in the best position will require the traveler to be set to the forequarter and out as far as possible, or barberhauled.

When the wind really starts blowing, your boat cannot handle the speeds the winds are trying to create, anyway; and your best bet is to head extremely deep, nearly dead downwind (watch for the accidental jibe), and get way aft on the boat. The deep heading will allow both hulls to be used and will make the boat more stable in a real blow.

Generally, your ability to get to the leeward mark before any other boat is premised on getting a full mainsail and a good complementary jib shape; reducing as much wetted surface as is safe; getting a good, readable telltale to suit you; deciding on the type course you want to sail; and walking that thin line, using the wind and waves whenever possible.

But all that still will not make you the victor without some strategy, so let's move on to the tactical side of downwind sailing.

## *TACTICS*

In general, you will have fewer tactical decisions with respect to other boats downwind than going to weather. The fleet tends to be more spread out on this point of sail.

### BASIC TACTICS

Therefore, you will be best benefited by observing the basic tenets of sailboat racing, which we spelled out in the weather leg chapter and reiterate here:

- √ Sail toward the side of the course having the best air and sea conditions.
- √ Tack on lifts and hold on headers (just the reverse of going to weather).
- √ Tack as little as possible, but do tack when you should. (Keep in mind that a jibe in a cat is much faster than a weather tack and will not cost you much distance.)
- √ All other things being equal, always take the tack that brings you more directly to the mark.
- √ Stay in clear air.

Let's look at how some of these basic factors can influence your tactical decisions downwind.

Picking out lifts and headers downwind can be done as illustrated with the grid in "The Weather Leg" (Chapter 10). Remember, however, that downwind the header will take you closer to the direction of the mark, and the lift will take you farther away from the mark.

Using the relationships to other boats not only points out what sort of shift you are on, but what you can do with it tactically. A caution, however: On the downwind leg there seems to be greater variation in sailing styles, and the fact that another boat is sailing higher or lower than yours does not necessarily mean it has caught a wind shift; it may just be the line the skipper chooses to take with the same wind you have.

The important thing is to watch for boats that are going both deeper and faster than you. If you can see no difference in boat or sail trim, try to get into the same air.

## DEFENSIVE/OFFENSIVE TACTICS

The four tactical situations presented in "The Weather Leg" also apply for the downwind leg, but the tactics you can use are far more limited. Defensively, there is relatively little you can do.

You can't get a safe leeward on another boat, because you have no backwinding position on the downwind leg. And residual wave action from your boat causes little, if any, problem for boats near you.

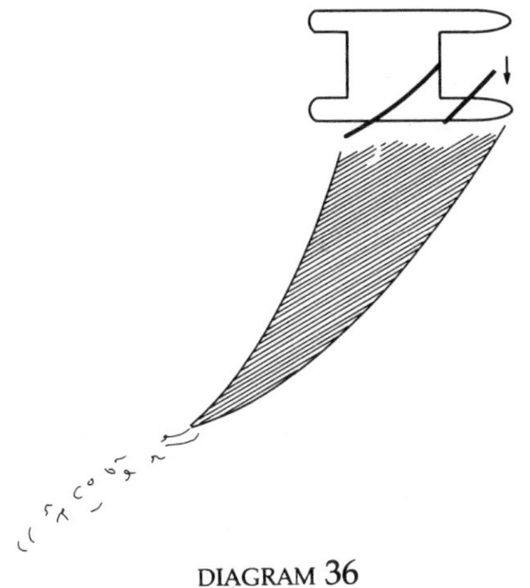

DIAGRAM 36
*An important tactical tool is the wind shadow that extends to the leeward of your boat, approximately as portrayed.*

The main tool with which you have to work downwind is the wind shadow thrown off to leeward and slightly aft. If you choose to use this weapon, keep in mind that the eddies and lack of air off to your leeward will fall at a point opposite of the direction of your apparent wind. If your stay telltales point at a 90-degreee angle from your hulls, then your shadow will be off to your leeward side at about that degree. (See diagram 36.)

You may use this wind shadow effect in deciding when to tack to cover a competitor. However, blanketing as a tactical tool downwind does not really come into play too much until you get into closer quarters—near a mark, for example.

Note that on the downwind leg, blanketing is an offensive tactic, whereas it is a defensive tactic going to weather. Off the wind, you must be behind the other boat (in relation to the mark) in order to blanket that boat.

Tacking to blanket a competitor can be disadvantageous, however, because you may then be blocked from tacking again yourself.

Let's take a look at the four tactical situations and how they apply to the downwind leg:

1. You are being overtaken from behind for reasons you do not yet know. (*Use defense.*)
2. You are leading and being challenged by one competitor. (*Use defense.*)
3. You are leading and being challenged by several competitors. (*Use defense.*)
4. You are behind. (*Use offense.*)

*1. You are being overtaken from behind.* Suppose you have rounded the weather mark and are off on a starboard tack, sailing as deep as you normally do while tacking downwind. The next boat around the mark sets up for his off-the-wind sailing and is heading 5 degrees deeper and going just as fast. (See diagram 37.)

If that competitor continues to sail deeper and as fast, then you must immediately make a decision.

One solution is to tack immediately, cross his bows and, if he remains on starboard tack, jibe back to starboard and stay between him and the next mark.

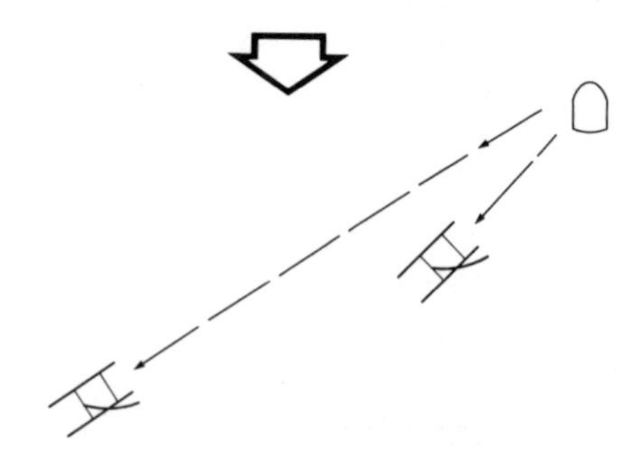

DIAGRAM 37

*PROBLEM: The following boat rounds the mark and sails deeper and as fast.*

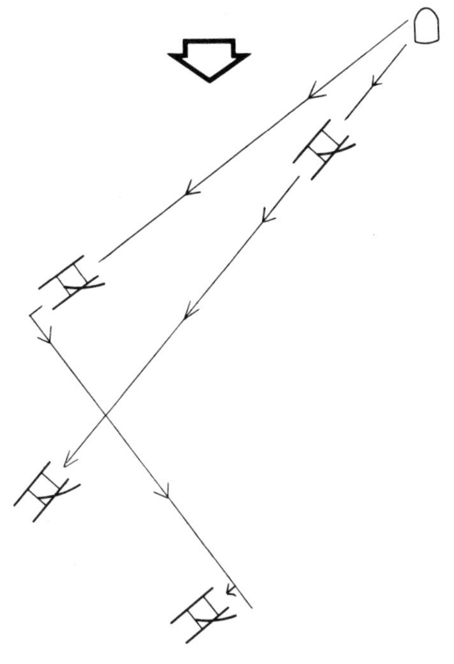

*SOLUTION 1: Jibe across his bows and then jibe again to stay between the following competitor and the mark.*

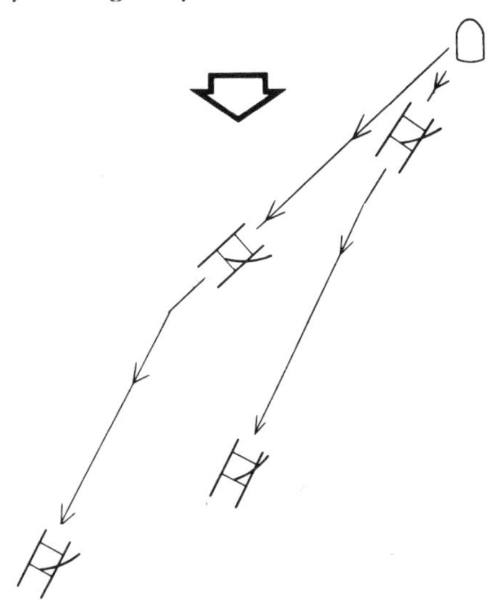

*SOLUTION 2: Hold the tack and hope the wind your competitor has reaches you before he does.*

You also could elect to hold the present tack with the hope that the wind he is getting will soon reach your boat and you both will be heading as deep, which will allow the competitor to gain but not overtake you.

If you wait too long to make a decision and, by tacking, would cross the other boat's stern, then you should hold the present tack and await a different wind shift.

*2 and 3. You are leading and being challenged.* Your only defense is to keep your boat between the competitors and the mark and attempt to stay in the same wind patterns and on the same side of the course as the competitors.

*4. You are behind.* As in going to weather, the best tactic is to do the opposite of the boats ahead of you. If the lead boat jibes to cover your splitting, you may then opt to hold the tack (being in clear air) or jibe.

Remember that the lead boat's covering on the downwind leg is not a blanket cover, as the lead boat is downwind. Still, the lead boat should try to remain between you and the next mark—he should not allow you to get in different wind patterns than those he has.

By holding the tack that you and the leading boat are on, and sailing efficiently, you may be able to drive deep and fast to get nearer to the lead boat. Your big hope will be to work down into a position where you may blanket him with your wind shadow.

Luffing up a windward boat is a defensive tool you might use to prevent a boat from passing to windward. Most commonly employed on reaches, it is occasionally used downwind. My advice on luffing matches is to avoid them. Both boats involved will lose too much ground to the rest of the fleet.

Generally, you are best advised to concentrate on sailing deep, fast, and efficiently on the downwind leg rather than worrying too much about tactics.

# 12

## MAINTENANCE

THE beauty is in the sailing, using the winds and the waves, the essence of nature, to soar with birdlike grace across the sea.

The satisfaction is in the racing, knowing you have used all your knowledge of the wind, the waves, the boat, and the tactics and that you did your very best.

The delight is in sipping a beer, enjoying the camaraderie of fellow sailors, talking over the day's racing—those elusive shifts, the close calls.

The gratification is in knowing the boat has this day thanked you for giving it loving care; she served you well and performed as best she could.

That loving care is what we must give her so that we will always be able to trust her to perform—if you take care of the boat, the boat will take care of you.

Preventive maintenance, a self-descriptive term, is often ignored, if even acknowledged. And yet, without preventive maintenance, your racing and sailing future will most certainly be in jeopardy. What you get out of the boat in performance is directly related to what you put into your boat—and most of the expense is in time, rather than money.

Starting from the beginning, assume you are pulling Old Faithful out of the garage and getting her ready for the first race of the season. Or maybe you are setting up a brand new boat.

Begin by lubricating everything that moves or on which something else moves. If it isn't mentioned in the following maintenance checklists, lubricate it anyway.

The most indispensable do-it-all for sailing is a can of spray lubricant. One simple yet remarkable can of lubricant can save you much time in repairs and can make the boat go fast and sail easier.

Many types of lubricants are on the market. Among the most popular are lubes like CRC and WD40, as well as the Teflon and silicone sprays. Try not to use petroleum- or oil-based lubricants, as they attract dirt and sand. Instead of freeing things up, you may be gumming up the works.

The Teflon or silicone sprays work really well, and many are nonstaining. The nonstain type may be used on the bolt rope of the mainsail, making it easier to hoist or lower, as well as making it easier to downhaul.

## *MAST AND BOOM*

1. Check all pulleys and swiveling apparatus and lubricate well. On roller furling jibs, spray the swiveling devices doubly well.
2. Check all shackles to be sure there are no signs of

stress. Replace any that might have bends or cracks or show any other signs of stress or strain.

3. Check rigging, stays, shrouds, and halyards, watching for kinks in the stainless cable and stress in the fittings; watch for frays in the halyards.

4. Check Nicro fittings and swagings to be sure they are showing no signs of stress. If so, replace.

5. Check any riveted fittings, pulleys, etc. If they show any signs of being loose, drill them out and replace them with stainless steel rivets.

6. Check all points of attachment, particularly those with pins held by circlips and/or cotter pins, and tape them in place to be sure they do not work loose or stick out into a position to tear a sail.

7. Coat your entire mast with a good coating of lubricant.

### *HULLS*

1. Turn the boat over and check the hulls for any scratches or gouges. Fill them with gel coat and sand hulls to remove all imperfections; then sand with 600 sandpaper for a fast hull. (By the way, do not drag the boat uncaringly across the beach unless you are fond of sandpapering.) Sanding strokes should be parallel to the water flow, not perpendicular.

2. On centerboard-type boats, a great deal of care around the trunk is mandatory. If there are gaskets, check to be sure they are glued extremely well. (Gaskets have a tendency to come loose and drag in the water.)

3. Check chainplates and all other attachment points for staywires to the hull. Repair and replace as necessary.

4. Check beam bolts to be sure they are tight. Many Hobie Cat skippers have epoxied their beam bolts, thus allowing a tighter boat overall. The problem is the boat will not come apart again. In lieu of epoxy, you might want to try silicone rubber sealant. Then you have a tight boat, and it can be taken apart as well.

5. Check rudder gudgeons and their attachment points.

If there is any looseness, repair. Do *not* use rivets. There is too much strain on these parts, which is then transferred to the boat's stern; therefore, through bolts must be used.

6. Lace the trampoline extremely tightly. This portion of the boat contributes to her stiffness overall. The trampoline and line seem to stretch, so tighten the trampoline often. If the lacings themselves are showing signs of wear, replace them with nonstretch line.

7. Double lubricate the main traveler track and any other traveler tracks attached to the hull.

8. Lubricate the mast rotation area as well.

9. Keep inspection ports open at all times when the boat is not in the water. This will allow air circulation in the hull to help it stay dry. Even with rain water, which will lie in the bottom, most of the glass will dry and the boat will be lighter and stronger. Fiberglass can absorb up to 25 percent of its own weight in water.

10. In some daggerboard trunks there is a great deal of roughness where the deck has been attached to the hull and the board trunk. This must be smoothed out. You might try reaching in with some sandpaper and smoothing out the spots, or use duct tape over them. You also might try using silicone rubber sealant, as it will set up as a soft, spongy surface, relieving scratches and nicks on the board.

## *BOARDS AND RUDDERS*

1. Check the boards and rudders for scratches and gouges, then fill and sand, finishing off with 600 sandpaper for that racing finish. First-timers with new Hobies should be aware that the trailing edges of both must be shaved down to a sharp edge and sanded; and the leading edge should be sanded to a smooth, rounded entry. Be sure sanding is done in the direction of water flow, leading edge to after edge or vice versa. Perpendicular grooves of any kind create water friction.

2. If your rudders have a great deal of play in the hous-

ing, you can shim them. There are kits on the market that cost too much and do little more than a Tupperware top. Butter container tops will work as well, but may not hold up as long.

In his book, Jack Sammons has recommended Formica, the type used on counter tops. If it becomes obvious that you need a spacer, it should be of a durable material that will allow the rudder to go up and down.

3. Check the rudder pintles and the rudder housing for cracks or signs of stress. Replace if necessary.

4. Many cats have a rudder-locking mechanism. Check to be sure the device will allow the rudder to stay down under normal sailing strains, yet will release upon hitting an unyielding object. In the Hobies there is a plastic cam that can easily be replaced if it is worn or faulty in any way.

5. Check connections of the tiller bar and tiller extension to ensure there is little slop. Replace, if necessary.

6. Rudder alignment should be checked after the boat is all up. The rudders should be lined up straight and even on each side. Some sailors recommend a slight toe-in. (This makes sense on the asymmetric-hull boats, as it would tend to elongate the curve that promotes underwater lift, as explained in Chapter 6.)

## *SAILS AND SHEETS*

1. Check for tears and rips in the sails. If there are any beginning, send the sails to your neighborhood loft for immediate repairs. Some tender spots on cat sails are along the luff of the mainsail, particularly where the batten pockets end. Due to the heavy tensions sometimes placed on the battens, the leading tip of the batten wants to pop out the front. Be sure the pockets are beefed up to take these loads.

2. The fully battened sail has a great advantage in that it can be stored very well by simply loosening battens and rolling it up. Battened sails stored this way last much longer than counterpart "monomaran" sails that are folded for storage. The jib sail should be rolled as well, rolling along the luff

and making it into a snake. They you need only coil it and safely place it away for storage.

3. Inspect sheets for extreme fraying. If in poor shape, replace.

4. Check all shackles on the sheeting systems to assure they are not stressed.

5. Lubricate all blocks and cleat swivels.

## *TRAILERS*

1. Check lights and wiring. If anything is faulty, repair or replace it.

2. Check wheel bearings and, if necessary, pack with grease. Also check springs and grease them if they are set up for such maintenance.

3. Lubricate the hitch ball and hitch with Teflon or silicone spray. The petroleum-based lubricants attract too much sand and dirt and eventually will cause even more wear than if the ball is not lubed at all. Be sure the safety chain is in good shape.

4. Overinflate small tires. Most tire specs call for less pounds per square inch (psi) than you should put in the tire. The usual small tire has a recommended psi of 60 lbs. Put in 70 psi, and you will find the tire will last longer and run cooler. Check spare tire, as well.

5. Check all boat rollers and lube.

*Note:* Never back your trailer into the water to the point where the wheel hubs or lights are submerged.

## *TRAVELING*

1. Be sure the boat is secured firmly to the trailer, with neither fore-and-aft movement nor lateral movement.

2. The mast should be tied fore and aft, with its extension no more than 3 feet behind the boat. Tie a red flag to the tip of it.

3. Stays, halyard, and shrouds may be coiled, tied securely in that coil, and then tied securely to the trampoline. Be sure nothing even has a chance to drag.

4. The rudders should either be taken off for transportation or secured so under no circumstances can they fall down into the vertical position. The Hobies can tie their tillers down to the rear beam, thus securing them from falling.

5. Daggerboards should be removed and stored carefully. They are difficult to tie successfully to the trampoline, so they should be bagged and put in the boat box or car.

6. Sails should be in the boat box.

# 13

## SAFETY

WHILE sailing is one of the most exciting and pleasurable experiences on one's list of fun things to do, as with most sports, it has its potential dangers. If certain safety rules are not attended to, that pleasure can turn into disaster.

Fortunately, sailboat racing has always been a relatively safe sport, with death or serious injury being a rarity. The reason for its good record is that most experienced sailors automatically adhere to the rules for safe sailing given in this chapter.

Probably the two most important general rules are:

√ *Never underestimate the power of the wind and the waves.*

√ *Know your boat's limits and don't try to push it beyond those limits.*

Keeping those basic axioms in mind, common sense dictates all the following advice:

1. Wear appropriate gear for the weather conditions. In cold water or low air temperature, wear a wetsuit or warm foul weather gear to avoid hypothermia.

2. Use some type of nonskid material on the rails or sides of the boat so your feet won't slip when you are trapezing.

3. Always have life jackets on the boat. (They are required, both by race committees and by the Coast Guard.) If you can't swim, wear your life jacket at all times. The race committee usually doesn't require that life vests be donned until the wind is around 10 knots or more. But don't let that stop you from putting them on sooner. An added advantage to wearing the vests is that it keeps them off the deck where they can get tangled in the sheets.

4. When racing, make sure your committee has provided for enough crash boats to handle emergency situations. In heavy weather conditions, if there are too few crash boats (or worse, none at all), object to the race committee. If the situation is not remedied, it would be a wise decision to sit out the race on shore and then protest to your class association.

5. Where there is thunder, there is lightning. If a thunderstorm or electrical storm is forecast for your area, postpone your sailing or racing until it blows over.

If you are out on the water and see a thunderstorm coming, head for shore as fast as possible. (Most race committees will abandon the race if they see lightning in the area.)

If you are caught, on the open water in the middle of a storm containing lightning, avoid sitting on or touching any metal parts of the boat, and do not put any part of your body in the water.

6. Make sure your crew knows enough about sailing to handle the boat alone in case you, the skipper, fall overboard or are injured.

7. Always be alert to what is happening on your boat as

well as to the relationship between your boat and others on the race course. Be prepared for a sudden change of course to avoid a capsize or pitchpole. Things happen fast on a catamaran, and you don't want to be caught off balance.

8. Make sure your boat and all its equipment are in top shape by adhering to all the maintenance suggestions in Chapter 12. A lot of people have watched their masts fall over during races, because of failure to realize you can't trust a ringpin (circlip).

Buy durable hardware for your boat. For racing, you want it to be lightweight, but it must be strong as well. Bad equipment can let you down at the wrong times.

9. Before each day's racing, check shackles, pins, and circlips and rigging (watch for wire strands broken or kinked) to be sure all are secure.

10. If you have diamond stays, be sure the adjustment barrels are tight, locked and secured by tying a length of line or wire between the centers of the two barrels. This will ensure they don't twist off more than a few turns. Otherwise, if a barrel comes all the way off, you will certainly break your mast.

11. Be sure your drain plugs are screwed in. A sinking boat is very slow, difficult to maneuver, and, if only one hull fills with water, could capsize.

12. If something goes wrong during a race (which it seems often to do), you can fix almost anything if you have along a Hobie key and a set of vise grips. The Hobie key is a very useful tool, as it serves so many functions. A set of vise grips is almost as good as having an extra hand along, and it usually has a wire cutter in its jaws, which can be used for cutting line. Armed with these two tools, you probably could take on an overhaul job.

It helps to carry a couple extra shackles, a piece of lightweight line, and an extra piece of shock cord as well, for those emergency jury-rig jobs on the water.

13. For racing, keep your decks as uncluttered as possible and free of extra debris (like beer coolers or extra clothing). It is an unfailing truth that whatever your sheets can get caught

on, under, or around, they will get caught on, under, or around. Tangled sheets have caused many a capsize.

14. Make sure your mainsheet and jib sheet cleats are positioned at an angle that allows you to release them easily, whether you are sitting on the deck or out on the trapeze. "I couldn't release the mainsheet" is probably the most common excuse given for capsizes.

15. Righting lines are a must for any small catamaran. In the chapter covering capsizing, a few methods of using righting lines are discussed. If you go over before you get your righting lines installed, all is not lost. In many boats the main halyard may be used; the mainsheet is another nice, long, available line that may be jury-rigged for righting the boat.

16. One of the most overlooked factors for safety in sailing, particularly racing, is the importance of being in good physical condition.

Catamaran racing can be and usually is quite demanding physically. After a tough race series, you may find yourself nursing aches, scrapes, bumps, and blisters.

That does not mean you have to be an Olympian to sail. However, it certainly is a good idea to be in good shape to prevent injuries and to improve racing performance.

For the top contenders to be in good shape is not just a good idea; it is an absolute must. Quite obviously, in heavy air it takes a lot of stamina and strength to sail the boats competitively. But even in light air it takes surprising strength and agility, for you must be able to react quickly to wind shifts or sit like a statue for long periods of time. Or you may have to move about the boat like a shadow, without disturbing the boat's attitude, its motion, or its sails. That takes physical ability—no room for a klutz here.

Physical conditioning is desirable for good sailing; but even more, it is a must for an emergency. It is amazing how fast your energy deserts you when you're being doused in cold, angry water, struggling to get your cat back on her feet again. The better your physical shape, the better your chances of getting the boat upright both quickly and safely.

Add to that the possibility of you or your crew drifting

away from the boat. Either of you must now call upon even more of your reserves to quickly right the boat alone in order to save the other from peril.

All these potential problems and stresses do require strength, and strength does not come to you in emergencies just because you are young and macho, or because you made the 1955 Keokuk, Iowa, All-City football selection. It comes from adhering to a continuing program of aerobic and muscle conditioning.

Many of the best ways of staying fit are almost entirely free: jogging, walking, swimming, and bicycling.

And there is no excuse for not getting in your daily dose on those ugly days when you do not want to leave the house. Now available are jogging treadmills, stationary bicycles, and rowing machines. A versatile but inexpensive device is the mini-trampoline on which you can bounce or run in place for half an hour a day to keep yourself in terrific condition.

A simple, home weight-training program of some sort is highly recommended to complement the aerobics.

17. The greatest number of deaths and injuries involving small sailboats, including catamarans, has resulted not from sailing or racing, but has occurred while the boat is still in the parking lot or rigging area.

Those accidents resulted from electrocution when the mast or part of the rigging came into contact with an overhead electrical wire. In a few cases I know of, the mast was not even in contact with the wire itself, but electricity arced from a frayed point on the wire to the mast.

So the MOST IMPORTANT SAFETY RULE is to look up and check for overhead wires. You see the notices and decals everywhere: "Extreme caution must be observed when launching and sailing near overhead wire. A mast near a wire could be fatal."

Heed that warning!

# 14

## CAPSIZE: PREVENTION AND CURE

A LASER can be capsized by simply sneezing in the wrong direction. And it is just as easily righted again.

But because of the inherent stability in a boat that is approximately half as wide as it is long, it is difficult to capsize most catamarans in light to moderate air. Wind alone usually will not do it—it takes a lot of weight in the wrong place to make it roll over.

Conversely, if you do manage to capsize in light air conditions, you probably will have difficulty righting the boat again.

In heavy air the boat is more easily capsized, but it is much more easily put back on its feet.

AXIOM: *If there is enough wind to blow you over, there is enough wind to right you easily; but if there is not enough wind to blow you over, there is not enough wind to right you easily.*

But why bother with righting at all, when capsize can almost always be prevented in the first place?

It is important to understand what causes capsize in order to understand how to prevent capsize. And since the situation almost invariably occurs in heavy air and seas, this chapter will relate exclusively to those conditions.

## *PHYSICAL FACTORS*

The two physical factors responsible for capsize are the boat's friction with the water and the heeling pressures of the wind on the sails.

Boat friction in the water becomes a factor because the sails are capable of going through the air much faster than the boat can go through the water. This can cause the boat to want to trip over its own nose and cause a pitchpole (capsize frontward).

This is counteracted by easing the sails a little to reduce speed and power or by moving the crew weight as far aft as necessary to keep the bows from tripping—or by a combination of the two.

The other factor is the wind pushing against the sails, trying to make the boat heel and fly a hull. When the hulls cannot go forward fast enough for the power generated by the sails, the boat will instead tend to be pushed over sideways. Again, this can be controlled by easing sails, getting weight as far outboard as possible on the windward side, or both.

If you begin flying a hull, once the hull gets up to a certain point, the wind pressure is no longer hitting just the sails, it is also hitting the underside of the trampoline, trying to push you over even more.

This same effect of the wind can work to flip you over backward if you are in irons in heavy air and the wind gets under the front of your trampoline.

Catamarans are no more likely to capsize (and perhaps less so) than monohulls in the same wind conditions. However, things do tend to happen faster on a catamaran, and reactions must be quick and instinctive. It is a high-performance critter that can easily get out of control in the hands of a novice going for the thrills before he learns the basics.

Experimenting to see how high you can fly a hull is a fun thing to do, but it is important to remember that at a certain point you will have gravity working against you in the weight of the mast and sails; and the wind will be working against you by pushing on the bottom of the trampoline.

## *FOUL-UP ON BOARD*

The two physical factors are always acting on the boat in heavy air and, when properly controlled, are not a reason for capsize. They are simply the ultimate cause when there is some foul-up in the control by skipper and crew.

Capsizes are more likely to occur during racing than daysailing, because the skipper is not free to pick an easier or less precarious point of sail; and he is pushing the boat to its limit, walking a fine line between preventing capsize and keeping the boat moving with the greatest possible speed and power.

The specific reasons and "excuses" for capsize are almost endless; but, generally, if a boat is well organized, it tends to get into problems much less than its more chaotic counterpart.

For example, you should have a clean deck, free from any clutter that may grab and foul a sheet at the wrong time.

Sheets should be tended constantly to ensure they are not washed overboard. An overboard sheet will not allow you to ease the sail. You see, the sheet comes directly from the ratchet block to your hand. If it is trailing in the water when you try to ease the sheet, the resistance of the sheet dragging in the water is as great as the tension on the block. As a result, the sheet does not go out; the sail is not eased; and the boat is in jeopardy of capsize.

The mainsheet, because so much of its length is loose on the deck going to weather, is easily washed overboard. A good way to keep the mainsheet on the boat is to tie a bungee cord across the trampoline about halfway between the fore and aft beams and through the loop of the mainsheet. (This is assuming your traveler line and mainsheet are continuous.)

Clear, crisp commands by the one in charge help define what is to be done aboard. Often, in heavy weather, the sounds of the sea and the wind can overwhelm softspoken orders, and mistakes are then easily made.

Actually, capsizes normally occur in only three major situations. In their order of probability, they are: (1) the reach; (2) the jibe; and (3) the tack.

## *THE REACH*

The cardinal rule for reaches (and this goes for sailing to weather as well) is never to cleat the sheets in heavy air. That extra moment of trying to snap the sheet out of the cleat may be just the moment that sends you into the drink.

In addition, by not being sheeted, you have a definite "feel" of the power of the wind in the sail, and you can react immediately to that "feel." When a hard puff hits you, you will already have felt its advance thrust and begun releasing the sheet.

By not cleating the sheets and by feeling the wind, you have reduced the possibility of capsize; you keep the boat in the proper attitude; and you keep her moving forward at optimum speed.

Often you will find the wind trying actually to trick you. You are reaching along when the wind swings to a header and dies a little. You probably sheet in and head down a bit. It then eases more and swings still more. You harden up still more, head down more, and start coming in off the trapeze.

And then . . . WHAMMO! The wind slaps you hard

from its original direction in a tremendous gust, blasting the sail at an angle too far perpendicular to give you thrust—only heeling moment. Hope the mainsheet was not cleated! Hope the jib sheet was not cleated, either!

Cleating can be a real problem, and it is unnecessary, unsafe, and unrewarding in winds over the moderate range. And it is not that difficult to hold the sheets. After all, we now have excellent blocks and ratchets, and we have a lot of sheet purchase.

You want to keep the boat at the proper attitude, as discussed in Chapter 8, "Weight Distribution." Flying a hull destroys forward speed and puts you in a position of possible calamity.

There are, however, going to be times when you still cannot react in time to save the hull from going up. If it starts flying, ease both the main and jib sheets until the ascent stops; then as it begins to descend, sheet in. This will give the boat a great surge forward, much like squeezing the seed out of a grape.

Your object is to catch the rise of the hull and, by quickly easing the sheets, stop the ascent. Do not let the boat get up on its ear. Getting the boat up high on its side is opening the door for still another puff to knock it completely over; besides that, you will have absolutely no speed.

## *THE JIBE*

Jibing can be a very hairy experience in heavier air; but if you are prepared, it becomes a bit easier. First alert the crew of the planned jibe, with crisp commands such as "Ready about" and "Hard alee."

With the crew duly alerted, bring the helm over fairly slowly until she is just about to jibe, then put the helm over hard, but be ready to bring it back quickly to head downwind again on the other tack as soon as the boom comes across.

The power of the sail striking hard on the opposite tack will try to round the boat up. You must stop that action by heading the boat down to stabilize it. Once it is stabilized, return to your normal handling of the boat while on the downwind leg.

Note that this jibing technique is only to be used in survival conditions, in order to reduce the possibility of capsize. In normal air, as the boat comes around on the other tack, you will, rather than heading down to stabilize the boat, head it up slightly above your normal course for a few moments to build up speed again before falling off to your normal heading.

If you find, after the jibe, that you are beginning to raise a hull, head it down quickly and get all your weight aft in the boat. By heading down, you will be utilizing the buoyancy of two hulls and not just the leeward hull. But the same force that began raising a hull may now try to dig the bows under water and cause a pitchpole. Getting your weight aft quickly should stop that threat.

Usually, however, the jibes should not be quite that violent, as you are getting pretty near the speed of the wind itself. As an example, when a monohull, limited to his hull speed of possibly 8 knots, jibes in winds of 18 knots, the difference in actual speed and wind speed is 10 knots. Therefore, there is a great deal of violence in the boom coming across.

In the catamaran, in the same 18 knots of wind, you may well be nearing the same speed as the wind, thus the boom is ushered across by a mere 2 or 3 knots difference. Hence, a more docile jibe.

But a caution: *If you execute your jibe too slowly and dally too long in letting the stern cross the wind, the stalled sails will slow down your boat speed, resulting in a proportionately more violent jibe.*

If you are sailing a boat with daggerboards or centerboards, it normally is recommended to raise them for downwind sailing, principally to reduce wetted surface. In heavy air, though, you sometimes get so busy there just isn't time to get to the boards.

With the boards left in the down position, you will find that steering the boat is much easier and rudder helm is better.

But the problem with that is the boat will tend to heel more easily. The boat offers an underwater resistance that allows the boat to raise a hull more quickly than with the boards up.

The best of both worlds would be nice, so raise the boards halfway, and you have a boat that steers fairly easily but has less tendency to fly a hull.

Perfection would be to sail with the leeward board up, the windward board down; but in a really hairy blow, who has time to find perfection?

## *THE TACK*

Tacking, the last and least of the dangers, can cause capsize only by major mistakes: by not making it to the new windward side; by cleating the jib in the backwind position; by getting tangled in sheets; by not being able to get unhooked from the trapeze on the previous tack; or by getting into irons and losing control of the boat.

Even if all goes well (see diagram 38), you can get caught in irons once in a while. If this happens, you will begin backing up, and you should immediately backwind the jib on the easiest side, while at the same time turning your rudders to the same side as the jib. The backwinded jib will bring the bow one way, while the rudders will push the stern the opposite way. When the boat is through the eye of the wind, quickly bring in the jib on the opposite side, bringing the bow still farther around. Then slowly bring in the main and steer the boat to close-hauled.

When you are caught in the irons position in a hairy blow, watch carefully that your weight balances the boat fore and aft, as well as side to side. The wind from ahead can easily get under the trampoline and blow the boat over backward; or if the boat suddenly comes out of irons and you are caught on the new leeward side, it will capsize sideways.

Whatever you do, try never to let a boat capsize during a race. It's not a good time to get in your righting practice. You probably have read that if you don't capsize once in a while,

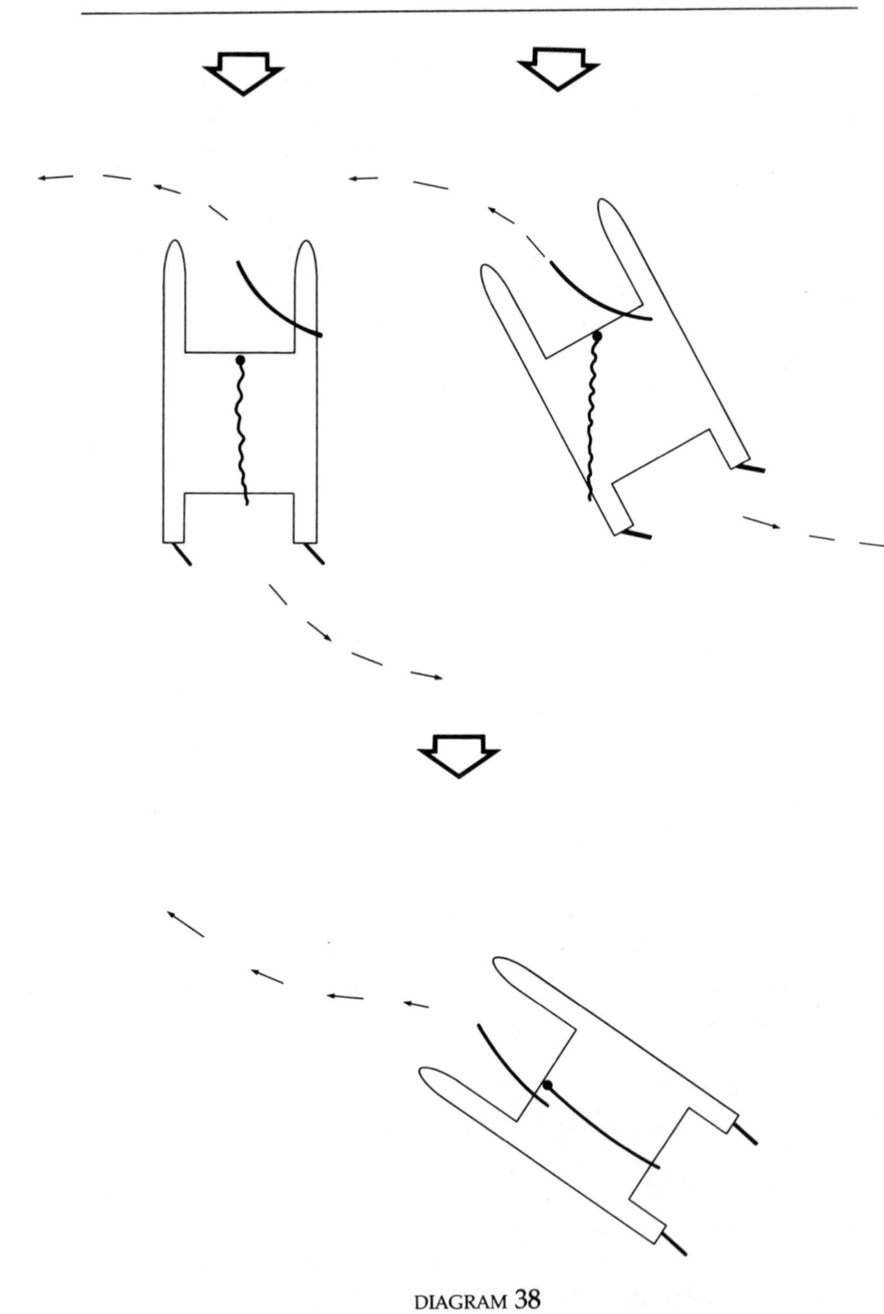

DIAGRAM 38

*This series of diagrams illustrates the procedure for getting out of irons by backwinding the jib.*

you are not trying hard enough. But I would suggest that you learn just how much you can get away with at some other time, not while you are racing.

Certainly, you should learn the characteristics of your craft and then push it to the hilt. But first learn where the hilt is.

## THE CURE

After you make that pilot error, which is usually the only reason you are capsized, you will probably find yourself upside-down, wondering what to do next.

But first, let us go back in time a little, to before you got yourself into this rather inefficient position.

Before even going out sailing, you should have installed some form of righting lines on your catamaran. There are

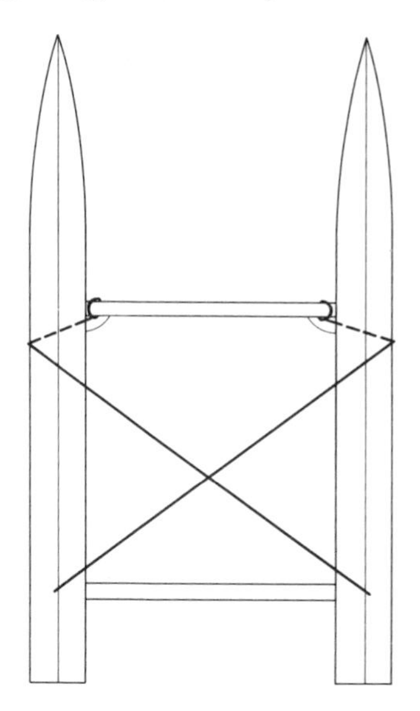

DIAGRAM 39

*A simple righting line system is to attach a line to each side of the forward beam, making sure each is long enough to reach over the hull and across the bottom of the boat to the opposite aft side, as illustrated. The lines are stowed on deck when not in use.*

many sophisticated rigging setups for righting lines. But since simple is often best, all you really need is a good, easily held line tied to the main beam on each side of the boat; each line must be long enough to go over the hull in a capsize position and reach the opposite aft side.

Now, as the boat is beginning to heel and fly a hull, you and your crew should be on the windward (rising) hull. Once the boat reaches a point-of-no-return angle on her side, she probably will go over due to the wind forces on the bottom of the boat and the weight of the mast, sails, and rigging. You might still stop the capsize at this point by getting your weight out to windward to counteract those forces.

But assume you couldn't stop the flow of capsize direction; the boat goes over. She will go over reasonably slowly. The phenomenon feels like a slow motion replay on TV. But instead of sitting there watching with interest, you should be clambering back over the windward side of the upper hull. (See diagram 40.)

Your object in going over the hull is still to attempt to equalize the pressures on each side of the lower hull's gunwale: The gunwale now is the fulcrum point for a teeter-totter.

Keep the boat balanced on that fulcrum by use of your righting lines and daggerboards or centerboards, if you have them. Boards make a fine place to sit to help balance the boat on the fulcrum point. However, usually the righting lines should be enough.

Bring the righting line over the high side of the upper hull. Hold onto the righting line from your position on the lower hull, and lean out away from the boat.

If you do not keep the boat on the fulcrum point, she will "turn turtle," that is, go totally upside down, with the hulls up and the mast pointing toward the bottom. This makes the boat more difficult to right, and can also damage your boat if the water is not as deep as your mast is tall.

If you keep the boat balanced on its side, the wind will blow the boat around, weathervaning it so that the mast will point directly into the wind. Once that has happened, you now have an additional ally in the wind. (It helped you go over, and now it will help you get back up.) The wind will

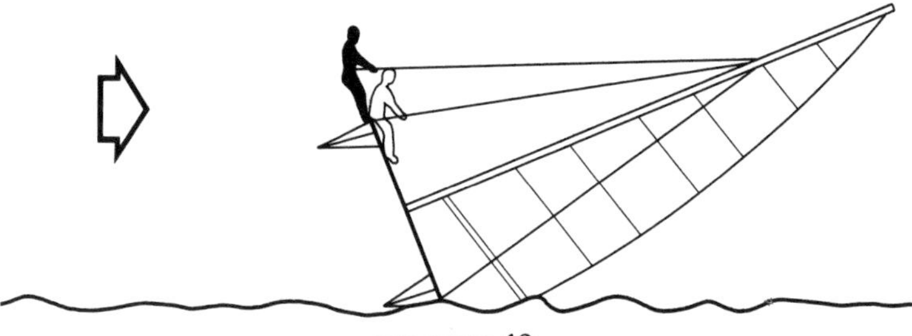

DIAGRAM 40

*Before going over, all sheets are released and your weight is out, but strong winds may still blow you over.*
*Immediately slide down to the lower windward hull, or boards, then begin pulling on the righting line to balance the boat on its fulcrum point to prevent turtling.*

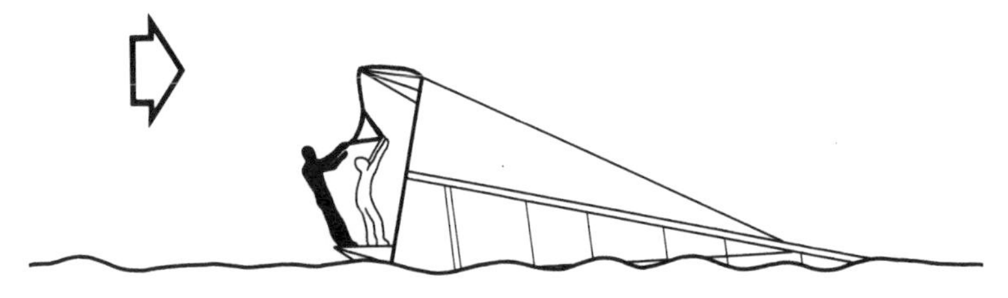

*Patiently balance the boat on the fulcrum point until the wind weathervanes the boat around. Once the mast is pointing toward the wind, the wind will push on the trampoline and soon will get under the sails. With the help of the wind and your pulling, the boat will be righted.*

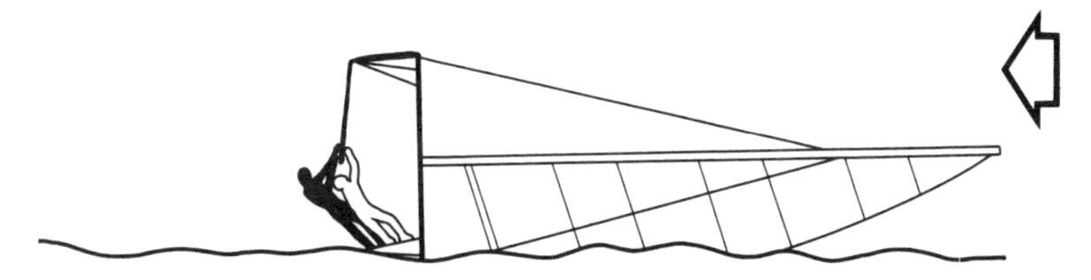

soon get under the sail and lift the boat back on her feet.

You should not have had the sheets cleated as you were going over. The fact that the sails are not sheeted will aid in righting the boat. (If the sails are still cleated, the water that gets on them cannot easily run off, and it is harder for the wind to lift the sails.)

*A boat can be pushed only so far and a hull only flown so high before the inevitable happens. In photos 1 and 2, these sailors were just showing off. In photo 3 they have reached the point of no return; and in photo 4, sure enough, they have capsized. Photo 5 has the crew digging out the righting line; and in photo 6 the boat weathervanes around, pointing its mast toward the wind. The crewmen are balancing the boat on its axis, allowing the boat to pivot with less drag. In Photo 7 the wind helps out and the boat comes up. (Courtesy of the Prindle Class Assn. Photo series by John Main.)*

But suppose you made two pilot errors: first, not preventing the capsize; and second, not preventing the boat from turning turtle.

You and your crew should place your weight at the stern of the boat on the upside-down hull that is the most leeward to the wind. Then start pulling on the righting line steadily. This should get the windward bow to come up out of the water quite a way; but as the wind gets under it, the bow will gradually start to come up more and more.

The higher the bow gets, the more the force of the wind and waves will help to start the boat up on its side. Once the boat gets near to being on its side, you should walk forward on the same hull and continue righting action as described above for the partial capsize.

These righting techniques are workable only for the smaller, beach-type catamaran designs, although they can be used to a certain extent for the older, larger, and heavier predecessors. However, once a larger cat turns turtle, it usually requires the assistance of another craft. The best way to right one of these boats is to tie a line from the mast base and bring it aft down the bottom of the deck or trampoline (which is facing upward) to the helping boat. Use a fairly short line; too long a tow line makes righting very difficult.

When the towing boat begins pulling, the crew should stand at the aft end of the overturned boat, forcing it down and forming a water break for the stern. A crew member also should hold the tow rope centered in the middle of the deck. The pulling boat, by applying steady yet increasing power, will pull the boat up end over end.

One advantage to capsizing a catamaran, compared to many monohulls, is that, once righted, it shakes the water off its sails and you are on your way again—not still sitting there with a boat full of water.

Some monohulls, even when upright again, have to be towed to shore because the gunwales are so low that waves keep coming over one side faster than the crew can bail water out the other side.

A review of this book's Chapter 13, "Safety," will help you prevent capsize . . . and help prevent serious consequences if one does occur.

# 15

## *CREWING*
*by Mary Wells*

MARY WELLS, whose family helped pioneer the introduction of catamarans into this country in the very early 1960s, has been under sail since the age of six, when her parents were racing a Lightning on Lake Erie.

Rodney MacAlpine-Downey had brought his Shark catamaran over from England for its first tour of the United States when Mary and sister Betty took a ride and convinced dad, Bill Wells, to buy one.

Bill and Betty went on to become a dominant force in the Shark fleet, both locally and nationally. Betty now skippers a Prindle 18, with her husband, Dick, as crew.

Mary, as helmsman with her father crewing, won two season

championships in the Lightning in their local fleet, skippered the Shark to numerous victories, and has raced a Dingo and a Laser.

She now crews for the author of this book on a Hobie 18 and admits she had a lot to learn about the front half of the boat. "When I was on the helm, I always thought the crew's main job was to keep the skipper dry by blocking waves."

Occasionally you'll run across a skipper who likes to run the whole show himself. His crew's job is to "be quiet; sit where I tell you; and don't touch a thing."

This skipper is a marvel to watch in action as he pulls in sheets with his hands, feet, and teeth and steers with the tiller tucked beneath his armpit.

This person either has a five-year-old child as ballast to make minimum weight or is simply afraid to delegate tasks and responsibilities. And probably this person should be sailing a one-man boat.

Most one-design catamarans racing today are two-person boats carrying a skipper and a crew. For some this means a master-and-slave relationship; but for most it is a partnership, a team effort, with both people working together toward the same goal: winning the race.

What is expected of a crew varies with every skipper. Some skippers like to give orders and make all the decisions, plan the tactics, and call the lay lines. Others like to delegate as much of that responsibility as possible to the crew, so they can concentrate on keeping the boat moving fast.

Some seem to be able to sail with a different crew every week and still win races. Others prefer a regular crew, so that a close teamwork can be established.

From talking to various skippers, I have gathered a composite picture of the perfect crew and broken it down into the following qualities.

*A GOOD CREW:*

1. First of all, knows how to sail the boat in case the skipper should fall overboard or be injured.

2. Has a winning attitude.

3. Doesn't argue with the skipper's decisions or carry on needless conversation that can interfere with the skipper's concentration.

4. Has enough strength, agility, and endurance to handle both light and heavy air conditions and to last through a grueling series of back-to-back races when necessary.

5. Is familiar with racing rules, tactics, and basic strategies.

6. Spots marks and is able to call lay lines and give the skipper input about what the competition is doing, wind shifts, approaching puffs, boats on the opposite tack, etc.

7. Understands weight distribution and knows what the proper attitude of the boat should be in the water.

8. Knows how the boat is put together and how all the rigging and blocks work.

9. Is a steady crew.

10. Is properly dressed and equipped, knows the crew responsibilities on the boat, and knows what to do on each leg of the course, completing all tasks quickly and efficiently without waiting for orders.

As I said, every skipper has different ideas of what he or she wants from a crew. But the "perfect" crew just described will be able to fill the bill, no matter what the requirements.

Let's examine each of these qualities.

1. Perhaps the most important requisite of all is for the crew to know how to sail the boat. If the skipper falls overboard, the crew must be able to maneuver the boat single-handedly to go back and pick him up.

Several skippers say the first thing they do is teach the crew to sail.

Not only is this important for safety; but the crew can do a much better job if he or she knows how the boat sails and what makes it go, rather than simply performing tasks by rote.

It makes the skipper's job easier if the crew understands the disastrous effects of a stall or of the jib backwinding the main . . . and the importance of keeping the slot open between the main and jib.

*Mary Wells*

For the first-time crew who does not yet know how to sail, it might be helpful to get a head start by reading this book's Chapter 2, "First Time."

2. A winning attitude and the crew's total involvement in the race are crucial to successful teamwork. You should have as much competitive spirit and desire to win as the skipper does. Probably nothing upsets a skipper more than feeling that the crew is daydreaming or not really paying attention. A half-hearted crew is not going to perform as well as one who is totally involved, mind and body, in the contest.

Hobie sailor Wayne Schafer's approach is "to try to make the race as interesting as I can for the crew. . . . I think one of the reasons the crew makes the same mistakes time after time is they're bored—they're not really into it."

He believes in getting the crew involved by giving them as much responsibility as they're capable of handling. "The more responsibility the crew takes for the race, the more equity they have in that race; and the more they want to win, the more they suffer along with you when you don't.

"Mistakes will be made, but you keep working at eliminating them. It's just like any sport, whether it's tennis or golfing; you know you're not going to play that perfect game; you'll have your highs and your middles and your lows, but you always play for that average.

"And I think the crew should participate in all that. So much energy and elation and anguish goes into a race that it ought to be shared."

He concludes, "If you're going to race, get involved in it. You'll have a lot more fun if you have an equity in the whole thing instead of saying, 'Oh, God, I have to ride around in this thing again.' "

3. One of the crew's foremost responsibilities is to help preserve the skipper's ability to concentrate fully on the race. When the skipper gives a command, it must be carried out instantly, without argument or discussion.

If the skipper blows a call with which the crew had not agreed, the crew must not start an "I told you so" debate. If the skipper expresses anger over a mistake made by the crew, the crew should let it pass without further comment.

It takes two to argue, and the sooner the mistake is left in the past, the sooner your team can resume sailing efficiently and the smaller the crack in the skipper's vital concentration.

The only conversation on a sailboat during a race should relate to the race itself. The skipper wants to hear only input that he can use in making decisions that will affect his course, tactics, and strategy.

Some skippers want more input than others. Nacra sailor Larry Harteck says, "Personally, I like someone who doesn't talk too much. Some people like a blow-by-blow description of everything that's going on in the race, but it's too much data for me. I need to concentrate."

There is never room for more than one skipper on the boat during a race. Orders must be obeyed, and difference of opinion should be held in abeyance until you're back on the beach.

4. Strength, agility, and endurance obviously are relative factors. A petite, 100-pound woman is not going to have the strength of a 160-pound man. But she can have the agility and endurance; and if she takes crewing seriously, she should work to develop her muscular strength to its full potential.

A crew does not have to be as strong as one might think, even in heavy air. The modern ratchet blocks for the jib and the degree of purchase on the mainsheet system make the sails fairly easy to sheet in and hold, even without cleating them.

If the crew wants to hand-hold the jib without cleating it, remember that with the ratchet block, the farther the sheet goes around the block, the more holding power the ratchet will have.

On the Hobie 18, for instance, if the cam cleat is set low enough on the block so the sheet can easily be cleated, it also becomes very difficult to hold without cleating it. If the cam cleat is set high, the sheet is allowed to wrap farther around the block, making it very easy to hold without cleating.

Many skippers require the crew to handle the mainsheet going to weather and on close reaches, especially in heavy air. If the main is too much for the crew to handle, add another block to the mainsheet assembly to provide more purchase.

All cat racers, both skippers and crew, men and women, need to adhere to a regular conditioning program that includes both aerobics and muscle development. Don't forget exercises to strengthen stomach and leg muscles, both of which can get quite a workout in heavy air when you are on the trapeze for prolonged periods of time.

5. The crew should be familiar with the racing rules and tactics and basic strategies. The more you know, the better able you will be to give the skipper information helpful in making tactical decisions.

Wayne Schafer wants his crew to know as much as he does about getting around the course. "The more the crew knows, the more they are able to understand what you are doing and the decisions you are making.

"At the point where you think the crew has enough knowledge and experience, you can shift the whole calling of the race strategy over to them, with you as the veto power, and let them call the race.

"I *want* them to call the race. I want them to call the lay lines; I want them to give me all the information of what's going on on the course, who's doing what. I will suggest back to them different options and alternatives, but I usually let them go ahead and make the calls.

"If I really don't want to do what they called, I tell them why and do what I want.

"In other words, I want the crew to take responsibility; if I decide to do what they say, I'm not going to criticize them.

"You may start out with the helmsman making seventy percent of the decisions and the crew only doing, say, thirty percent. Now, if we can get that down to the sixty-forty or even fifty-fifty range, then I think you're coming close to a combination that's going to win the regatta.

"The crew is afraid of making a mistake and incurring the wrath of the skipper. But the skipper shouldn't get mad unless the crew is making the same mistake year after year. Then you need to find a new crew."

Randy Smyth concurs. "I make the ultmate decisions, but I want a lot of input from my crew. I like to reserve my concentration for making the boat go fast."

6. A good crew should locate the weather mark as soon as possible and keep track of where it is. When the boat is getting within range of being able to "lay the mark" (make one more tack to sail straight to it), the crew may be expected to call the lay line and tell the skipper when to tack.

You have, in most cases, reached the lay line when the mark is on a direct line sighting perpendicular from your boat to windward. When you make your 90-degree tack, you should be heading right for it.

However, you as crew must also keep in mind such factors as waves that might push the boat below the lay line and through which the skipper may not want to point as high. Also take into consideration current or tides that may cause the boat to drift either to or away from the mark.

You also must consider the degree to which your boat is

capable of pointing. Some can point a little higher than 45 degrees and some point lower. This, of course, will influence the lay line angle.

The most important rule, in calling a lay line, is NEVER OVERSTAND THE MARK. If you go too far before tacking, you will have to fall off to get to the mark and are covering more distance than the boats that did not overstand.

If the skipper expects input, the crew should also be able to keep him informed of how other boats are doing in relation to your boat.

Watch for boats on opposite tacks. If you are on port, make sure you can clear their bows; if not, alert the skipper. If you are on starboard, be ready to hail approaching port-tack boats so they can avoid you.

Observe other boats on the same tack. If others are pointing higher and going faster, they may be in a different wind pattern that your skipper should know about; or an adjustment may be needed on your boat.

You should understand wind shifts and how they affect the relationships between boats on the same tack. If you appear suddenly to gain considerably on boats to windward of you but fall behind boats to leeward, you probably are on a header. If you appear suddenly to fall behind boats to windward but gain on boats to leeward, you are on a lift.

The normal procedure in going to weather is to hold on a lift and tack on a header, so the skipper should be notified of these wind shifts if he has not observed them himself. (For a more complete explanation of wind shifts, see the grid illustration on page 150 in Chapter 10 of this book.)

Observation of other boats can also help you judge the varying velocities of the wind on different parts of the course.

If you see boats to windward of you start flying a hull, alert your skipper that a puff is coming so you can be ready to convert that power into speed instead of being knocked down.

7. Whether the skipper considers the crew to be a partner on a team or merely so much movable ballast, it is important for the crew to understand the principles of weight distribu-

tion. Read this book's Chapter 8 on that subject to get an overall understanding; but there may be variations you should learn about for the boat on which you are crewing.

The crew plays an important part in keeping the boat at the proper attitude in the water because you usually are much more free to move around the boat than is the skipper.

In erratic air you may have to dance fore and aft along the rail on the trapeze, or swing in and out like a yo-yo.

On a screaming reach, the skipper may be sitting on the hull, with the crew straddling him on the trapeze, forward leg braced to avoid flying forward against the pull of the wire.

In light air the positioning of your weight will be even more crucial, and any movement to change position must be delicate to avoid shaking the wind out of the sails.

You may find yourself perched precariously out on the forward bow wondering how long it will be before you roll off into the water.

No one ever said a crew's job is easy . . . or dry.

8. The crew should know how everything on the boat is put together, how it works, and what is most likely to go wrong. He or she should carry a Hobie key or similar tool and know how to use it on shackles and bolts.

It is a good idea to carry a couple extra shackles as well. The day will come when a spare shackle means the difference between winning a race and dropping out to make a pit stop at the beach. Carry them on the lanyard with your Hobie key or attach them somewhere on your person or on the boat.

Also bring along a piece of small-diameter line and an extra piece of shock cord. Both can be remarkably useful for jury-rigged repairs on the water.

During the race the crew should keep an eye open for the things most likely to come unscrewed or untied or jammed or bent, so problems can be prevented.

It goes without saying that any sailor should know how to tie at least a few basic knots, like a clove hitch, double half hitch, and bowline.

Randy Smyth said he counts on the crew to help him with prerace maintenance checks. "My crew helps make up for my lack of organization."

9. For many skippers, the perfect crew is the steady crew.

Schafer said, "I marvel at the people who can sail with a different crew and do well time after time.

"I try to get a good, knowledgeable, steady crew when I can. They get to know my style and what I want out of them; and I know what I can expect out of them, and I don't have to learn that through a regatta. It helps when you get on the boat and you already know each other's styles."

And Randy Smyth goes a step further. "On the Olympic level, the only way to succeed is to have the same crew all the time. There is no room for teaching there."

Smyth and crew Jay Glaser have been a winning combination in both the Prindle 18 and the Tornado; and Smyth has dominated the Prindle 16 class for the past few years, sailing that boat exclusively with his wife, Susie.

Among those who do well with different crews is Hobie Alter, Jr. Because his racing is sporadic and usually involves traveling to far-flung places, he has had to gear his style to accommodate the problem of often sailing with a strange crew. He sometimes meets his crew for the first time on the beach before the race.

Therefore, he has gotten into the habit of making most of the decisions—calling the lines and generally accepting most of the responsibility for the race.

One "problem" with having a steady crew, as Schafer points out, is that "As soon as the crew knows as much as you do about racing, they can sail their own boat, and you sometimes lose them."

10. Last, but certainly not least, we come down to the nuts and bolts of what the crewing job is all about.

Each crew should find out what the skipper expects; but basically, as Larry Harteck describes it, "The crew is responsible for running the front half of the boat."

The crew will be handling the jib sheets; adjusting the barberhaulers; running the jib traveler fore or aft, inboard or outboard; making sure the mast rotates to the proper degree and, if necessary, holding it there; raising and lowering daggerboards or centerboards; adjusting luff tensions on the main and jib; and possibly tightening or releasing the main outhaul. In addition, the skipper may require the crew to handle the mainsheet, especially in heavy air.

After sailing with the same skipper a few times, the crew should know without being told how much to raise the boards and what to do with the various adjustments for each point of sail.

Besides the tasks involved with actually sailing the boat, the crew is sort of the "housekeeper" and should take on the task of making sure the decks are always as free of clutter as possible. Keep all gear stowed out of the way or tied down securely. Make sure all lines and sheets are running free—watch for those insidious kinks that begin to develop in sheets before they can get jammed in the blocks.

Every time you race you will discover something new that can go wrong. You will learn how your jib sheet ties itself magically into knots or loops itself around the block or feeds itself double through the block.

If you have a mast-rotator wishbone on your boat, your jib sheet will try to catch on it as you tack. It is your job to find a way to prevent this from happening. A blown tack can cost you the race.

In light air particularly, keep an eye on the upper part of your jib to make sure it does not catch on the mast spreader arms. Not only does this result in an unproductive jib shape, it can tear the jib.

You are more likely to be a happy, productive crew if you are comfortable, warm, and properly equipped for the job. Among the items you will need are:

√ A good wetsuit or one of the newly popular, one-piece "dry suits." It is extremely important to stay warm. When you are very cold, your body does not respond quickly and efficiently. Besides that, it can make racing a very miserable experience.

Even on a warm day you can get cold with the wind blowing on your wet skin or clothes. And remember, it's much cooler out on the water than it is on the beach.

√ Wetsuit boots. I categorize this separately, because you may want to wear them even on days when you leave your full wetsuit behind. They are great for improving traction on a slippery deck and for trapezing. They also prevent wear and tear on your ankles when you use hiking straps.

√ A life jacket that is as streamlined as possible and fits well. Make sure it is Coast Guard–approved. The race committee will allow you to wear one that is not Coast Guard–approved, but the law still requires an approved jacket to be on board for each person. You don't want to carry any unnecessary extras during a race.

√ Sailing gloves. These are used by both men and women. Some people swear by them; and some never use them. If you don't use them, expect to be nursing some blisters until your hands get calloused.

√ A trapeze harness. For the crew particularly, I strongly recommend a full trapeze harness rather than the popular butt bucket belts. The butt bucket does not support your back well enough to allow extended trapezing in the proper position. (The ideal is to have your body straight out, perpendicular to the side of the boat.) It is difficult, if not impossible, to achieve and maintain this position for any length of time with a bucket belt.

Make sure your harness fits snugly but is large enough to go over a wetsuit and any additional clothing you may need to wear under it. (Most people put their life jackets on over their harnesses.)

√ A Hobie key or similar tool for opening shackles and tightening bolts or other minor repairs that may have to be made on the water. A Swiss Army knife also can come in handy.

√ An optional item is either a starting watch, a watch with a sweep second hand, or a digital watch that displays seconds. The crew should use the watch as a backup for the skipper's starting watch. Two second hands are better than one—especially if one stops working.

The crew also may want to do a few things to the boat

(with the skipper's permission, of course) to make his or her job easier.

√ If there is no nonskid tape on the side of the boat where your feet will be when you are trapezing, you should ask the skipper about the possibility of getting some. The Hobie 16s go so far as to put carpeting on their rails. Wearing wetsuit boots will help your traction, but the nonskid tape adds some extra security.

Some skippers do not want anything on their rails, as it can cause friction and drag if that part of the leeward hull gets under water in heavy air.

Another option is to use surfboard wax or paraffin, but this will wear off quickly and must be reapplied frequently.

√ Adjust your trapeze ring to the height at which you can get in and out smoothly and comfortably. Keep in mind that in heavy air it helps to hold the boat down if your ring is set lower than normal; but, on the other hand, if the ring is set too low, waves may keep hitting you and trying to knock you off the boat.

The ring itself can be important to the ease of trapezing. Most crews prefer a large, open ring, as opposed to the "dog-bone" type, which is more difficult to hook onto your harness.

√ If cam cleats are mounted on your jib blocks, set the jaws at the angle that will allow you to cleat and uncleat the sheet easily from your position on the trapeze as well as on deck. If you do not plan to cleat the jib, turn the jaws up as high as they will go. This gives your sheet more purchase around the block and makes it much easier to hold.

√ The Hobie 18 jib blocks tend to flop around quite a bit, so to keep them in one position, many crews like to run a shock cord across the deck between the two blocks.

With each race you probably will find new things you can do to make your job easier and to reduce the potential for mistakes and foul-ups.

One of the crew's jobs is to be an efficiency expert, always looking for faster and simpler ways of doing things on the boat.

You should know your job on each leg of the course. A triangular course usually includes a weather leg, a reaching leg, and a downwind leg, not necessarily in that order. Cat races usually are set up to emphasize the weather and downwind sailing, and the course can even be a simple windward-leeward rather than a triangle.

## *PREPARATION FOR THE START*

Before the start the crew should always make a point of noting the course number (if it is posted on the committee boat) and make sure the skipper knows what the course is.

If paper course charts are handed out, you will be responsible for keeping it dry and in a convenient location. Put it in a see-through plastic bag and keep it on your person, or secure it to some part of the boat with tape.

Be familiar with warning signals and with the various other pennants that may be flown from the committee boat.

If you are not conversant with basic starting strategies and how to determine which is the favored end of the line, read this book's Chapter 9, "The Start." You should know why the skipper is doing things, so you can better anticipate the boat's movements.

Some skippers require the crew to carry the starting watch and do an audible countdown from the five-minute signal to the start. If this is the case, know in what increments the skipper wants the countdown.

Ideally, the skipper should let the crew know what the starting plan will be so the crew can be prepared. You don't want to leap out on the trapeze at the starting gun, only to find your skipper plans an immediate tack to port.

During the five minutes leading up to the start, the crew should be on the boat (not on the trapeze), concentrating full attention on the jib. Timing is crucial at this point, and the skipper will need to move the boat foward quickly, stop suddenly, make abrupt course changes, park temporarily, or creep forward slowly. The jib should not be cleated at any point during these maneuvers and must be played constantly, as it is an important tool for changing course as well as speed.

If it is necessary to luff the jib to stop or park, keep a close eye on the sheets where they go through the blocks. The commotion of the jib jerking the sheets and blocks can easily cause the sheet to tie itself into a knot or wrap itself around the block, preventing you from sheeting in the jib.

During starting procedures, it is important to listen carefully for the skipper's commands. It is difficult to hear when the sails are flapping—both yours and those of other boats around you. In addition, the skipper tends to speak in a lower voice when in close quarters with competitors, because he doesn't want them to know what his next move is going to be.

At the starting signal the sails should be set for going to weather, and unless the skipper decides to tack right away, the crew should immediately get in the proper position for the wind and water conditions.

In light air, you probably will be on the leeward side of the boat with your weight forward to depress the leeward bow. In heavy air, you probably will be getting out on the trapeze immediately.

## *GOING TO WEATHER*

On the weather leg, if the air is light, you will have relatively little to do physically except keep your weight in the proper place to maintain the boat's proper attitude in the water. The jib probably will be cleated so the skipper can sail by it.

You should be lying down, keeping as low a profile as possible to reduce wind resistance. And whatever you do, stay out of the slot—the opening between the jib and main—because you do not want to disturb the air flow that comes off the windward side of the jib and across the leeward side of the main.

In light air, you also must be careful to move around on the boat as little as possible. Any necessary movement should be done slowly and gently, because in light air the wind can very easily be shaken out of the sails, slowing the boat.

In heavy air, on the other hand, you probably will be out on the trapeze on the windward side and will adjust your weight fore or aft to keep the bows the proper depth in the water. If the water is flat, you can keep your weight relatively far forward with the bows fairly deep. If there is chop, you may want your weight farther aft, to keep the bows a little higher so the waves won't slow the boat.

In erratic, gusty winds, you may be required to move constantly fore and aft, inboard and outboard.

It is preferable not to cleat either sheet in heavy air, both as a safeguard against capsize and so the sheets can be eased and tightened as necessary to keep the windward hull from flying. However, if the skipper requires you to work the mainsheet, you will have to cleat the jib.

Learning to pump the main will take some practice, as the goal is to keep the boat at the same attitude all the time. You don't want the windward hull going up and down, so you must anticipate the puffs and ease the main just enough to prevent the hull from rising. Then sheet it again as soon as the puff has passed over, so the hull won't settle down into the water.

Some skippers prefer to leave the main set and counteract the puffs by easing and sheeting the jib.

Aside from weight distribution and sheet handling, on the weather leg the crew is in a much better position to do some "sightseeing" than is the skipper, who should be concentrating on his jib telltales and keeping the boat driving and working up to weather.

You, on the other hand, should keep your eyes peeled for wind shifts, note relationships to other boats, locate the weather mark, watch for approaching puffs of wind, and feed all this information to the skipper.

Tacking involves a lot of personal preference in style and technique on the part of both crew and skipper. If you are sailing with a skipper for the first time, be sure to practice tacking techniques prior to the race. Different boats also require different techniques, as do different weather conditions.

Some of the guest contributors to this book have described the tacking technique they prefer on the boats they sail.

Bascially the difference will be in how soon you should come in off the trapeze, how soon to release the jib, and how soon to sheet it on the new side. Again, this requires a few practice tacks.

A normal procedure is for the crew to come in off the wire first (before the skipper), get the sheets ready by uncleating the sheet on the side the jib is on, and getting the slack out of the sheet from the opposite side.

Do not release the jib until the bow of the boat has crossed the eye of the wind. Then let it go, and quickly sheet in on the new side. Take care not to crank it in too flat too fast, or it will keep the boat from building up speed again on the new tack.

Most skippers will want you to move somewhat aft on the deck during the tack, as the boat can pivot more easily with the bows lifted a little higher. This takes careful positioning and synchronization with the skipper so you don't inadvertently bump him off the back of the boat.

Crucial to successful tacking in heavy air is the crew's ability to get in and out of the trapeze quickly. It is no time for floundering around. To get out, hook the trapeze ring to your harness, slide outboard as far as you can until you can put your aft foot on the rail and push yourself the rest of the way out.

To get back in, some people just lift both feet off the rail and swoop in. I take a more conservative approach, letting my front leg come in on the deck straight and bending my aft leg until I am within sitting distance of the deck.

Develop a style that works for you, and practice until the whole tacking process, wire to wire, is smooth and instinctive.

Keep in mind that it is sometimes more difficult to tack the boat in heavy air and/or big chop or waves. In those conditions it may be necessary to backwind the jib by waiting until the bows are well across the eye of the wind before you release it.

### HOMING IN ON THE WEATHER MARK

As all the boats begin homing in on the weather mark, the crew must be even more alert in watching for boats on opposite tacks. If on port tack, you should watch for boats on starboard and carefully judge whether your boat will be able to cross the next boat's bows or will have to dive behind its stern or tack to avoid it.

If it is going to be close and the skipper chooses to fall off and go behind the starboard boat, you should be prepared to help the skipper make your boat fall off. It probably will be necessary to ease the jib, and in heavy air it may be necessary to get your weight back to give the boat more steerage.

If your boat is on starboard and port boats are approaching, the crew should hail the port-tack boats by calling "Starboard" until certain the other skipper has heard. Although the port-tack boat has the obligation to give you right of way, the starboard boat still has an obligation to avoid collision.

As you approach the weather mark, the crew should be aware of what point of sail the next leg will be, should already have spotted the next mark, and know what direction the boat will be going.

## *REACHING*

If the next leg is to be a reach and the wind is heavy, the crew and/or skipper may or may not have to be on the trapeze. On a fairly close reach, you may have to move your weight very far aft on the windward side.

On the other hand, if the air is light, you may need to be on the leeward side and forward.

On a reach, the skipper can sail a course directly to the next mark; therefore, it will be necessary for the crew to "play" the jib to compensate for any variations in wind direction. Watch the telltales on the jib at all times, and constantly adjust the jib to keep the telltales flowing properly.

If the telltale on the windward side of the jib acts up, you should bring the jib in a little; if the telltale on the leeward side acts up, you should let the sail out a little.

This requires intense concentration by the crew; on this leg there will be no time for "sightseeing" at all. You must have tunnel vision, focused on that jib.

If you are sitting on the leeward side of the boat, remember to stay out of the slot.

## *SAILING DOWNWIND*

Let's say the next leg is going to be downwind. As you round the mark, you may have several tasks to perform within those first few seconds.

First, you will ease your jib very far out, making sure there is enough slack in the sheets so that the leech is not hooked in toward the main. You want the clew of the jib as far outboard as possible, with the jib assuming a nice, full, deep curved shape.

In all but extremely heavy air, the crew should have gone immediately to the leeward side to hold that jib clew outboard at arm's length, so that you are in effect taking the place of a whisker pole or barberhauler.

Once the jib is set to the skipper's satisfaction, it should be held in that position without deviation if the skipper sails by the jib downwind. On the other hand, if his technique requires you to play the jib, you will work it by watching the telltales just as on the reach.

Other chores you may have to perform at the start of the downwind leg include raising the daggerboards or centerboards (if the boat has them), releasing the outhaul on the main, overrotating the mast, and possibly adjusting luff tensions for the main and/or jib.

But of primary importance is to get the jib full and pulling and set immediately. It may then be necessary to cleat the jib for a few seconds while performing the other tasks.

When holding the jib on the leeward side, you are in a perfect position to make sure the leech of the jib is complementing the curve of the leeward side of the main.

If sailing by a permanently set jib, as in going to weather, the crew will again have time to look around and, instead of daydreaming, should be noting relative speeds of other boats, whether they are sailing higher or lower, possible wind shifts, and keeping an eye on the mark.

## JIBING

Most cats tack downwind, so you will be jibing to make 90-degree course changes in your progress toward the mark. Jibing is much easier and faster than tacking, and the crew's job is fairly simple.

As the jibe begins, the jib will cross to the other side of the boat by itself. The crew must feed sheet through the blocks to give the jib all the slack it needs to go far out on the other side. The crew should try to arrive at the new leeward side at the same time as the jib, catch the clew, and instantly get it full and pulling again.

When approaching the leeward pin, the skipper will begin ordering the preparations for going back to weather. The outhaul must be tightened again on the main; the boards must be dropped; if luff tensions were loosened, they must again be tightened.

As the boat rounds the mark, you must bring in the jib at the same rate as the boat is coming up into the wind and immediately get your weight in the proper place for the wind conditions, whether that is the trapeze for heavy air or the leeward bow in light air.

Now we've been once around the course, and we've covered the basics of your job. Too much detail about execution has been avoided because each crew will develop his or her own style and way of doing things.

Crewing can be as simple or as refined as you want to make it. Just remember that the more you know and the more skilled you are, the more of an asset you are to your skipper.

Also remember, however, that your skill and knowledge do not give you license to argue with the skipper's decisions. If you find yourself constantly disagreeing and wishing it could be done your way, maybe it's time for you to get your own boat and start training your own "perfect" crew.

## *A WORD TO THE WOMEN*

This is directed primarily to the woman who will be crewing for the first time. (The veteran female crews already know all this, or they probably wouldn't have become veterans.)

Those of you who are advocates of equality for the sexes will find that crewing is the perfect way to prove you mean what you say. "Crew" is a unisex word, and when you crew on a racing catamaran with a male skipper, you are no longer a "woman" in his eyes.

So throw glamor to the winds. Braid your hair and dab some zinc oxide on your nose, because by the time you get into your wetsuit, trapeze harness, life jacket, and boots, you're going to look like a pregnant frogman.

The qualifications for the "perfect crew" apply equally to both men and women. Woe to the woman who doesn't take this seriously and thinks she can get by on her bikini.

Once the race has begun, the gender of the crew is the farthest thing from the skipper's mind, and it is not a good time to remind him of it.

If you want a long-term crewing job, display competitive spirit, do your job, and keep a low profile during the race.

The woman who is crewing for her husband or boyfriend has a most difficult task because she must completely forget about the man–woman aspect of their relationship. Out there on the water they are skipper and crew, a team working toward the same goal.

An aggravating factor is that although women no longer promise to obey their husbands in the marriage vows, the crew must make this promise to the skipper. Many good relationships have been destroyed completely; others have been saved only because the couple stopped sailing together. These unfortunate situations occurred in many cases because it was impossible for the woman to wear two different hats.

When her spouse or boyfriend, normally even-tempered and good-natured, suddenly becomes so totally involved in the competition that he shouts or loses his temper, it is difficult for the woman to realize he is not angry with her personally.

He is angry at the "crew" . . . or he is angry because of some mistake he made himself and has to let off steam . . . or he is angry at the sails or the wind or any number of things—all of which are totally unrelated to his feelings for her as a woman.

Back on shore, he will have forgotten it all. And if she does not forget it as well, it can lead to continuing arguments, hurt feelings, and damage to the personal relationship.

It will help to eliminate many of these problems if the woman gets as strongly involved in the race as her skipper and has that winning attitude. She should strive to acquire all the characteristics of the "perfect crew," as outlined at the beginning of this chapter, perhaps paying special heed to the warning not to argue with the skipper and to avoid needless conversation.

On catamarans a male skipper often will be inclined to choose a woman for a crew because of the weight factor. For that same reason a female skipper might choose a male crew. Two women would be too light for most cats; two men may be too heavy.

Thus, cats have gained a reputation for being couples boats. And this very factor has helped promote their popularity and the social as well as competitive success of the racing programs.

Sailing is one of the few sports where a man and woman can perform together as a team and do equally as well as the all-male teams.

It works for many couples. Larry Harteck's crew, Eloise, has been with him since 1976. She started out as his girl friend, and now she's his wife. Randy Smyth and wife, Susie, are an unbeatable combination on the Prindle 16.

So unless you really are happier watching the races from the beach, leave your false eyelashes and "I told you so's" behind and go for it.

# 16

## ON THE NACRA FAMILY
*by Larry Harteck*

- √ Four-time winner of the PMA (Pacific Multihull Association) championships in California, sailing in Nacras
- √ Nacra California state champion four years in a row, 1978 through 1981
- √ Runner-up in the North American Nacra Championships, 1977 and 1979. Placed sixth in 1980 and 1981, and third in 1982

LARRY HARTECK has been with Nacra since its beginning.

One of those kids who get into boats rather than cars when they are teenagers, Harteck began racing an 18-foot Alpha Cat when he was fifteen. He made an easy transition to Nacra 5.2 when the Alpha Cat's builder unveiled Nacra in 1975.

At age twenty-four he has already had substantial success racing Nacras, as is apparent from the above credentials.

Harteck now works for Nacra, primarily in research and development. He designed the 5.0 meter, which recently hit the market; and he has raced extensively, both personally and on behalf of the factory, in the 5.2 and 5.8.

He sails mostly in the waters off his home town of Santa Barbara, California.

In the early 1970s Tom Roland had a dream—a dream of a professional catamaran racing circuit, one where the best sailors from around the world would compete on a regular basis for prizes. Large corporations would sponsor the boats and place advertising on their sails. Eventually, races would be seen on television, and catamaran racing would be brought into homes around the country.

Roland was not the first, and surely not the last, to have that dream. What made his dream different was the boat they were going to race. It was like nothing ever built before. The boat was a very large racing catamaran, with specifications that boggled the mind. Two lightweight, sleek hulls 36 feet in length, connected by two 20-foot-long, 6-inch-round beams. The platform supported a 50-foot mast with 500 square feet of main, and open headsail dimensions.

The crew of three was spread from wire to wire across the trampoline while sheeting the 27-to-1 mainsheet system. Headsail winches could be tailed from the trapezing position. The boat was extremely fast, with speed capabilities of 40 knots.

The first one was launched in the summer of 1974 in Santa Barbara, California, and was called Nacra, which stands for North American Catamaran Racing Association. An airbrushed Playboy logo on the sail attracted the attention of sailors throughout southern California.

But for Roland to race it officially against other large cats, he would have had to load it down with safety gear. Performance would be sacrificed. Therefore, Nacra was the unofficial renegade in many offshore races.

In the 1975 Newport-Ensenada Race, Nacra finished in record time, being the only boat ever to complete the course the day it started. The win was unofficial, and so the new time never entered the record books. Roland didn't care; that kind of racing wasn't his goal.

Time passed and Roland's attempts to lure sponsors for Nacra failed. He realized that the United States wasn't ready for professional catamaran racing. But that didn't put an end to his dream; it just changed it.

During the time Nacra was being conceived, Roland was also busy producing, on a limited basis, the Alpha Cat, a very fast, powerful, 18-by-10 cat. Unfortunately, the Alpha suffered from being too wet due to bow spray, and its 10-foot width reduced marketability.

Roland scaled down his Nacra to a 17-by-8-foot two-man sloop-rigged speedster. If one converts feet to meters, one arrives at 5.2. That was the name of the new boat, which was then produced by Nacra with immediate success. Many of the design concepts of the original, 36-foot Nacra were used in the 5.2, along with some hardware components from the Alpha Cat. In a matter of a few years, 5.2's were racing throughout the United States, Australia, and Japan.

Racing has been very competitive, making the 5.2 a very fast handicap class as well as an excellent one-design. The 5.2 was more sophisticated than most other production catamarans at the time because of its many adjustments and settings. The result was that sailors were going fast but had different ways of doing so.

A good example of the differences is found in the tuning of the mast. Some would sail with loose diamonds and lots of mast rotation; others had tight diamonds and little rotation. But most would still manage to sail around the course rather fast.

As the class developed further, sailors would change their settings from one race to the next, depending on conditions, instead of using what they thought was fast for all conditions.

A key trouble spot for them was when it came to tuning and how to control mast bend. Some sailors thought you wanted a nice full sail in light winds, but the tendency in the last few years has been to use flatter sails in all conditions.

Full sails are more powerful than flat sails but suffer from having too much drag. They are attractive to the novice racers, since they have a wider range of adequate headings with decent boat speed.

The flat sails, on the other hand, are less powerful, but don't have much drag. Their potential speed through the wind is greater, but it requires a more skillful helmsman to keep them working all the time.

The Nacra models now on the market only allow stock sails to be used; you can't buy a flatter cut, and you are stuck with the sails you have and the adjustments allowed by class rules.

Since the luff of the mainsail is not straight from head to tack, you really don't want a straight mast, either. The amount of sail forward of the head-to-tack is called luff curve. If you have a mainsail with a good amount of luff curve and hoist it up on a mast that is stiff, you will end up with a full sail. By allowing the mast to bend more, the sail will tend to become flatter.

If the sail has little luff curve, the mast must be stiffer for the sail to be efficient. The well-designed boat has a mainsail with a luff curve that matches the bend characteristics of the spar.

A catamaran that allows you to control mast bend through the use of a mast rotator and diamond wire spreader system will be efficient in a greater variety of conditions. So in controlling mast bend it is important to realize that you must combine the effects of rotation and diamond wire tension.

There are two forces at work producing the bend in the mast: downhaul and mainsheet tension. Even though the downhaul does produce some bend, it is not nearly as powerful as mainsheet tension.

Most masts have an elliptical shape in cross-section, consisting of a major and minor axis. They will bend much more easily when force is applied along the minor axis. As the mast is rotated from zero to 90 degrees, the ratio of the major and

*Larry Harteck*

minor axis changes with respect to the direction of force.

If one can imagine that the mast bends the least when the rotation angle is zero, and the maximum when perpendicular to the center line, then it's obvious that the more one rotates the mast, the flatter the sail becomes.

At low angles of mast rotation, there is a "depowering effect," due not necessarily to a flatter sail, but more to a disrupted airflow around the mast-sail junction.

In extremely heavy air, one can counterrotate the mast, giving a good depowering effect. Not only will the luff area of the main be stalled, but the top of the mast bends off to leeward, reducing power aloft. One must be careful not to break off batten tips or lose the rig itself, as this places high compression loads on the mast.

The degree to which a mast will bend is controlled by the length of the diamond wires, which are usually adjustable. This bending effect, however, reaches a maximum when the mast is rotated to 90 degrees, as the mast is supported by the diamond spreader wires along the minor axis.

As we rotate the mast back in toward the center line, diamond tension is less of a controlling factor in mast bend. In other words, at low angles of mast rotation, the difference in mast bend between loose or tight diamonds is not readily apparent. Rotating near 45 degrees with loose diamonds will cause the center part of the mast to bend to leeward. This will, in effect, choke off the slot, resulting in the jib backwinding the main.

So if you're going to sail with loose diamonds to flatten the sail in heavy air, make sure to rotate a lot or not much at all.

Another problem with sailing with loose diamond wires is that when the mast bends, the mast hound is lower. With the lower hound, the rig becomes looser and the forestay may sag off to leeward with the jib sheeted hard.

Most Nacra sailors sail with a rather tight rig for those reasons—some with their rig so tight that the mast is bent out of column due to the downward pulling of the stays, even without the sail up.

The hotter Nacra sailors are raking their masts aft. They feel this helps stabilize the boat better in heavy air; it utilizes the rudders to stop leeway and allows the boat to point better.

In November of 1982, the international 5.2 class voted in double trapezing for class racing. Prior to that, all major 5.2 races only allowed single trapezing, as does the Tornado. Now, with the double trapezing, the boat will be driven much harder when the wind picks up, and it will not be necessary to depower as much.

Another spinoff on the original Nacra was the 18-square-meter class. It had its beginnings back in 1974, when Roland modified an Alpha Cat 18 to what was called the Alpha Centauri. It was 18 feet long, 10 feet wide, very lightweight, and it was a main-only sail plan.

It was raced in *Yachting* magazine's one-of-a-kind in 1974. It was so sexy-looking and such a gas to sail that people were standing in line to take a ride. Diego Carr of Newport Beach, California, made the comment that the Centauri was like sailing a Formula One car.

The seed was planted, and talks started: "Let's take the specs and construct a formula class around it." A meeting of some Pacific Multihull Association members was held, and the specifications were drawn up as follows: a one-man, wind-driven watercraft, with the combined sail and spar area not to exceed 8 square meters (which is under 94 square feet). Hull length was not to exceed 5.5 meters (18 feet). And so the 18-square-meter was born.

The first Nacra 18-square-meter was cat-rigged, with 5.2-meter hulls and a 10-foot-wide platform. Being a foot shorter than the maximum allowed didn't seem to hurt the Nacra until some newer, custom, light boats like the Climax and Coyote came along with superior speed.

Nacra then redesigned its 5.2 into an 18-foot version, the Nacra 5.5. It was light and could race competitively with the most exotic of the 18-square-meters.

Always staying in the forefront of experimental catamaran design, Nacra introduced two new one-designs during 1982.

The Nacra 5.8 is a two-man sloop-rigged cat, 19 feet long and 8 feet wide. The Nacra 5.0, also a two-man sloop rig, is 16.7 feet long and 8 feet wide.

Both are boomless rigs.

# 17

## *TUNING AND RACING THE HOBIE 16*

*by Wayne Schafer*

- √ Hobie 14 national champion, 1974 and 1976
- √ McCulloch Trophy for best all-around sailor in a Hobie 16, Lake Havasu, 1971
- √ Retired the Ancient Mariner Series trophy at Newport Beach after winning it three times
- √ Hobie 16 Southern California Divisional Champion, 1979 and 1981
- √ Past runner-up in the Hobie 16 Nationals
- √ Runner-up in the Hobie 14 Worlds in the Canary Islands in 1977

√ Qualified for the 1983 Hobie 18 Worlds by placing in the top ten at the 1982 Hobie 18 Nationals

WAYNE SCHAFER, silver-haired but still as trim as a teenager, races and wins against skippers twenty and thirty years his junior.

He considers himself a "seat-of-the-pants" sailor and credits his racing success to a "lot of time in the boat."

One of the early cat sailors, Schafer's sailing experience actually began back in 1951 in a Rhodes 32. He was converted to multihulls four years later when he started sailing with a friend on a 16-foot outrigger.

He raced P-Cats for a time before getting into the Hobie 14 in 1968 and the Hobie 16 in 1971. He still races both boats and recently began trying his hand, with his usual success, on the Hobie 18.

Schafer's home waters are off Capistrano Beach, California.

## *TUNING*

### MAST RAKE

I almost always sail with my mast raked aft. There is the rare occasion, say a drifter on a small inland lake with smooth water, that I might get the mast up there more. But ninety-eight percent of the time I will sail with the mast raked aft.

How much it should be raked is kind of hard to say, since it depends on your style of sailing, your crew weight, the wind and wave conditions. I just know where to rake it from the feel of the helm.

To find the right spot for your own boat and conditions, I recommend starting with the mast perpendicular. Sail with it that way to see how it feels; and then start gradually raking it back one hole at a time until you find the point where your boat performs best.

Basically, three things happen when you rake the mast aft.

First, the weight aloft in the length of the mast itself makes the mast act as a levering tool. When it is straight up and down and you add wind power, it forces the leeward bow down with all that power. The aft rake acts to take that leverage off the bow and frees it up some. In choppy situations, hobbyhorsing will be even more pronounced with the mast straight up and down. If you move that weight back, the boat will balance much, much better.

Second, with the mast back you somewhat depower the sail. You allow the wind to strike the sail in a less powerful way, allowing the boat to be more controllable.

Third, you are moving the center of effort aft toward the lateral resistance supplied by the rudder, letting it act much like a daggerboard. The boat then becomes much more efficient to windward, sails through the chop better, and will point higher.

Some of what you gain going to windward, you will lose when you begin your downhill run, especially in light to moderate air. However, it has been my experience that you won't lose as much downwind with an aft-raked mast as you would going to weather with a perpendicular mast. And if you are sailing well enough, you should be able to hold onto what you have on the downwind leg.

The harder the wind blows, the less disadvantage you will have downwind. In heavy air the aft-raked mast helps to keep the bows from digging in.

Ideally, you would like the mast aft upwind and more forward downwind. The Hobie 14 can be sailed that way, but you cannot do that in the Hobie 16.

Crew weight is an important factor in mast rake. We try to stay at around or under 300 pounds overall (minimum weight on the Hobie 16 is 285 pounds), and we feel that we can handle both light and heavy air with our mast aft.

However, if the crew weight starts getting up there, like 310 or 320 or more, then you want more power and can move the mast more forward. Still, those same guys will sail with their mast back in heavier air. It is a matter of style. You should go out and experiment with it.

If you do rake the mast back, you definitely will have more weather helm, but you will go to weather better. If your helm is really excessive, then your rudders probably are out of alignment. You shouldn't get an overwhelming helm. Some guys say that if you have helm, you have a lot of drag; but I think some helm is good on the 16, and it doesn't seem to slow down the boat.

But helm also can be corrected now with the new adjustable rudders that can be raked forward under the boat. By raking them under the boat, you eliminate almost all that controversial helm, anyway.

Before the adjustable rudder, a lot of guys used to plug the holes of the rudder axis points and then redrill them to rake the rudders forward, thereby eliminating helm. But others just didn't want to go to the trouble of doing all that, and they still did well.

With the new adjustable rudder, however, Hobie has opened up whole new terrific avenues for tuning. The combination of rudder rake with mast rake probably will have the boat going a lot faster in the near future. If you can get the combination that fits your style of sailing and your crew weight, it's going to make a world of difference in the performance of this boat.

### MAST ROTATION

How far you want to rotate your mast is a matter of taste. The stock rotation is fine, but it gives you a stiffer mast to work with, one with less bend. If you overrotate the mast, you get a much wider range of sail shapes to play with. You will have a bendier mast, and then it depends on your sheeting as to what kind of sail you will have. And, of course, downwind the overrotation gives you a much better entry into the wind. So I go with the overrotation.

When I want a fuller sail, I do not sheet as much. When I want the sail flatter, I sheet more. With the bendy mast, I can do these things with the sheet.

You have to be careful, though, when cutting off the mast rotation stops. Take off very little at a time; otherwise, you will have overdone it, and you will not be able to build it back up very easily. And you know you cannot use a wishbone mast-stop like the Hobie 18 has.

I wouldn't overrotate to more than between 60 and 80

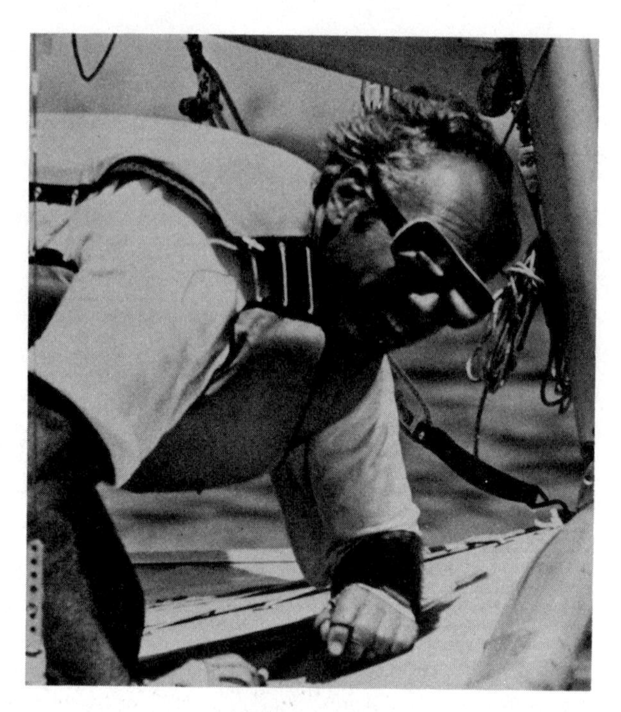

*Wayne Schafer*

degrees. A good way to see what is happening is to put telltales on your mast and note the wind flow around it. The best way is to shave a little bit off at a time and sail a little bit. See how it does, check the telltales on the mast to see what they are doing. The telltales should be placed right at the front of the mast, a little to each side. You should see an eddy on the windward side; the leeward side will tell you a lot.

MAINSAIL

People ask me whether I want my mainsail draft full or flat, forward or aft. I'll tell you, I have been all over the map with those questions.

At first we started sailing them as they were, with the draft cut way forward at about 33 percent. They seemed to be fine that way.

But then we got to fooling around with untapered battens and getting the draft back to 40 to 45 percent. And theoretically, that should work great; the air should attach longer to the mainsail; it opens up the slot; and just generally it made a lot of sense. But the catch was, it didn't work any better than with the draft farther forward.

So now we are back at the original 33 percent, and we are using tapered battens. This configuration, to me, seems to give a little more power; it seems to get through the chop better and generally has a little more punch. It also gives me a wider range of sail shapes. Off the wind it seems to have more power as well.

Of course, that is just my opinion at this time, and it may well change next year.

As for the fullness or flatness of the sail, here in California we usually sail in medium air, and we shoot for the optimum weight of 285 to 300 pounds. In these cases we want a moderately flat sail.

If the wind blows hard, we depower the boat somewhat by loosening the rig. The slack allows the mast to fall off to leeward a little and helps the lighter crews hold the boat down. In this heavy air you do not need power at all; you want to get the boat to where you can control it. So you want the sail flat, mast aft, and rig loosened. All these things are depowering the boat to the point where you can handle it better in wind over 20 knots.

Some guys play around a lot with battens, weighing their poundage and tapering them very finitely to a point where they are a perfectly balanced, matching set. And that is fine, if you have the time and the desire. But all I do is try to play around with them once in a while so the sail looks good. I taper here and there, but I do not make a science of battens.

Generally, I put the battens in with enough pressure to take the wrinkles out. Then, to get sail shape, I use the downhaul, outhaul, and sheet. If it looks as though there may be some uneven battens, then you can either tighten or loosen a batten or so, to get a smooth mainsail.

On the downhaul: Once I set the luff, I leave it. In the morning when I first raise the mainsail, I won't put a lot of tension on the luff. I don't want to honk it down yet; I prefer to let it gradually start stretching. I go out on the water with it that way.

Then after the wind hits it and stretches it, and after I see what the actual conditions are in which I will be sailing, then I tension the luff for the conditions. Basically, I am just taking the wrinkles out; and if the sail looks good, that is where I leave the luff tension.

I usually use a tight outhaul going to weather, because the Hobie 16 needs to have a tight leech. Leech tension is what makes the boat go to weather. By helping the wind, and therefore pressure, adhere to the windward side of the main to as far back on the sail as possible, more load is put on the rudders, so they can help resist leeway and keep the boat pointing higher and driving nicely.

The leech and rudders work together in very close partnership to get you to weather. This partnership can easily be destroyed by either oversheeting or undersheeting—the two major sins on the Hobie 16. It is really hard to find the perfect sheeting spot.

If you are undersheeted, your rudders will not be loaded enough, and you will tend to sail a lower course and maybe make more leeway.

If you are oversheeted, you will still be going to weather, but the boat will feel a little doggy, your rudders will be overpowered, you will have too much helm, and you will make more leeway than you would normally.

Because it is easier to feel oversheeting than undersheeting through the helm, I start out sheeted tightly. If I feel the symptoms of oversheeting, I let off a little bit and I am right on the money.

Leech is an area that's very hard to read; telltales don't read very well there. The only way you can tell what the leech is doing is by what you feel on the helm. But you have to have enough tension on that leech, and there's no way to tell anyone how to set it. You have to feel it and learn this by time on the boat.

It is hard to decipher and coordinate all this, and it takes a lot of experimentation. As a matter of fact, I am still playing around with it myself after all these years of sailing.

JIB

I like my jibs cut a little on the flat side. If the jib comes to me on the full side, I take it to a sailmaker and make adjustments within the rules to get it flatter. A fuller-cut jib does not do as well on the 16. In fact, the jib is usually just in the way, despite the fact that you do need it. So a fuller jib probably won't work well for you.

In the 16 we just try to get upwind any way we can. The boat is a reacher, and weather work is a struggle. With a full jib you won't point as high; and if there is wind, you probably will have to sail a lower course in order to carry the weight of the crew on the trapeze. The flatter jib seems to have a better entry angle into the wind; it allows the boat to drive better and is more controllable.

Another advantage of the flatter jib is that you can now taper the jib battens, giving you a wider range of sail shapes for your jib. The fuller jib, with tapered battens, comes off looking like a big sack.

The draft location of the tapered-batten sail will be up around the 33 to 35 percent area. If you prefer, you can extend the taper farther back on the battens, or you can just thin the battens out for their full length and let the sail cut dictate to the battens where the draft will be located.

Jib sheeting is very tender on the 16. I use a low-profile set of blocks, which can be bought through the "Hobie Hot Line," and attach them to the lowest or next to lowest hole in the clew plate. This pulls the jib more on the foot than on the leech. If you were to put the jib blocks in a higher hole, you would be pulling tighter on the leech and the sail will cup more, throwing the wind into the main, closing off the slot.

As for the traveler: Going to weather, I leave the jib leads in pretty close to the mast in lighter air. If the air begins to come up, you can move them out a little; it doesn't hurt, as you can always sail on the main alone.

And if it is really blowing hard, I'll just move the traveler all the way out and not worry about the jib. After all, you have so much air blowing through there, anyway, backwinding your main and blowing your mast out of column. That's worse.

You cannot be too dependent on the jib going to weather. The main is the big engine.

Off the wind, however, the jib is everything. The boat won't do anything on this point of sail until the jib is set all the way out.

As for the luff tension, I put quite a bit of pull on her. If the luff is too loose, the sail will curve off and will not present a good entry into the wind and will not be an efficient profile for the weather leg.

## *HELMSMANSHIP*

### TO WEATHER

Going to weather I usually sail with my main traveler set out at about 3 to 6 inches, depending on the wind condition. That allows for the loaded hook of the leech. If you have a tendency to oversheet, then certainly leave the traveler off a little bit. If you want to sail a higher line but do not mind sacrificing some speed, then you can pull the traveler in to the center.

The leech is what is getting the boat to go to weather (through its effect on the rudders), but if it is pulled too tight, it will hook back to windward and will slow your speed a bit. It will point higher, but you are looking for the ability to go high and yet as fast as possible.

In heavy air, put the traveler out to the point where you can make the boat controllable. If you keep flying a hull, you must still spill some wind up high by easing the sheet. The Australians put a lot of mast rake in and sheet block to block. When you're in that position, your main is not fully sheeted and the wind will be spilled up high, keeping the drive down in the lower section of the sail. They are very good at doing this.

Air spills off the upper part of the sail because it twists to leeward more than the lower section of the sail. The top does not offer as much drive as the bottom, anyway; but it does try to heel the boat over, which is something you just don't need in heavy air.

I prefer not pinching, because otherwise you create so much leeway. If you drive off more, you get to the same place and much quicker. Occasionally, when it is just too heavy for me, I will be forced to feather up.

As a steering guide, I do have a bridle fly, but I only use it to get general directions of the wind. Mostly I sail by what the other boats are doing. Of course, I look at my jib, the telltales, and the bridle fly; but mostly I just sail in relation to the competition. If they are pointing higher and going faster, then I adjust. I really do key off them.

### TACKING

Tacks can be difficult if a person doesn't work on smoothing them out. The first thing to do is alert the crew of the tack, so he or she can get off the wire and get the sheets organized. And the crew should know not to cut the jib loose too soon.

The skipper should stay on the wire and put the helm over and come in when the boat comes head to wind. Tension on the main also should be released when the boat comes head to wind. As you cross over, the crew should be watching the bridle fly; and when the fly is past the centerpoint of the boat and 15 to 20 degrees on the other tack, the crew should cut the jib loose from the previous tack and *quickly* sheet in from the new side.

In other words, for the jib the secret is "Slow to cut, quick to pull." The jib really does all the work in getting the bows across the wind.

During the tack the crew also should come aft on the trampoline as far as possible without impeding the skipper's progress across the boat. That can take some practice. If the crew comes back too far, you will collide. If the crew is too far forward, the boat will stay into the wind. By getting the weight aft, you are shortening the water line, allowing the boat to pivot on the back part of the hulls.

Once the bows are about and the jib brought in, then you can sheet in on the main. However, if the wind is heavy, both the jib and the main should be brought in together. The main should never be brought in ahead of the jib, as it will cause the boat to weathervane right back head to wind, and you will be in irons.

### DOWNWIND

On the downwind leg I generally put the main traveler out to near the hiking straps. The jib traveler goes all the way out. I do not want the main traveler all the way out, because I want some twist in the sail. If the boat feels good to me (balanced without too much helm), then I begin concentrating on the waves. If the helm is too great, I probably will ease the sheet some. Occasionally, I will let the traveler out more. It all seems to depend on the feel of the helm.

I usually try to sail as deep as I can, but not so deep as to sacrifice speed. The lighter the air, the closer to the rhumb line I sail. I figure that the wind is shiftier and less predictable, and it is very difficult to make up the extra distance with the speed. The more the air is blowing, the more you want to sail by that apparent wind. That is what catamarans are all about. Apparent wind must be made use of, and so you will sail a higher course.

Good downwind sailors will work closely with that apparent wind; and when they are getting too high a line, they will jibe. They will not sail down into a stall. But jibes hurt, too. They are faster than tacks, but you still lose a lot of distance on a boat that is moving.

I sail wing-and-wing only in winds of 5 mph or under. In that kind of condition, by sailing straight for the mark, you are assured of not making any mistakes. It's not much fun sailing straight down there, and you may feel like a dunce, but you may surprise yourself. When the air lightens or dies, aim at the mark or as close to it as you can.

The big telltale downwind is my bridle fly. I use it exclusively. Sometimes I sail with it pointing between 85 and 90 degrees. Do not let the fly point any further forward than that, as you will stall the boat and will have a hard time getting it going again.

It takes a lot of concentration to keep the fly just where you want it, but that is the big fun on the Hobie 16. That is really what it is all about.

Downwind is my favorite point of sail on the race course.

# 18

## *WINNING ON THE HOBIE 18*
### *by Hobie Alter, Jr.*

- √ National champion Hobie 14, 1978,
- √ National champion Hobie 16, 1979, 1980, 1981, 1982
- √ Champion of Champions winner, sailing a Prindle 16, 1979
- √ National champion Hobie 18, 1978, 1981
- √ World champion Hobie 16, 1982
- √ Winner, Worrell 1000, 1982

SAILING ability must come with the name. Hobie Alter, Sr., and his three children—Hobie, Jr., Jeff, and Paula—all have had remarkable racing success. So far Hobie, Jr., has racked up the most impressive list of credentials, but brother Jeff is coming on strong. In fact, he beat his older brother to win the Hobie 18 Nationals in 1982, with Junior placing third.

Hobie, Jr., now twenty-five, started his career when his mom signed him up for a summer sailing course at the age of eight. "We had class for a week and then a race. My boat cleaned everybody in the race, and I got my first taste of sailboat racing. I said, 'Hey, this is fun.' "

At about the same time his father bought a P-Cat, which they played around with in the Laguna Beach area of California. His dad designed the Hobie 14 when Junior was ten, "so it was kind of a natural for me to start sailing that."

He said the key to success is getting to know your own boat and acquiring a feel for what makes it go faster, rather than worrying about what other people are doing.

## *TUNING*

### MAST RAKE

Although my mast is not as far aft as many, I do rake my mast aft on the Hobie 18. It seems to be a bit easier to sail that way than with it perpendicular, and I want to put the lateral resistance load on the rudders as well as the boards.

Overall, I like the steerage much better with the aft-raked mast, as I feel the boat more acutely through the helm. There is more helm, but it is not excessive.

As to how far back I rake the mast, there is no sure measurement that I use. I judge by the distance between the blocks when the mainsail is in and fully sheeted. Then I look for about a foot or a little less between the blocks. If that distance is about 6 inches, then I feel that the mast is back too far.

There are times when I will rake it a bit farther forward: in flatter water and lighter winds. In these cases there is no worry about the bow diving, and a bit more power does not hurt, either.

Some sailors think that off the wind you sacrifice some power with the mast raked aft, but I do not think so. If you drive the boat well and do not sail too deep or too high, then it will sail just about as fast as a boat with forward raking.

The rake I have downwind may change from the weather leg, however, as I do not use a tight rig. It isn't really sloppy, but it isn't tight. That way the leeward shroud will give some off the wind and allow the mainsail to twist off nicely and fill out, rather than have an inverted crease running down its length caused by the shroud pushing back on the mainsail.

Also, the slackened rigging allows the mast to stand up straight for off-the-wind sailing. So maybe that is why I am not getting hurt on the downwind legs.

### MAST ROTATION

The mast controls the fullness and flatness of the sail by degrees of rotation. The less rotation you use, the fuller the sail and the more power. The more you rotate the mast, the flatter the sail will become and the less power you will have, although the sail will be capable of faster speeds.

If I want the sail full, I will set the mast rotator at about 70 degrees. If I want the sail flatter, I set the rotator at about 90 degrees. Should a required sail shape be somewhere in between, then I would set the rotator between 70 and 90 degrees, wherever I thought the sail looked right for the condition.

### MAINSAIL

The sail should vary in draft as you go up. For example, the bottom part of the sail should have a moderate draft located about 45 percent back in the sail, the draft working gradually forward until, at the top, it will be located farther forward, at around 33 percent, and it will be a little fuller.

I like the leech to flatten out somewhat, and that is why at the top the draft must be farther forward. The distance fore to aft at the top of the sail is so short that the draft must be forward in order for the leech to develop any flatness. I want it flat so there is no chance of the leech hooking to windward, causing flow detachment and increased drag.

I run the diamond tension fairly tight, compared to everyone else. The measurement to the point where I can press them against the mast is about a foot. That way I get a fairly uniform mast bend. Some people run them up to two feet, but I think that is too loose.

As for the battens, I really don't put much work into them. In the Hobie they all come the same way, so there isn't much you can do with them, except taper them.

The bottom six battens should be left untapered, as they are already flexible enough and the untapered battens allow the draft to be located at about 40 to 45 percent in the sail, which is what you want.

The higher up the battens, the shorter, and there you should taper them so the draft will be up to 33 percent in the sail.

Overall, I just look for a good sail shape, and if the battens need to be tapered to accomplish that, then I do it. So the shape I want is moderate at the bottom, with the draft at about 45 percent, and progressively fuller and farther forward—up to 33 percent—as you go up the sail.

As for batten tension, I simply snug them into the pocket just enough to take the wrinkles out of the sail. The sail material should be taut, but the battens should not be jammed in. You see, actually the batten, loose or tight, does not have that much to do with the curve of the sail.

The really important sail-setting devices are the downhaul and outhaul.

In light air, or when I want a full sail, I do not downhaul that much—just enough to get the wrinkles out. The outhaul I ease off a bit to get a little shape in the lower batten.

If the air becomes moderate, then I harden down the downhaul and take the outhaul out farther.

In heavy air I really honk down pretty hard on the downhaul and take the outhaul car all the way out.

### JIB

The one thing I do that other people do not do is set my luff tension on the beach. Since I carry a looser rig than most, I do not know how tight to set the jib luff control without sheeting the main. So I sheet in the main and then go up and set the luff tension. I do not like a tight luff control on the jib; I set it just enough to take out the wrinkles. There is not a great deal of tension on it. In fact, I have accidentally set it so that there were wrinkles, and it sailed just as well, if not better.

By setting the luff tension in this way, you know exactly what it is going to look like going to weather. If you set the jib luff too tight, the sail will tend to cup up front, causing a distorted sail that breaks funny and whose telltales do not read right. Overall, that is hard to sail by.

With the moderate setting of the jib, you have a flatter entry into the wind, a better profile.

The draft is something I do not worry about with the Hobie 18 jib, because they all come the same way. If I had my choice, I would prefer the draft a bit farther forward; but since that cannot be done, I sail with what I have.

My jib settings are set in the middle of the track at almost all times. I do not deviate much from that, since I don't think the jib lead tracks do much good, anyway—they don't give much variation to the lead angles.

Some people, I have noticed, run their jib leads aft in heavy air; I, on the other hand, tend to run mine forward. Moving the slide forward is similar to running the traveler outboard on the Hobie 16; it opens the slot a bit more. If it is heavy air, you are not sheeted hard, anyway; and by sliding it forward and slacking the sheet, you open the slot.

## WEIGHT DISTRIBUTION

Upwind, I like the bow down into the water, with the average water line running about halfway up the bow. If the air is pretty light and the seas smooth, then you can dig in the bow more.

In trapeze weather you want the bow still taking the average water line at about halfway up the bow. In lighter air you want the crew on the leeward side and forward to get the bow down deep.

*Hobie Alter, Jr.*

Off the wind I do not like to get the bows too deep, particularly in heavy weather. But in lighter air I want to balance right over the rocker of the boat, so that the sterns are out of the water.

In light air, on all points of sail, you must be sure that you do not get too much weight on the windward hull. The weight must be dispersed so that the boat is well balanced.

## *HELMSMANSHIP*

### TO WEATHER

The traveler is always set right in the middle. The only exception to that is when it is really blowing hard; then I would let it out 4 to 6 inches. I do all my sail trimming pretty much with the sheet tensions.

In heavy air I carry my jib sheet tension really soft and work the main extensively. I figure the thing that makes you go faster than the next guy is to work harder: dumping your main more and pulling it in more often, really working the mainsheet.

The farther out you put the traveler, the less you have to work. With the traveler in the middle, you have to work that much harder. The twist off the top is far better, the power low in the sail is better, and the boat definitely goes faster and higher. But, again, you do have to pay for it in labor.

Pointing high or driving off really do not enter my mind while sailing in trapeze weather. I just try to hold the boat down. If I fall off too much, I cannot hold the boat down without easing off the sheets or traveler.

On the other hand, if I am holding the boat down with no problems, then I will pull the main in good and tight until the boat begins to come up again. The technique is sort of a combination of how hard you sheet in and how high you fly the hull. You want to balance the boat and the sheet to get the maximum forward and windward effort.

You do not want to lift the hull up, but you must be sure you have enough power to do so whenever you want.

In heavier air I simply use the hulls and the feel of the boat and its speed to determine my point of sail. I do not really use a telltale or anything. I just keep the hull kissing the water, assuming that the sails are all set properly.

When the air lightens up and it is no longer trapeze weather, then I begin sailing by the telltales on the jib and the main. First I set the sails where I want them; and then instead of changing settings, I steer by the telltales on the sails.

### TACKING

In the Hobie 18 I turn pretty fast, using the speed of the boat to get through the wind quickly. You must not exaggerate the quickness of the turn to the point where you stall the rudder in the process, but you do want a quick turn. Some sailors seem to pinch up for a while or start up so slowly that they bleed off all their speed before getting into the turn itself; then they do not go through the turn fast enough.

Backwinding the sail should only be done in choppy seas. I normally have the jib cut loose right away.

Holding the rudders over at the turn angle all the way through the turn is a must. If you let go of the rudders and they straighten out during the turn, you have blown the tack. They must be held in the proper arc all the way through the tack.

Sometimes, in the heat of the race, your mind is so involved on the race and the tactics that when you get ready to tack, your mind is still on something else. You cannot do that. I just tell myself to forget the race and make this particular tack a good one; and then, after the tack is completed, I get my mind back into the race. That way you concentrate on the tack itself, and chances are you will not blow it. A blown tack can cost you a lot of ground.

As for weight distribution in a tack, I get right back on the after beam and stay there, while the crew is located right around where the jib sheet blocks are. This gets the weight pretty far aft, allowing the bows to get out of the water, and you develop really good relative steerage between the rudder and the board.

## DOWNWIND

When sailing downwind on the Hobie 18, I let the main traveler out to a point just inside the hull. The traveler does not easily go all the way out, anyway. Then I cleat the sheet with the sail twisting off at the top. That means the mainsheet is pretty slack.

Generally, the main does not flow that well when sailing downwind. The telltales never seem to make much sense, which really makes it difficult to know exactly where to sheet the main. It seems as though if you ease off the sheet until the back side flows, then the windward side would be luffing. So according to the telltales, it appears that the main is oversheeted a bit, but that allows the jib to set properly and flow the air through the slot.

For my course downwind I sail at about 90 degrees apparent wind. I will sail a bit higher to get the boat speed and then fall off to somewhere below 90 degrees, but not into a stall. If I start to get too deep, I head it up quickly to get the speed back again.

My primary telltale is my jib. I use it as a guide for sheeting; and then once it is set, I sail by the jib, keeping the jib telltales flowing. It seems to be very important to keep a good slot between the main and jib as well. So I set the jib, then adjust my main to complement the jib.

Another good telltale is my bridle fly. I will keep the feather running at about 90 degrees to the boat. That will change a little bit, depending on conditions.

If I catch a wave, I will just run deeper downwind. If it's choppy and I get a better speed by going a little higher, well, then I go a little higher.

It still all relates to feeling the boat and getting the most speed. You might take a few seconds and ease the main and see if you can feel any difference. If it is slower, then put it back to where it was. If you harden up the sheet and it feels faster, leave it there. You have to keep experimenting to get the most boat speed at all times.

### JIBING

There is no really hot technique for jibing. The big secret to a good jibe is timing; that is, mastering WHEN to jibe. Unless you are forced to jibe quickly, you should wait until you are driving off and heading deeper than 90 degrees. That way all you have to do is to drive off a little deeper yet and round it to the other tack. You keep a fast line that way.

If you jibe from a high position on the wind, you have farther to go around than if you tack when driving off. And, of course, if you catch a wave and are going very deep, that is an excellent time to jibe, as the wave will surf you through the jibe.

Generally, I would say that to win a lot you have to have a "seat of the pants" feel for the boat. It is something that requires time in the boat and some natural ability.

The worst thing some people do is always worry about what the "hot skippers" are doing, rather than about themselves. They are always looking for some trick or go-fast, thinking that maybe the hot skippers are using something that they are not. What they should be doing is looking at what they are doing themselves.

If more sailors would work with their own sheets, their own sails, their own helmsmanship, they would develop their own "seat of the pants" sailing technique. That would be better than looking out ahead of themselves and saying, "What are they doing that I am not doing?"

Instead of concentrating on the boat ahead of them, they should concentrate on their own boat.

# 19

## *THE PRINDLE 16—TALES AND TIPS*
*by Tom Tannert*

√ Winner of the Prindle 16 Midwestern Championship, 1977, 1978, and 1979
√ Winner of the Prindle 16 Nationals in 1979

LIKE many of the top racers today, Tom Tannert started out in a monohull. In 1960, while still in his early teens, he began racing a Pintail, a small, family daysailer in the Midwest.

He sailed in four Pintail national championships, never placing worse than fourth.

In 1975 he converted to catamarans, with the Prindle 16. Tannert is now a dealer in Akron, Ohio, selling Prindles, Hobies, and several other lines of sailboats. He is an active supporter of local fleet racing, but still manages to hit the campaign trail for the bigger cat races once in a while.

He races primarily on Lake Erie, Sandusky Bay, and various small inland lakes in Ohio.

The Prindle 16 catamaran is one of the new breeds of lightweight, durable, asymmetric-hull catamarans. It was developed in 1974 by Geoff Prindle as a couples catamaran. Geoff wanted a catamaran that could be easily handled and raced competitively by crews who weighed around 260 pounds.

As shown by the fact that eight of the first nine national championships were won by husband and wife teams, the Prindle 16 has proved to be a successful design.

Crew weight and placement are critical performance factors on the Prindle 16. The common view is that crew weight must be under 300 pounds and close to the class minimum of 260 pounds in order to be competitive.

The proper fore-and-aft trim on the Prindle 16 is to keep the leeward bow 6 to 12 inches out of the water. Many Prindle sailors put tape on the inside of each hull 6 to 12 inches down from the deck so that they can more easily judge hull trim.

In extremely light wind it usually pays to try to reduce drag by lifting the stern clear of the water. Position the crew forward of the main beam on the leeward hull. As the wind increases, the crew should move back and to weather to keep the boat in proper balance.

The idea on asymmetric-hull catamarans is to sink the leeward hull deep into the water in order to reduce side slippage. Raising the weather hull just barely out of the water sinks the leeward hull and reduces wetted surface, and thus frictional drag through the water. Your goal should be to keep the weather hull just kissing the crest of the waves.

The successful Prindle sailor doesn't cleat the mainsheet but is constantly pumping it in and out, anticipating gusts and lulls in the wind to avoid having the weather hull fly up and down. The weather hull is just barely out of the water at all

*Tom Tannert*

times, keeping the boat in the most efficient trim nearly 100 percent of the time.

There has been an evolution in the Prindle class in recent years concerning mast rake. Several years ago the theory was to set the mast straight up and down. But the European racers would come to the United States national championships with stories of great success using radical mast rake in the heavy winds and waves of the North Sea.

Most of us were quite skeptical of their theories until the 1980 national championship at Hilton Head Island, South Carolina, where Randy Smyth and Menno de Boer convinced most of the rest of us that raking the mast a lot was the only way to go, especially in winds over 10 to 12 knots.

In 1980 and since, Randy, with his wife, Susie, as crew, have totally dominated the championships, using a great deal of mast rake. Mast rake wasn't the only reason they won, of course. Randy and Susie sailed a tremendous regatta utilizing super starts and superior tactics as well. But they sure did seem to have an advantage in boat speed with their mast rake.

Menno de Boer's performance was even more impressive to me. In the race with the heaviest wind, Menno had a poor start. With his rig raked aft he was able to keep the boat driving through the waves at top speed without burying his lee bow. He passed most of the "gold" fleet to round weather mark in second place and held on to finish second to Randy and Susie in that race. His boat speed was startling. Menno, from Holland, converted me to the European theory of mast rake.

Most of the Prindle racers sail with their rigs tight. My normal approach in most conditions is to tension the rig so that I've got it as tight as I can get it, yet the mast will rotate freely. By keeping the rig tight you keep the forestay from sagging, which helps windward performance.

At the Prindle Nationals in 1979 in the Pacific Ocean off La Jolla Point, we experienced some conditions that were unusual for most areas of the country but somewhat common in my stomping ground of Lake Erie. The winds were light and fluky with a lot of choppy waves.

A large school of highly regarded game and eating fish called Yellowtails just happened to make a long-awaited appearance right off La Jolla Point during our championships.

Dozens of charter fishing boats with twenty or so fishermen hanging off each side were trawling all around the race area, providing the contestants with waves from every direction imaginable. It was enough to make even Ted Turner nauseous.

As in Lake Erie, I had good results sailing with a loose rig. Off the wind the loose rig allowed the jib to become a little fuller, giving my son Tom, Jr., and me extra power to drive through the waves. Upwind, we could use the mainsheet to pull the mast back, making the forestay tight in those light wind conditions.

On the Prindle 16, as on most other catamarans, it is imperative that you keep moving with good boat speed while beating. If you try to point too close to the wind, the boat will start crabbing or sliding sideways.

The Prindle racer must develop a feel for how much boat

speed he should have for the wind and wave conditions. If you feel that the boat speed is too slow for a certain wind and wave condition, you must let the sails out a little and fall off away from the wind slightly in order to build the speed back up again. Once boat speed is back up to where you feel it should be, you can sheet in a little and point back up.

Most successful Prindle racers have a little alarm built into their heads that goes off whenever the wind and their boat speed don't correlate.

People who have trouble sailing a Prindle 16 to weather usually are too hung up on pointing. The only time that it seems to pay to pinch up a little is on inland lakes with extremely flat water. With any wave action at all, the waves will actually stop your boat. Fall off enough to keep your speed up and keep it driving.

The Prindle 16 is a relatively easy boat to surf. But surfing the boat well enough to compete with the Hawaiians, the Californians, and the Floridians is a different matter.

The first time I raced with the surfers was in 1978. I had decided that I was going to race in the national championships for the first time that year. They were held in the Gulf of Mexico off Treasure Island near St. Petersburg. We had gone down to Florida a few days before the racing was to start and had entered a local fleet race to see what we could learn.

I had an excellent start in the first race and rounded the first weather mark with a 100-foot or so lead and was starting to feel pretty good. That was before I looked back to see Jorn Curtiss coming up on me like a freight train. Try as I might, there was nothing that I could do to hold him off. He was surfing three out of every four waves, while I could only catch maybe one of four.

Since the Prindle Association insists on sailing their national championships in open water, the flat-water sailors like myself must take advantage of every opportunity to practice surfing.

In my opinion, it is nearly impossible to be competitive in Prindle racing with stock sails. Even the hot-shot racers from the factory use custom racing sails for major events. Sails by

Smyth of Huntington Beach, California, and Echles Design Sailmakers of Ventura, California, are two of the sailmakers that have been at the forefront of Prindle sail design for several years. To try to win a major Prindle event with stock sails is like trying to win the Indianapolis 500 with a stock Ford.

In addition to custom racing sails, the prospective Prindle racer will want to add most of the following items to upgrade his stock boat:

When you talk to the sailmaker about your sails, don't forget to mention foam sandwich battens. They are much lighter, reducing weight aloft where you don't want it, and are tapered to allow the sail to take the shape that the sailmaker designed into it. Your new sail should be cut to match your new battens, so it is best to buy them at the same time from the same sailmaker.

In order to be competitive in heavier winds, you will want to add a second trapeze rig. The rig that comes with the boat is the one that I prefer, with one difference. I like a half harness or butt bucket. This is only a personal preference, and you should make sure that your harness is comfortable to you.

The stock tiller is not at all suitable for racing. It is too short and does not allow you to get forward far enough for proper boat trim in light air. It's also a little short for proper trapezing. The tiller to look for is made of fiberglass and telescopes from about 54 inches to about 97 inches. When the aluminum telescoping tillers dent, they won't telescope. The fiberglass tillers have about the same resistance to breaking, but they won't dent and will last years instead of weeks.

In order to trim your jib properly, you'll want to add a barberhauler. The barberhauler allows you to trim the jib out toward the end of the forward beam when sailing on reaches, just as the main traveler does on the rear beam for the mainsail. Most Prindle dealers will be able to help you select and install a barberhauler.

It is important that you eliminate as much play in the boat as possible. The stiffer the boat, the less drag it will have going through the water. The first place to eliminate play is in the area where the main beams bolt to the hulls. Once you are sure that the boat is settled into its proper alignment, remove the trampoline and the forward beam. Put an ample amount of mold release (or if you don't want to get too fancy, auto wax) on the beam where it touches the hull. Lay in a bed of epoxy resin mixed with the proper amount of catalyst, and bolt the beam back down. Now do the same thing to the rear beam, and you'll have the stiffest hulls around.

The play in the rudder system can be removed by adding any of the rudder shim kits that are on the market. You can also make your own shim kit out of plastic coffee can lids.

When aligning the rudders, I prefer to adjust the built-in alignment screw on the connecter bar so that the rudders are parallel, but any play that is in the rudder system will go toward toe-in. The theory is that any toe-out is really bad; a little bit of toe-in won't hurt and may be good.

One cheap little addition that seems to work extremely well for me is the shock cord inhaul on the boom. When you want to make the bottom one-third of the sail a little fuller, the easiest way is to bow the bottom batten out from the boom.

Unfortunately, that batten won't stay bowed. Attaching a piece of shock cord to the outhaul car and putting it under tension to the outhaul cleat or an eyestrap that you've added for this purpose will keep the batten in the position that you put it.

Most new Prindle sailors tend to oversheet the jib. If you pull it in too tight, you will cut off the flow of air through the slot between the jib and the mainsail. This drastically kills the power of the mainsail. Position the jib bridle rope through the grommets in the trampoline. Then allow the leech of the jib to follow the contour of the mainsail when the jib is pulled in just firm, not tight.

In other words, keep the slot open.

# 20

## *OUT FRONT ON THE PRINDLE 18 . . . AND THE TORNADO*

*by Randy Smyth*

√ Prindle 16 National Champion, 1980, 1981, and 1982
√ Prindle 18 National Champion, 1980, 1981, and 1982
√ Tornado World Champion, 1981 and 1982
√ Tornado National Champion, 1980, 1981, and 1982
√ Tornado European Champion, 1982
√ Pre-Olympic Champion, last two years, 1981 and 1982
√ Yachtsman of the Year, 1983

RANDY SMYTH has been the hottest sailor around for the past three years, dominating three classes simultaneously. In contrast to the winning sailors who "do what feels right," Randy takes a more technical and scientific approach to both his equipment and his racing.

At twenty-eight, he already has more time on the water than many of the old veterans. He started sailing a dinghy at the age of seven and won his first trophy when he was eleven, racing an Aqua Cat to Catalina Island, with his little brother as crew.

He looks a good bet to represent the United States in the 1984 Olympics.

His interest in sailing is financial as well as fun, as he operates a successful sail loft (Sails by Smyth), which he opened in 1976 in Huntington Beach, California.

## *TUNING THE PRINDLE 18*

### MAST RAKE

I rake my mast aft on the Prindle 18. The primary reason is that the Prindle has asymmetrical hulls without centerboards and therefore derives its lift from two places: first, from the hull design itself; secondly, from the rudders, which on the 18 are very efficient, very deep, very high aspect, and have a very nice cross-sectional shape. I prefer to put a fair amount of the leeway load on the rudders, rather than on the hulls.

That is an overall picture of why we rake our mast aft. As to how far aft, we have a bunch of numbers to help us find the mast position we want in an unfamiliar boat, which is about all we seem to sail.

What we do is measure the forestay length on the Prindle 18, assuming the bridles are all equal. Last year we set our forestay length at 21 feet 11⅞ inches; and this year we are setting it 1¼ inches longer. Then we simply tighten the two side shrouds down until the rig is tight.

To digress a moment, I should elaborate somewhat on the right rig. It really does not make too much difference going to weather because your leeward shroud will still be slack, and due to the tension of the mainsheet, the forestay will be tight and not sag.

*Randy Smyth*

But the true advantage is off the wind on reaches and broad reaches, where you get a moderate amount of wind and a lot of waves—sloppy conditions. Here I want a tight forestay and do not want the jib slacking off. I steer exclusively by the jib, so if the jib is flopping around due to a loose rig, then it would be very difficult to steer the boat accurately.

But getting back to the aft mast rake, besides the advantage of loading the leeway power on the rudders, there is the added advantage that it opens up the slot between the main and jib. That is especially good in heavy air, as it allows all the wind to blow through there much easier than with a vertical mast.

With the vertical mast you tend to close the slot somewhat and cause a sort of stagnation of the flow on the leeward side of the main. We are really trying to increase the velocity of the wind flow across the leeward side of the main, and so we do not want anything to be hampering the basic flow of air between the jib and the main.

Many sailors think that while they may go better to

weather with the aft-raked mast, they will lose some speed on the downhill leg. However, you will only lose speed off the wind if you are sailing with the apparent wind aft of 90 degrees.

You see, if you sail with the wind coming more from the aft of the boat (in other words, you are sailing deep and in a stall), the wind does not really have any release with the mast way back. The wind sees a shorter rig, it sees less sail area, and it seems to stagnate in the mainsail, not being able to release and flow as it should.

Sail the boat with the mast rotated to 100 degrees, and sail with the apparent wind never aft of 90 degrees. Then you keep the flow on the main at all times. Now, the wind sees the sail at 90 degrees, and the mast rake doesn't affect the speed of the boat. You must keep the speed, though, in order to utilize the aft-raked mast properly while off the wind.

So you are not really sacrificing anything with the aft-raked mast, unless you sail the boat with the apparent wind aft of 90 degrees and do not allow the wind to flow across the mainsail; in that case you are allowing the main to stall.

### MAST ROTATION

The mast rotation on the Prindle 18 is a very critical adjustment. The mast is a near copy of that of the Tornado—a long, thin, teardrop-shaped mast with its chord considerably longer than its breadth.

So the more you rotate the mast, the more flex you will have.

This is an aspect of the mast that you must keep in mind. If it is very windy and the top of your sail is very full, rotate the mast more to flatten out the top of the sail.

To determine how far to rotate it, I use a rather unscientific method. I just put my hand up where the mast and the sail join on the leeward side and feel if it is a smooth transition. If here is any concave or convex feeling, it is a reliable sign that the configuration will have a hard time keeping an attached flow across the leeward side. What you need is a good "fair curve" on your leading edge. I look for this configuration under any point of sail and any circumstance.

I feel that fullness and flatness of the mainsail should be dealt with in a way other than mast rotation. If you reduce mast rotation to 45 degrees, then you will most certainly have a concave configuration between the mast and the sail. Again, I feel the primary reason for mast rotation is to develop that fair curve and contour that shows the wind a good leading edge.

## MAST BEND

I like to split mast bend into two regions: the top of the mast and the bottom of the mast. The top is controlled by two things: the mainsheet load and mast rotation. The bottom of the mast is totally controlled by the support given by the diamond wires.

As for the top, by rotating more, you allow the top of the mast to flex more. Mainsheet load also bends the top of the mast, which flattens the top of the main.

The diamonds, if tight, will not allow the lower section of the mast to bend; so the lower section of the sail will remain full. If the diamonds are loosened, the lower portion of the sail will be much flatter.

Basically, what you want to do is tune your mast to your sail. If you want the fullness out of the bottom of the sail, you loosen the diamond wires. If you want the fullness out of the top of the sail, you rotate the mast. Of course, if the effects you desire are opposite those, you reverse the action.

On the Prindle 18, if you loosen the diamond wires more than 40 inches up from the tangs, you are getting close to a risky extreme of mast bend—risky to the point that it may break.

## MAINSAIL

The magic word in mainsails is "versatility." You do not want the same sail upwind as you do after you round the weather mark. The key there is to have controls on the boat to adjust the sail and to have a sail that can be adjusted. Relatively speaking, you want a flat sail going to weather and a full sail downwind.

That is rather basic; specifically, the shape of the mainsail will differ considerably.

For example, on the downwind leg the sail should be more of a circular shape; the leech should look a lot like the luff. That is, neither the luff nor the leech should have a flat shape; both should have a fair curve.

Upwind, you will want the draft a fair amount aft in the bottom sections, simply because the jib overlaps there. You do not want a full draft forward right where the jib is throwing air across the main. That would shut off the slot. I would say the mainsail would work better with the bottom draft being located at 50 percent aft.

However, as you get up to the numbers or the "P" on Prindle sails, the draft will be a bit farther forward, since there is not so much influence from the jib. Here the draft should be around 40 percent aft.

Both the bottom of the sail and the top should be very flat. The bottom, because of the jib overlap. The top, because flatness allows a little more twist in the top of the sail and your apparent wind up there is quite a bit farther aft—it is not being backwinded by the jib. With that combination you seem to get a much more even flow from top to bottom, according to the telltales. So I think the ideal sail is flat at the bottom, medium in the midsection, and flat again at the top.

You may wonder why this sail shape would work in light air where you would want a full sail. Take a look at the top batten: It is only 22 inches long, attached to a mast which has a chord 6 inches long. So although the sail material itself will show no camber, the combination of the mast and sail will still have a very deep draft within a relatively short span.

In order to have a reasonable shape, to your eye it should appear that the sail is very flat. If the top of your sail looks full and then you add the 6 inches of mast camber, which is also part of the foil, you have a real bag! A lot of problems.

BATTENS

All my battens are measured for deflection and tapered in matching sets for my sail. I want stiffer battens in the top and softer ones in the bottom of the sail. In the top the deflexion weight is about 9 pounds, while in the lower pockets I use much lighter battens that deflect at about 2 pounds.

The bottom battens are soft, because stiff battens tend to inhibit versatility. However, the top ones have to be relatively stiff, because they have to support some of the roach at the top.

Batten tension is a very poor way to adjust sail shape. If you have a flat sail and in trying to make it full you opt for tightening in the batten very hard, you will bow out the batten in the batten pocket. But what about the cloth in between? It does not bow out with the batten. So you end up with a scallopy-looking sail, probably not as good as what you started out with.

My philosophy is to tighten the batten into the sail until it removes the wrinkles from the pocket itself under a very mild tension.

MAIN LUFF TENSION

Luff tension is very critical. When the hull starts coming out of the water, it is time to yank on the downhaul. Generally I set the downhaul tight enough to make the sail look smooth—no wrinkles. This should give you a fuller sail, for those times when you need the power.

But when the wind picks up and you are constantly raising your hull and not going anywhere, it is a good sign your downhaul is too loose.

What the downhaul does is distort your sailcloth in such a way that it flattens the top of the mainsail. If you pull it even more, it will not only flatten the top, but will flatten the sail on down to the numbers, or to below the "P." Flatten it still more; it will begin to open the leech at the top of the sail, allowing the power to spill off where the sail has the most leverage for heeling the boat.

What you end up with is the excess power going off the top; the boat begins to sail flatter and doesn't fly a hull. You will not have to ease the sheet much, either; therefore, the forestay stays tight, allowing the jib to continue working and letting you point. The lower part of the mainsail leech will still be pointing you high.

### OUTHAUL

In a sloop-rigged boat, the outhaul should be pulled all the way out while going to weather. Even in choppy seas I will use the downhaul to shape the middle of the sail, but I keep the bottom of the sail very flat.

### JIB

I like the shape of the jib to be fairly full at the bottom and progressively flatter as you go up toward the head of the sail.

The fullness at the bottom is beneficial, because the boat does need a fair amount of power. You know that you do not want to pinch the boat, and you want to drive it; the fullness is then quite advantageous.

The flatness near the top gives the sail a little twist, which gives you a parallel gap between the main and the jib.

The draft location in the jib should be just under 40 percent back from the luff, pretty much the same configuration as in the main.

### JIB LEADS

Jib lead locations should always be set well aft; on the Prindle 18 I use the stock inboard-outboard locations. Usually I keep the jib blocks in the farthest aft position on the stock boat, putting the sheet load on the foot and not so much on the leech of the jib.

Downwind, we use the barberhauler, so the leads move out to a forward and outboard position. We usually set them almost all the way out. Then we set the jib sheet so that the telltales at the top and the bottom break evenly.

### JIB LUFF TENSION

The draft of a stock, colored sail, particularly up near the top of the jib, will drift aft as the wind picks up, and so luff tension must be added in great amounts. I build the vertical-seam jibs, and the tension is not so critical, as it stays right around the seam.

### WEIGHT DISTRIBUTION

Going to weather, the Prindle 18 is rather specific in where it wants you to be. In pictures of us sailing, it appears that we are too far aft on the boat, sailing with the bows up and are sinking the sterns. That attitude normally is not fast, but it is on the Prindle 18.

There are two reasons for sailing the boat in this position. One is that the boat creates pretty big bow waves, and those waves hit the little lips where the hull forms the deck. You do not want these lips to hit the waves; they can create a lot of drag. So we make sure they are well out of the water.

The second reason requires some explanation. If you would look at a Prindle hull from behind, you will find the keel line is not exactly straight. It has a little outward twist to it in the aft three feet; and if you sink it deep in the water, the back three feet of the hull can develop a great deal more lift in that short area than does the rest of the hull. Also, with our weight aft, the rudders are very efficient and deep.

In essence, you sail this particular boat with a bow-up attitude.

Downwind, however, you sail like any other boat, with your weight far enough forward to keep the sterns out of the water, so there will be no turbulence off the transoms.

## *HELMSMANSHIP ON THE PRINDLE 18*

### TO WEATHER

The traveler is always set in the middle when I go to weather, no matter what the conditions. I did lay it off about 4 inches once, when it was over 30 knots of wind. But, then, that is a lot of air; it is near the velocity where your main concern is survival.

In boats that come with stock sails, they sometimes have to let the traveler out just to hold down the boat, because by easing the mainsheet the sail becomes fuller. The only way that type of sail can be flattened is by using mainsheet load. So when a puff hits and they ease the mainsheet load to relieve the power of the puff, the sail actually becomes fuller, thereby making things worse—more heeling moment at the top of the mast, more hull flying, and less forward thrust.

In our own sails we use a lot of downhaul, flattening out the top of the sail and allowing the leech at the top to open up and spill off excess power in the puffs.

We sheet very hard when conditions require us to be on the trapeze, and utilize all the power we have. When the conditions exceed that, we tighten the downhaul and ease the sheet.

I have my crew handle the mainsheet in heavier airs, and his job is to see to it that the windward hull is just kissing the water—never quite into the water, except a few inches, and yet not flying a hull. Then I steer by the jib.

I like to make the boat go fast and totally forget about pointing too high. Time and time again I have looked back to see someone pointing higher, and time and time again I go ahead and sail the way I know I should: driving the boat and keeping the speed. After a while I'll look back and the other boat still will be aiming higher, but it will be farther back than it was before.

Just because you're pointing the boat higher doesn't make it GO higher. The faster you go through the water, the more lift you get—and less leeway.

As I said, I steer by the telltales of the jib. I keep the windward telltale dancing and the leeward telltale flowing. That is all I look at.

Since I steer my boat by the jib, I rely on how the jib is set. If the jib were to be let out, I would be sailing at an angle considerably off the wind. If it were tightened, I could head up. Basically, you set the jib at what you think is the proper angle to steer the boat toward the weather.

If it's too tight, you will point high, but you will develop too much leeway and boats will beat you to the mark. If it is too loose and you must drive, you will realize that right away from the other boats around you, as you won't be pointing as high as they are.

Once we have the jib set the way we want it, then I use only one telltale on the main in order to set it to the jib.

There is a telltale just below the "P" on the Prindle 18 mainsail and about 10 inches back. I simply sheet the main in until the leeward mainsail telltale stalls, then ease it back out until the telltale just begins to flow; then I know that is all the power we are going to get out of that particular boat and sail on that particular day.

Now, if the jib sheeting is changed, it will affect the telltale on the main as well, and a mainsheet correction must be made. So whenever possible, I want the jib held solid in order to keep the sails complementing one another and to have the constant jib by which to sail.

### TACKING

Like most catamarans, the Prindle 18 likes to go straight. The idea, when going into a tack, is to trick the boat into believing that you are not really tacking. All you have done is pushed the helm somewhat—you are both still in the trapeze and sheets are taut. It should be a smooth turn up into the wind (not a jamming turn).

You and the crew should keep your eyes on the jib. It will start to luff, then luff a little more, and just as it starts to backwind, that is your cue to begin activities.

The crew and skipper should come off the wire. The main should be eased. Both people should take their time on the old windward hull, fairly far aft.

You are depressing the soon-to-be-leeward hull and

pivoting the entire boat on that one point, until the boat is around and through the eye of the wind and pointed in the direction of the new tack angle. Then we sheet in and very quickly scurry over to the new windward side all at the same time.

What we have done is pivoted the entire boat on the old windward hull. (By being far back on the one hull, we have reduced the waterline length and so had to turn only one hull instead of two, as the other hull is barely in the water.)

You really have to take your time about this maneuver in order for it to be effective. But once the hulls are around, you must be very speedy about getting across to the other side and getting sheeted in and moving.

In essence, this is a form of roll tack. *Caution:* If you wait too long, you will capsize. This may take a bit of practice to perfect.

## DOWNWIND

As in weather work, on the downwind leg I like to set the jib first and begin sailing by it. We set the barberhaulers, then trim the jib, and then I steer to get the telltales working the way I want them to. Then we begin trimming the main to where we want it.

The main is really what develops your speed. I set the main off the wind the same way I do when going to weather. With the jib telltales flowing just right and the main traveler almost all the way out, I then look at the leeward telltale on the main, located about 10 inches aft of the mast and just below the "P" on the Prindle mainsail. I try to make sure that telltale is flowing. If you have trouble keeping it flowing, it is a good sign that you need more mast rotation.

With the apparent wind at 90 degrees, I feel the mast rotation should be more than 90, perhaps 100 degrees. Now, once the leeward mainsail telltale is flowing, you are sailing by the jib, and the mast is rotated a lot; then if the wind is blowing pretty hard (say 15 mph or better), you can yank on the traveler up to 12 inches to increase speed without losing any downwind pointing ability.

I sail at about 90 degree angles to the wind, although it appears that I sail pretty high. After first rounding a weather mark, I start off pretty high, then bleed off speed and get down to a proper angle. The worst thing you can do is to head right down, because you'll immediately lose all your speed and never get your flow attached. The secret is keeping your flow attached.

I never sail an efficient catamaran wing-and-wing, so I cannot really talk about it. There are some pretty inefficient boats that could probably use that style of sailing.

### JIBING

The mistake most people make is getting the jib sheet in before setting the barberhauler. The barberhauler should be brought in and then the jib sheeted, preferably at the same rate of speed as the skipper turns the boat.

As for the actual steering, the turn should be a very gradual turn, and you should turn farther than you might think you should. A good way to gauge your turn is to look back in the water. You should see an "S" wake. You make your initial turn and keep on going beyond the normal curve, then begin the last half of the "S" to bring the heading back down to a normal course.

In this way you are heading a little higher on the new course to develop speed and then falling off to the normal course.

## *. . . AND THE TORNADO*

The Prindle 18 and the Tornado share many similarities, as do most catamarans. Therefore, to eliminate redundancy, I am here discussing only those aspects of tuning and helmsmanship on the Tornado that I handle differently from what I do on a Prindle 18.

### MAST RAKE

Even on the Tornado I rake my mast aft. The old tradition was to use the centerboards for lateral resistance. But now the theory is to balance the load on the centerboards and rudders. So we are now asking the rudders to help out with the leeway load.

Weather helm will result from raking the mast aft, and the simplest way to judge it is to look back at the rudder blade; if it is going through the water at an excessive angle, say 5 degrees, then you have gone too far with the mast rake. Normally, the angle through the water should be about 2 degrees.

I really do not go by the feel of the helm. I do not want excessive drag to result from the aft-raked mast, although a couple of degrees of rudder angle will not hurt. And the added lift I now get from the rudder more than makes up for the little drag I have created.

### JIB LEADS

On the Tornado we use the inboard-outboard jib lead locations extensively. In the lighter airs we have them set about 12 inches inboard from the hull; if we begin to trapeze, we yank them out to about 9 inches inboard from the hull; and when it gets really choppy or windy, we get them out to about 6 inches inboard from the hull.

We do not adjust the fore-aft leads at all, but opt to leave them far aft at all times. I want to make sure the slot is not closed.

### WEIGHT DISTRIBUTION

The Tornado gets a fair amount of lift from its very deep, knife-shaped bows, so the best place to keep your weight is forward of the middle of the boat. Of course, if it gets windy and choppy, you do have to keep the bows free of the waves. So then you must get your weight farther aft.

DOWNWIND HELMSMANSHIP

The main difference between the Tornado and the Prindle is that we never let the traveler all the way out anymore on the Tornado. The most we let it out is about 8 inches from the end. We play the traveler a lot off the wind.

In any kind of air we yank it in to about 2 feet inside the hull, using a lot of twist off the top. We then get a lot of forward apparent wind and are sailing very fast, but surprisingly still tack at about 90 degrees. The apparent wind runs at about 80 to 85 degrees.

I still sail by the jib, however.

# *GLOSSARY*

ABAFT—aft of; toward the stern, at the stern.
ABEAM—at right angles to the line of the keels.
ADRIFT—afloat without being anchored or moored; also unsecured, as in the case of gear tossing about a boat.
AFT—in or near the stern.
AFTER—toward the stern.
ALOFT—overhead, above the decks.
ALONGSIDE—by the side of, side by side.
AMIDSHIPS—in or toward the center of a boat; between bow and stern.
APPARENT WIND—to those aboard a boat in motion, the direction from which the wind appears to blow.
ASHORE—on or to the shore.
ASPECT RATIO—the length of a luff of a sail in comparison to the length

of its foot. The luff of a high-aspect-ratio sail is very long, compared to the foot.

ASTERN—toward the stern; behind a boat; opposite of ahead.

ATHWARTSHIPS—at right angles to the fore-and-aft line of the boat.

BACK—to force a sail against the wind when maneuvering (a jib is "backed" when you want to force the bow to fall off the wind); see *backwind;* to allow or cause the boat to move backward with the bows pointed into the wind.

BACKWIND—to impair the effectiveness of a mainsail by sheeting in the jib so far as to deflect a stream of air against the lee side of the mainsail, thus destroying its partial vacuum. Also, see *back.*

BACKSTAY—a supporting wire cable for a mast, leading to deck well abaft the mast (not used on most catamarans).

BAIL—to dip water out; also a ring or hoop or partial hoop designed to support something.

BALLAST—weight on a boat to give it stability.

BARBERHAULER—a device of lines and blocks for changing the jib lead point.

BARGE—to reach off for the starting line in a sailing race and force room illegally at the windward end of the line.

BATTEN—a piece of wood or plastic inserted in a sail pocket to stiffen and hold the sail shape.

BEAM—the width of a boat at its widest point.

BEAM REACH—the point of sailing with the wind directly abeam, or 90 degrees from the keel.

BEAM SEA—a wave or waves striking a boat broadside.

BEAMY—wide, as describing a hull.

BEAR DOWN—to head down a boat to leeward.

BEAR OFF—to head away from the wind more.

BEAR UP—to head into the wind more.

BEARING—the direction of an object or the course of a boat, usually stated in compass degrees.

BEAT—the act of sailing a boat close-hauled to windward.

BECKET—a rope's dead-end attachment point, mounted on the bottom of a block.

BELAY—to make fast a line by taking turns around a pin or cleat.

BERTH—sufficient maneuvering space.

BILGE—the turn of the hull below the waterline.

BINNACLE—a compass case.

BITT—an iron or wooden head set vertically to which mooring or towing lines are made fast.

BITTER END—the end of a line.

BLOCK—a seagoing pulley.

BOLLARD—a vertical head or post of wood or iron on a pier to which mooring lines are made fast.

BOLT ROPE—a rope sewn into the leading edge of a sail to strengthen it.

BOOM—a spar to which the foot of a fore-and-aft sail is attached.

BOOM VANG—a block-and-line device, attached between the underside of the boom and the hull or foot of the mast, that stabilizes the boom in offwind sailing.

BOW—the forward or front end of the boat.

BOW LINE—a mooring line attached to the bow of a boat.

BOWLINE—an excellent knot for putting a loop in the end of a line, used extensively for sheets.

BOW WAVE—a continuing wave that forms on each side of the bow when a boat is in motion.

BOWSPRIT—a spar extending forward of the bow of a boat to take the jibstay of a sailboat.

BREAK OUT—to bring something out of stowage, such as a sail from its bag or food from a cooler.

BREAKING SEAS—waves curling over at their tops as the water shoals.

BREAKWATER—a structure to break the force of waves and to protect a harbor or beach.

BRIDLE—cable wires running from each hull to the forestay.

BRISTOL—describing the ultimate in a neat, trim boat; shipshape.

BROACH TO—to swing or slew around toward the wind when running free and thus come broadside to the sea. Broaching to is usually caused by bad steering or by the force of a heavy sea or surf.

BROAD REACH—any point of sailing between a beam reach and quartering the wind aft.

BROADSIDE—the entire side of a boat, from stem to quarter.

BULKHEAD—a vertical partition separating compartments in a hull.

BURDENED VESSEL—a boat not having the right of way.

BY THE LEE—a critical point of sailing on a run, when the wind is allowed to strike the forward surface of the mainsail, causing it to waver with the possibility of a jibe; this is sometimes called "sailing by the lee."

CANVAS—a general term referring to sails.

CAPSIZE—to overturn.

CAST OFF—to let go a line.

CATAMARAN—a twin-hulled boat with a deck between the hulls for carrying the crew.

CATBOAT—a sailboat with only one sail.

CATSPAW—light air ruffling the surface of the water during a race.

CENTER OF EFFORT—the center of the combined area of all sails on a boat.

CENTER OF LATERAL RESISTANCE—the center of area of a hull's underwater profile.

CENTERBOARD—a board that passes through a slot in the keel to provide lateral resistance for a sailboat. It is enclosed in a waterproof trunk and may be raised in shallow water.

CHAINPLATE—a metal strip bolted to the hull of a sailboat to which one of the shrouds is attached.

CHEEK—the side of a block shell.

CHOCK—a lead for lines that go over the side.

CHORD—a straight line intersecting a curve.

CLEAT—a device used to belay or secure a line.

CLEW—the corner of a sail at the juncture of the leech and the foot.

CLOSE-HAULED—sailing as close to the wind as possible, with all sails trimmed flat; see also *beat.*

CLOSE REACH—a point of sailing between a beam reach and a beat.

COCKPIT—a space that accommodates the helmsman and crew.

COME ABOUT—to tack.

COURSE—the direction steered by a helmsman.

DAGGERBOARD—a nonpivoting board passed down through a slot or trunk in the keel of a sailboat to provide lateral resistance.

DINGHY—a small boat usually used to tend a larger boat; any of several small sailing boats that have developed into one-design racing classes.

DISPLACEMENT HULL—a hull designed to pass through the water rather than skim over the surface.

DOWNHAUL—a line for putting downward stress on a sail at the luff; the act of tightening the downhaul.

DOWNWIND—sailing with the wind.

DRAFT—the fullness of a sail.

EASE—to reduce the amount of pressure on a sheet or on the helm.

EYE SPLICE—a loop or a ring in the end of a cable or line.

FALLS—lines rove through blocks to form tackles.

FATHOM—a unit of depth measure equalling six feet.

FEATHER—a telltale made of feather material; also, to head up into the wind and bleed off air when close-hauled.

FEND OFF—to push a hull away from an object or another boat.

FLAW—a gust of wind heavier than the prevailing breeze.

FLY—a small pennant used for telling apparent wind, usually

mounted on the masthead or the forestay bridle.

FOLLOWING SEA—waves approaching from astern.

FOOT—the bottom edge of a sail.

FOOTING—sailing to windward slightly less than close-hauled on the theory that the added speed more than offsets loss in pointing.

FORE-AND-AFT—running, acting, or lying along the general lengthwise line of a boat.

FORESAIL—the first working sail immediately forward of the main; the jib.

FORESTAY—a mast-supporting cable on which the jib luff is attached.

FORWARD—at, near, or belonging to the fore part of a boat; also, more toward the bow than the stern.

FOUL—an error in a sailing race.

FOULED—tangled or caught, e.g., a fouled line or sheet.

FOUNDER—to fill with water and sink.

FREEBOARD—the area on the sides of the hull, from the water line to the gunwale.

FREE—to sail with the wind well aft, as in "running free."

FRESHEN—to increase in wind strength.

FURL—to roll up a sail and secure it to a spar.

GEAR—a collection of items such as canvas, ropes, spars, etc.

GEL COAT—the final resin gloss coating of a fiberglass hull. It contains the color pigment.

GENOA JIB—a large, overlapping jib with peak hoisted to the masthead.

GHOSTER—a sailboat capable of comparatively good speed in very light air.

GHOSTING—sailing in very light air.

GO ABOUT—to tack.

GOOSENECK—a metal device used for securing the boom to the mast.

GROMMET—a metal eye fitted into the sail, used to take the wear of a line.

GROUND SWELL—a heavy roller caused by a distant wind.

GUDGEONS—socket fittings on the transom to accept rudder pintles.

GUNWALE—the junction of the side of the boat and the deck.

GUY—a rope that steadies or supports a spar; usually a line leading aft from the outboard end of a spinnaker pole to its after control position.

HALYARD—a line for hoisting or lowering a sail.

HARD ALEE—a warning called by the helmsman just as he puts the helm over to come about.

HARD CHINE—an abrupt angle at the intersection of topsides and bilges.
HARDEN—to trim sheets and sail closer to the wind.
HARD OVER—the extreme position of the helm.
HAUL—to pull with force; to remove a boat from the water; to sail closer to the wind.
HEAD—the upper, top section of a sail.
HEAD BOARD—a stiffening board inserted in the head of a sail.
HEADER—a wind shift that makes you steer down from your normal course to avoid luffing or losing speed.
HEADING—direction of travel of a boat; a course, normally expressed in compass degrees.
HEAD OFF—to steer away from the wind.
HEADSAILS—any sails forward of the mainmast.
HEAD-TO-WIND—with the bow headed into the wind.
HEAD UP—to steer the boat toward the wind.
HEAVE—to draw on; to pull or haul; to push.
HEAVE TO—to head into the wind; also, to keep a boat nearly stationary and headed into the wind, as when riding out a storm.
HEAVY WEATHER—strong winds and rough seas.
HEEL—the lateral rotation of a sailboat under pressure of the wind.
HELM—the tiller by which the rudder is controlled; pressure on the rudders, as felt through the tiller, tending to pull the boat either to weather or to leeward.
HELMSMAN—one who steers a boat.
HIKE—to position your weight as far to windward as possible, leaning out over the windward hull.
HULL—the main body of a vessel.
HULL SPEED—the maximum speed to which a displacement-type hull can be driven. It is limited by the length of the hull's waterline.
INBOARD—inside the hull(s), or more toward the inside than outside.
IRONS—luffing into the wind and unable to bear away on either tack.
JIB—a triangular sail attached to the forestay and forward of the mainmast.
JIB SHEET—a line for controlling a jib.
JIBE—passing from one tack to another by swinging the stern of the boat through the eye of the wind.
JURY-RIG—rig for temporary use.
KEEL—the lower edge or backbone of a vessel extending along the center of the bottom from bow to stern. A sailboat's keel extends to greater depths to provide lateral resistance and ballast.

KNOCKDOWN—to be heeled over or capsized by a sudden flaw or squall.

KNOT—the speed of one nautical mile per hour.

LANYARD—a cord or braid around a sailor's neck to secure his knife, starting watch, or Hobie key.

LASH—to secure by binding with rope.

LATERAL RESISTANCE—the ability of a hull, by means of the area of submerged surfaces, to resist being driven sideways by the wind or the pressure of wind on the sail.

LAUNCH—to put a boat in the water.

LAY LINE—a direct course line to a mark or the finish line requiring no tacking or jibing, as in "lay the mark."

LEADING EDGE—the forward edge of a sail.

LEE—the side of a boat away from the direction of the wind (opposite of weather side).

LEE BOARDS—boards projecting downward from the gunwales to provide lateral resistance.

LEECH—the after edge of a sail.

LEECH LINE—a small line in the leech of a sail used to make a sail fuller by tightening.

LEE HELM—a tendency to bear off the wind due to poor sail balance. It is caused by the center of effort being too far forward of the center of lateral resistance.

LEE RAIL—the rail away from the wind.

LEEWARD—the direction away from the wind.

LEEWAY—the amount a boat is pushed sideways by the wind.

LIFT—a wind shift that requires you to sail a higher course in order to maintain the same angle with the wind.

LINE—every rope used on a boat except a sheet or bolt rope.

LIST—a lateral inclination.

LOSE WAY—to stop.

LUFF—to take the wind pressure off a sail by easing the sheet or by heading into the wind, causing the sails to flap. Also, the forward edge of a sail.

LUFF ROPE—the rope sewn into the luff of a sail.

MAINSAIL—the large, principal working sail, attached to the mainmast.

MAINSHEET—the line for controlling the main boom and mainsail.

MARK—a turning point for a leg of a race course.

MAST—the vertical spar to which a sail is attached.

MAST BUTT—the lower end of the mast.

MASTHEAD—the top of a mast.
MASTHEAD FLY—a telltale mounted in a swivel at the top of the mast. It reveals apparent wind.
MOLDED PLYWOOD HULL—a hull made by gluing successive wrap layers of thin wood together over a male mold.
NAUTICAL MILE—a distance equal to one minute of arc of a great circle of the earth (actually 6,080.20 feet, but usually given as 6,080 feet). When reading a chart, it's handy to remember that a nautical mile equals one minute of latitude.
OFF THE WIND—sailing any course other than to windward.
ON THE WIND—sailing a course that is close-hauled.
OUTBOARD—situated or extending outside of the hull(s).
OUTHAUL—a line for hauling out the clew corner of a sail to the end of the spar.
OVERCORRECTING—swings the helm farther than necessary to bring a boat back on course.
OVERLAP—the positioning of two boats in close proximity on the same course, the bow of the boat astern extending past the stern of the forward boat. An overlap can be used tactically.
OVERLAPPING JIB—a jib sail that overlaps the mainsail.
OVERSTAND—to sail farther past a mark than is necessary before tacking for it or rounding it.
PAINTER—a handling line attached to the bow of a small boat.
PAY OFF—to ease off a rope.
PENNANT—a streamer or bunting; a small flag used for signalling.
PINCH—to steer the boat too close to the wind while sailing close-hauled, thereby luffing somewhat and retarding speed.
PINTLE—an upright pivot pin that forms a hinge on a rudder.
PITCHPOLE—to capsize a boat frontward.
PLANE—to elevate a hull so it skims along the surface instead of plowing through the water.
PLANING SPEED—the speed at which a planing hull rises to the surface.
POINTING—a boat's level of efficiency in sailing to windward; also, sailing as close to the wind as the boat's design will allow.
PORT—the left side of a boat.
PORT TACK—sailing with the wind coming over the port side.
POUND—to strike the waves with a jarring force, as is characteristic of some hulls.
PREVAILING WIND—the usual wind direction for the area and season.
PRIVILEGED VESSEL—the boat having the right of way in a meeting situation.

PURCHASE—an increase in applied power through use of a mechanical device such as a tackle.
QUARTER—the part of a boat between the beam and the stern.
QUARTERING SEA—waves striking a boat on its quarter.
RAFTING—tying two or more boats alongside each other.
RAIL—the top of the bulwarks or gunwales.
RAKE—the inclination of a mast fore or aft, away from the perpendicular.
REACH—all points of sailing between a beat and a run.
READY ABOUT—the last warning call given by the helmsman before putting the helm over to come about on the other tack.
REEF—to shorten sails.
REEF POINTS—small grommets in the sail located in a row parallel to the foot and used for shortening sails.
REGATTA—a series of boat races on one day or on consecutive days.
RESIN—the cohesive plastic used in constructing reinforced fiberglass hulls.
RHUMB LINE—a straight line between two points.
RIG—the type of sail arrangement; also, to step the mast and attach shrouds and stays while fitting out.
RIGGING—any rope, wires, or cable used to support (standing rigging) or control (running rigging) masts, spars, or sails.
RIGHTING MOMENT—a disposition of weight in relationship to buoyancy, tending to prevent a boat from capsizing and to return her to her normal attitude of flotation.
ROACH—that portion of the leech of a sail that extends aft of an imaginary line from the head to the clew.
ROCKER—a hull characteristic, low in the middle and sweeping upward at the ends, such as a rocker sheer or rocker chine.
ROLLER REEFING GEAR—a device for rolling a sail up on its attachment point (forestay or spar) like a window shade.
ROOSTER TAIL—a high plume of water rising from the stream of fast waves meeting astern.
ROUND UP—to head into the wind.
RUB RAIL—a molding around the hull to prevent it from being damaged.
RUDDER—broad, flat, movable shapes hinged vertically from the stern of the boat and used for steering.
RULES OF THE ROAD—laws covering the right of way of boats in meeting situations.
RUN—the point of sailing with the wind free and pressing directly from behind; sailing downwind.

RUNNING RIGGING—all sheets, halyards, guys, backstay lanyards, and other lines used to control spars, sails, or the support of spars.
SCULL—to move a boat forward by moving the rudder back and forth, creating the effect of a propeller.
SECURE—to make fast.
SELF-BAILING—designating a boat capable of draining any water from its cockpit.
SELF-SAILING—capable of sailing with helm unattended.
720—the act of sailing in a 360-degree circle twice.
SHACKLE—a U-shaped piece of metal with a pin through the end, used for securing lines and parts together.
SHEAVE—a wheel inside a block.
SHEET—a line for controlling a spar or sail in relation to the wind.
SHIPSHAPE—everything neat, clean, and orderly; in "Bristol" fashion.
SHORT TACKS—coming about frequently when sailing to windward.
SHROUDS—the wire rope stays supporting the mast laterally.
SKIN FRICTION—surface resistance of a hull as it passes through water.
SKIPPER—the master of the boat.
SLACK—to pay out or ease a line; the amount of play in a line that is not tight.
SLOOP—a single-masted sailboat with a large mainsail and a single working jib.
SLOT EFFECT—the acceleration of wind passing through the opening between a mainsail and overlapping jib, creating increased pressure differential between the windward and leeward side of the mainsail.
SPAR—any mast or boom that supports or extends the sail on a boat.
SPINNAKER—a large light, triangular sail used off the wind and set opposite and forward of the mainsail.
SQUALL—a sudden and violent burst of wind.
STALL—the slowing effect from sheeting the sails too tightly in relation to the wind direction or falling off without easing the sails.
STANDING PART—the part of a line made fast to something.
STARBOARD—the right side of a boat.
STARBOARD TACK—sailing with the wind coming over the starboard side.
STAY—a wire rope used to support a mast or other spar.
STAYSAIL—a sail with its luff attached to a stay.
STEERAGE WAY—having enough way (speed) for the vessel to respond to the helm.
STEM—the foremost timber (or steel bar) in a vessel.
STEP—to set and afix a mast in position.

STERN—the after end of a boat.

STERNWAY—moving in reverse.

STERN WAVE—a continuous, V-shaped wave forming from the stern of a boat on each side while the boat is moving forward.

STOW—to store or put away.

SWAGING—a fitting for cable attachments.

SWELL—a heavy undulation of the sea, with long fetch, caused by a strong wind blowing at a distance. It is often a harbinger of a major storm.

SWIVEL—a rotating fitting used to prevent a line from winding up.

TACK—the corner of a sail at the juncture of luff and foot.

TACK—to come about; to change the course of the boat by bringing the bows through the wind so that the wind is now on the opposite side. Also, the relationship of a sailboat with respect to the wind. If the wind comes over the starboard rail, the boat is on starboard tack; if the wind comes over the port rail, the boat is on port tack.

TACKLE—a purchase, consisting of one or more blocks and connecting falls, for multiplying the power of or changing the direction of a line.

TANG—a metal mast fitting to which a stay is attached.

TELLTALE—a short piece of ribbon, plastic, or feather attached to sails and/or shrouds for the purpose of reading wind direction and for monitoring sail trim.

TIE-DOWN—a line or lacing used to secure something to a deck or for holding down a boat to a trailer.

TILLER—a steering handle attached to the rudder(s).

TOPPING LIFT—a line by which the outer end of a boom is supported.

TOPSIDES—the sides of a hull from the chine or the turn of the bilge to the sheer line.

TRAVELER—a horizontal track mounted astern with a movable car that is connected to the mainsheet for the purpose of controlling the boom and sail trim; also used for fore-aft and inboard-outboard jib lead locations.

TRIM—to haul in on a sheet; also, to set the sails at their optimum position for efficiency; also, to balance the hull in a proper attitude in the water.

TROUGH—a hollow between waves.

TRUNK—a shaft in which daggerboards and centerboards are lowered and lifted.

TURNBUCKLE—a mechanical device, consisting of end screws of opposite threads, connected to a center barrel that can be rotated for adjusting the slack in a stay.

UNDER WAY—in motion over the water.

UPWIND—sailing close-hauled toward the wind.

VANG—see *boom vang.*

VEER—to change direction (as the wind).

VEERING WIND—shifting wind.

WAKE—the temporary track left by a boat in the water.

WATERLINE—the line of intersection of a hull with the water when the boat is in its normal attitude.

WAY ON—moving through the water.

WEATHER—indicating the side toward the wind, also known as windward; "to weather" is to windward.

WEATHER HELM—having a tendency to head into the wind.

WETTED SURFACE—the total submerged area of a hull or its appendages.

WHISKER POLE—a spar used as a boom to hold a jib or spinnaker guy out and away from the boat.

WINDAGE—the amount of area presented as a target to the wind.

WIND SHIFT—a change in wind direction.

WINDWARD—toward the wind.

WING MAST—a one-piece mast and sail molded or constructed from a rigid material.

YACHT—any pleasure boat.

YAW—to go off course or swing from side to side, normally associated with running before the wind in a sea.

# INDEX